The Dialogue Comes of Age

CHRISTIAN ENCOUNTERS WITH OTHER TRADITIONS

Edited by John B. Cobb Jr.
and Ward M. McAfee

Fortress Press
Minneapolis

THE DIALOGUE COMES OF AGE
Christian Encounters with Other Traditions

Cover image: *Arrival* by Helena Wadsley, 2008.
Cover design: Kevin van der Leek
Book design: PerfecType, Nashville, TN

Library of Congress Cataloging-in-Publication Data

The dialogue comes of age : Christian encounters with other traditions / edited by John B. Cobb Jr. and Ward M. McAfee.
    p. cm.
  Includes bibliographical references.
  ISBN 978-0-8006-9751-8 (pbk. : alk. paper) 1. Christianity and other religions. I. Cobb, John B. II. McAfee, Ward.
  BR127.D5395 2010
  261.2—dc22
                        2010019115

Manufactured in the U.S.A.

14 13 12 11 10 1 2 3 4 5 6 7 8 9 10

Contents

Introduction

John B. Cobb Jr.

Today many of us Christians live in intimate relations with persons who belong to other religious communities. Many of these people draw forth our respect. Sadly, some Christians think that they are betraying or watering down their own faith when they feel admiration for other forms of faith. This book argues quite the contrary. Faithfulness to Christ leads us to such admiration. The question for us is how Christians are called to rethink our faith in light of the challenges posed to us by other traditions.

The authors are "progressive" Christians. This is the label that has been adopted by many Christians who, like us, seek both to continue and to modify our "liberal" heritage, which adjusted Christian thinking to the discoveries of the sciences and the growing understanding of history. We are heirs of the "Social Gospel," a movement that was widespread early in the twentieth century, which understood Jesus' central proclamation of the "Kingdom of God" to direct his followers today to work for peace and justice. We have internalized the criticisms of this movement by Reinhold Niebuhr and the theologians of liberation to such an extent that we need a new name by which to call ourselves. We have also expanded our understanding of God's purposes for the world by appropriating the concerns of the ecological movement.[1]

The authors of this book have found our own commitment to Christianity deepened by our interfaith involvements. Some Christians who seek a new relation to other religious traditions want to emphasize what all religious traditions have in common and to deemphasize, or even abandon, what is distinctive in the Christian tradition. We reject this approach. We do not serve humanity best by abandoning the distinctive wisdom and truth that has been entrusted to us. We do not ask such a sacrifice of any other community. We enrich one another through our differences.

As Christians we approach other communities from our Christocentric commitment. It is our effort to be faithful to Jesus that leads us to repent of our sins against other religious communities and to open ourselves to learning from them. In this learning our faith is changed. We believe that through this change we become more faithful.

We are convinced that it is not enough to develop a new stance toward "other religions" in general. They vary greatly, and our relation to each requires separate consideration. We need to understand the teachings and practices of other traditions and also the often ugly history of our relation to them. Only then can we rethink our own teachings and reshape our relations with them. Accordingly, much of the book deals with the past.

If by "religious pluralism" we mean only the recognition that there is a diversity of religious traditions and communities, then Christians have always lived in the context of religious pluralism. There have always been other forms of religious life and community in the world inhabited by Christians. The existence of these others has always been important to the Christian imagination.

Indeed, this experience was most vivid in the first centuries of Christian history. It became an important topic for theologians in the nineteenth century and for Christians, on a wide scale, in the twentieth century. Only in this period did the contemporary meaning of religious pluralism emerge: a multiplicity of religious movements through which people find authentic meaning and valuable truth. It is out of the nineteenth and twentieth century reflection on this topic that our own views have been shaped.

The positive appreciation of others has roots in the early centuries. Christians were appreciatively aware of the religious philosophies of the Greeks. These they did not dismiss or view with contempt. Sometimes they claimed that Greek philosophy was inspired by ancient Hebrew wisdom, but even when they recognized its separate origins, they admired its insight. The New Testament itself is influenced by it, especially by Stoicism. Early Christian thinkers adopted and adapted Platonic and, later, Neoplatonic thinking. What emerged as official Christian theology in both East and West was a synthesis of biblical and Greek philosophical insights.

However, the general attitude to the religious practices of others was negative. Jews and Christians saw the surrounding religious culture as idolatrous and polytheistic. Christians followed Jews in rejecting this culture and insisting that there is only one God, a God who cannot be depicted in a statue.

The most difficult problem was the demand of the Roman Empire for worship of the Emperor. Jews refused so stubbornly that the empire gave them special dispensation, although they were not free from persecution. During the period of Paul's missionary travels, the Jews were expelled from Rome. Christians gained some protection from persecution by claiming to share in the Jewish exemption from worship of the emperor. But persecution of Christians was, from time to time, quite severe.

The remaining issue was how to understand Judaism. This was the most difficult question. For a couple of centuries, Christians understood themselves in sibling rivalry with Jews. Initially, the Christians had no scriptures other than the Jewish ones. The new movement was a Jewish sect, with its distinctive interpretation of these writings.

Sadly, this closeness did not lead to harmonious or even friendly relations in many instances. Sometimes Jewish leaders punished those Jews who joined the new sect. This led to bitterness on the part of Christians. The extremely harsh statements about Jews in the Gospel of John may have been in response to such treatment. All the Gospels shift much of the blame for the crucifixion from the Roman authorities to the Jews. These distortions often poisoned Christian thinking about Jews and continue to do so even today. Increasingly, Christians defined themselves over against Jews, claiming the divine covenant for themselves and accusing the Jews of the terrible crime of killing their messiah.

The medieval period added Islam to this list of "others." The Muslims, like the Jews, were called "infidels" because they did not believe that Jesus was a divine being. There were occasional examples of good relations between Christians and Muslims, but these were more likely to be in contexts where Muslims were in control, especially in southern Spain. The dominant history was one of warfare. Christians fought Muslims for the Holy Land, and Muslims conquered much of Spain and the Balkans. Few kind words were spoken about the military enemy! At the same time, Christians drew heavily on Muslim scholarship for their knowledge of ancient Greek philosophy and science.

During the era of exploration and colonization, Western Christians encountered in Africa and the Western Hemisphere indigenous people with religious practices that the Christians regarded as "heathen." The response was to enslave and convert them. Centuries passed before Christians began to appreciate the spiritual wisdom in those cultures.

In South and East Asia, on the other hand, they encountered civilizations whose religious and philosophical ideas they could not so easily dismiss. Although these encounters affected the experience of most Christians only marginally, they did raise important theoretical issues for a few. The most important, historically speaking, was the status of Confucianism.

Christian theology was formulated in such an exclusivist way that if Confucianism was understood to be "a religion," then a convert to Christianity must reject it altogether. However, although Confucianism certainly had a religious tinge, its primary role in China was social, ethical, and political. Chinese society and government was Confucian through and through. Really to reject Confucian practices and teachings would be to separate oneself quite radically from Chinese life and society.

The Jesuits saw that asking the Chinese to abandon Confucianism in accepting Christianity made the acceptance of Christianity extremely difficult. In the seventeenth century the papacy recognized the need of adapting to local cultures in East Asia, and the Jesuits gained great influence in the Chinese court. However, the Dominicans objected strongly to what they saw as heathen practices allowed to Christians, and they persuaded the Pope in the early eighteenth century to forbid Christians to participate in basic Chinese ceremonies. This led the Chinese emperor to withdraw support of Christianity. If the popes had followed the Jesuit lead, the Chinese court might well have become Christian, and many of the people might have followed.

In general, however, the Catholic missions of the sixteenth and seventeenth centuries and the Protestant missions of the nineteenth century assumed that to become a Christian required abandonment of previous religious commitments. Catholics were more willing than Protestants to include existing practices of converts in the new churches. But the assumption was that salvation was only through Christ. Only in the twentieth century was serious consideration given to the saving power of traditions other than Christianity.

Despite the long-held assumption that universal conversion to Christianity is the one goal in relating to those who are not already Christian, these brief comments show that Christians have always dealt with diverse "others" in different ways. These differences came strongly into view again in the twentieth century. In that century the study of world religions or the history of religions became a standard part of Western college education. Within theology the "theology of religions" gained increasing attention. This book is a contribution to this new discipline.

With regard to the theological issue of how Christians should understand others, however, there continues to be a tendency to ask the question in quite general ways. How should Christians view "other religions?" Some leading scholars in the field of theology of religions tell us that we should choose our answer from among such options as exclusivism, inclusivism, and pluralism. Exclusivism means that we continue the view that however interesting other religious traditions may be, they cannot offer salvation. Only Christians can be saved. Inclusivism is the doctrine that Christ has been savingly at work not only among Christians but in other religious communities as well. In this context "pluralism" usually means that Christianity is one of several paths up the mountain of salvation. These options are often discussed in some abstraction from the detailed study of the other religious traditions.

Fortunately, alongside this abstract discussion of the Christian response to religious diversity there is a large amount of literature dealing with the relation of Christianity and specific other traditions. The most extensive literature has dealt with Judaism. Probably Buddhism comes next. Today Islam has become a topic of special interest. Hans Küng has produced a series of excellent volumes that deal with these relations one by one.

This book is a contribution to the task Küng has pioneered so richly. It makes no pretense of exhaustiveness. We are asking a quite limited question. What can we, as progressive Christians, learn from our study of the history of the relations of Christianity with other traditions and from their unique wisdom? How can we help to reformulate the Christian faith in light of what we learn?

The first chapter opens the discussion by reflecting on our current situation, especially where the authors live, in southern California, where the experience of religious diversity is part of everyday life. The chapter calls for mutual appreciation and openness, and it argues that this is faithful to Christ. It offers biblical interpretations supportive of this view. And it points out that our task is to think through our relations to each of the other religious traditions in their distinctive terms. So many persons were involved in its writing that we have not listed an author.

Although there are many traditions, and each poses different challenges, we believe that carefully chosen examples will suffice to indicate the sorts of changes progressive Christians need to make and to commend to Christians generally. For example, there are indigenous cultures around the world—each of which has its distinctive insights and experience with Christianity. Of these, we deal only with Native Americans. This is not at all to say that we do not have much to learn elsewhere, from the indigenous traditions of Africa, for example, or from Korean shamanism, or from Japanese Shinto. We encourage continuation of studies and encounters with all of these and others. Still we think our example suggests the kinds of challenges that are posed.

We have dealt similarly with the great religious traditions of South and East Asia. We have chosen Buddhism and focused on just one of its many forms. Clearly much additional interaction with these traditions is desirable and enriching. But we think that Buddhism serves to indicate something of the nature of the challenges they pose.

Our treatments of these two traditions are themselves quite different. This is partly a matter of chance due to the perspectives of the authors of the two chapters. But it also expresses our sense of the profound difference in the current relation of Christianity to Buddhism and to Native American traditions. Buddhism is now a strong missionary movement in the United States. There are many dialogues going on between Christians and Buddhists. Dickson Yagi, the author of the chapter on Buddhism, has lived in the midst of this situation. He is a Christian who grew up in a Buddhist family in Hawaii, spent much of his life as a Baptist missionary in Japan, practices Zen meditation, and engages in extensive dialogue with Buddhist thinkers. He shares his experience and reflection in the midst of this internal and external dialogue. The reader is invited into this thoughtful and richly informed conversation.

Ward McAfee has written the chapter on the Native American challenge in close relation to Jack Jackson, a Christian Native American. We thought initially that we needed to retell the story of the genocidal treatment of Native Americans and their culture by our Christian ancestors. But Jackson thought that would serve little purpose. It would challenge us to express shame and regret but little more. Jackson believes that Native Americans understand at a deep level what is lacking in Western Christianity. He wanted us to learn from Native Americans, some of whom are Christian and some of whom have rejected Christianity. They challenge us to reimagine and rethink the world in ways that we can now, at last, recognize as urgent.

Our chapters on the other Abrahamic traditions seemed to require a very different treatment, focusing on the history of our relations. It is our current awareness of how our teachings have contributed to the horrors of this history that primarily challenges us to change. Further, we did not feel that we could select just one of these siblings to represent them both. The historical relation of Christianity to Islam is profoundly different from its relation to Judaism. This leads to important differences also at the present time.

Eva Fleischner, the author of the chapter on Judaism, has devoted much of her professional life to spreading and deepening an appreciative understanding of Judaism, especially in her Catholic context. Her work has been recognized and affirmed by the Vatican. She was one of three Catholics appointed along with three Jews to study the record of papal actions in relation to Jews during the Nazi period.

The author of the chapter on Islam, Ward McAfee, has been mentioned above in connection with his work with Jack Jackson to make the challenge of the Native American thought come alive in the Christian sensibility. He has recently retired from a career as a historian, especially of the United States, but also of world religions. Currently he works as a United Methodist lay person in relating his congregation to local Muslims and issues involving Islam.

The very different character of the treatments of other traditions serves to emphasize our opposition to the one-size-fits-all approach to a theology of religions. Further, we are saying less about our theological understanding of other traditions and more about how we need to change and rethink ourselves in light of our encounters with them. This topic appears, at least implicitly, in the four chapters that follow the more general one. However, since we consider this to be the primary focus of the book as a whole, it is the single topic of the concluding chapter.

The senior editor of this volume and the writer of the concluding chapter is John B. Cobb Jr., a retired professor of theology from the Claremont School of Theology. He has been active in interreligious dialogue with Buddhists, Jews, and Muslims. Among his previous books, two are particularly relevant to this one. They are *Christ in a Pluralistic Age* and *Beyond Dialogue: The Mutual Transformation of Buddhism and Christianity.*

These chapters were written by members of the Reflection Committee of Progressive Christians Uniting. They have all been extensively discussed in the Committee and rewritten several times. This has been a rich learning experience for the members of the Committee, who no doubt are those who profit most from the work on these topics. When the Committee is ready, the papers are sent for approval to the Board of Progressive Christians Uniting, a primarily activist organization that works closely with churches. It takes stands on issues and engages in programs that official church bodies have difficulty in treating. When the Board is satisfied, these essays become position papers of the organization. They, and the books that contain them, belong to Progressive Christians Uniting.

Two other volumes of the work of the Reflection Committee have been published. The first, *Progressive Christians Speak,* is a collection of position papers on current issues. The second book, *Resistance: The New Role of Progressive Christians*, is a more integrated volume that undertakes to redefine the relation of progressive Christians to American culture. The present volume locates progressive Christianity in relation to other religious traditions. We hope that it advances this discussion in ways that will prove helpful to many Christians.

ONE

Rethinking Christian Faith in the Context of Religious Diversity

John B. Cobb Jr.

The Story

"I was all set to choose Yoko—she knows the job and she seems like a good person to work with. But I don't see how we could have a Buddhist as the financial secretary of a Methodist church. The financial secretary has to interact with our members. How would Mrs. Stanhope feel if she knew she was talking to a Buddhist?"

"But you said that Yoko was by far the best qualified of the applicants. Of course our financial secretary needs to work with our members—to respect them and their religion. How does she feel about working in a church?

"She told me that some of her family are Christians, but that when she began to think for herself, she found more depth and reality in the old tradition of her grandparents. She doesn't seem at all defensive or want to argue about religious differences."

Yoko was hired, and five years later, the church administrator made the following comment: "How good that we chose Yoko. All this time she has kept our accounts perfectly. She says she is an even stronger Buddhist than she was when she came to work for us, but she always has shown respect for our ways too. We have grown to trust each other, not only about money but about understanding each other too. I think that most of our members have come to respect her kind of faith a lot more than they did at the start."

Introduction

Few questions are more troubling to Christians today than how to understand our faith in relation to the diversity of ways our friends and neighbors think and live. From the Reformation down through the nineteenth century, in the Christian West the issue of religious diversity was chiefly a matter of the multiple forms of Christianity; and after a period in which Christians fought against and persecuted one another over their differences, they agreed to live and let live. In the U.S. Protestants developed an understanding of "denominations" as Christian organizations with particular and distinctive emphases that recognized one another as equally Christian bodies. Of course, not all Christians have accepted this solution. There are still Protestant groups that are far more exclusivist, believing that the rest of us are committing serious errors that cannot be tolerated. And while Roman Catholics and Eastern Orthodox have accepted the role of being denominations among others for practical purposes, their official positions are not this egalitarian. Nevertheless, the problem in its acute form, both sociologically and theologically, has been largely resolved for many Christians. For them ecumenical dialogue has replaced hostility or isolation.

Today, the burning issue for Christians in America, as for Christians in Asia and Africa, is the relation of Christianity to other religious communities. We Americans now live in a much more religiously diverse society. This diversity is especially marked in California. Since the student body of seventeen thousand students at the Irvine campus of the University of California is the most culturally diverse in the system, the school annually holds a Religious Diversity Faire in which many religious traditions have opportunities to present themselves to the general public in panels, lectures, and demonstrations led by educators and theologians, who are clergy, lay, and Catholic sisters. Events like these heighten awareness that southern Californians live among Protestants, Catholics, Eastern Orthodox, Jews, Muslims, Bahá'ís, Hindus, Sikhs, Buddhists, Confucians, Taoists, and Native Americans who practice their traditional ways.

The awareness of religious diversity leads some Christians to intensify their view that only through belief in Jesus Christ can anyone be saved. Others assume that this is what a Christian must believe and, for just that reason, distance themselves from the church altogether. We believe that a vital Christian faith calls for positive appreciation of other religious traditions and for rethinking tradition to make this explicit.

This chapter is divided into two major parts. The first part describes ways in which Christians can respond to this awareness of religious diversity in faithfulness to scripture and tradition without negative teachings about other traditions that have characterized most of our past. The second part offers resources for understanding the richness of the diversity within which we live. It sets this in the context of a history of the increase of religious diversity in the United States. The brief accounts of nine religious communities (other than Christian ones) have been developed in careful interaction with persons who participate in these communities or have strong sympathies toward them. The paper concludes with practical proposals of actions that congregations can take to express their appreciative relation to other religious communities.

Transforming Christian Teaching

Biblical History

The Jewish scriptures that have been transformed into the Christian Old Testament are not preoccupied with the question of religious diversity. They focus primarily on issues internal to Israel. Here there is a strong emphasis on devotion only to Israel's God and condemnation of any worship of the deities of other peoples. At least by the time of Jeremiah, the prophets were not only opposing the worship of other deities but also denying their reality. Most emphasized that the one true God worked in and through people who were even outside of the Jewish community. Some dreamed of a time when people from all over the world would come to Jerusalem to worship God and learn Torah.

For many Jews the conviction that they alone were worshipping the true God led to an intensification of their devotion and willingness to sacrifice for their faith. The stories of Joseph, David, and Esther encouraged Jews in diaspora to remain monotheistic. The prophets often spoke of God's working with foreign forces. Jews resisted any interference in their religious observance so fiercely that they won special consideration from their Roman rulers. Some Jews drew the conclusion that they should also seek to convert gentiles to the Jewish faith. Jesus is quoted as having been sharply critical of Jewish missions of this sort (Matt 23:15). In any case, many gentiles were attracted to Jewish synagogues apart from missionary efforts.

Jesus, like most Jewish teachers of his time, addressed himself primarily to other Jews. He had definite views about what God required of them, and he was sharply critical of what he saw as distortions of true Jewish teaching and practice. Under special circumstances, he extended his ministry to gentiles who asked for his help.

The first communities of followers were Jews. They contested with other Jewish groups, especially the Pharisees, for influence among the Jewish people. This conflict led to strong language by Jesus' followers against their Jewish rivals, condemning them for their refusal to accept Jesus as the Messiah. Exclusivist statements were made implying that those Jews who rejected Jesus could not be saved. Some of this language was attributed to Jesus himself.

The writings that became the Gospels grew, in part, out of these inner-Jewish controversies. Taken out of their context in the struggle of a Jewish sect against more powerful groups of Jews, they have led later generations of Christians to extreme forms of anti-Judaism. This problem of Christian anti-Judaism is so distinctive and so important that it requires separate treatment beyond what can be said here.

At a very early stage in the development of the Jesus movement, the conviction that Jesus had freed his followers from Jewish ceremonial law led to the removal of the barriers that Judaism in general had placed in the way of gentile conversions. The greatest barrier had been the requirement of circumcision. The decision that this was not necessary made the Jesus movement attractive to the gentiles who were already associated in a secondary status with Jewish synagogues dispersed throughout the Roman Empire. It also freed members of the Jesus movement, such as Paul, to express the missionary logic of the belief that the God of Israel was the only true God. Hence, it was in its Christian form that the Jewish heritage spread throughout the Roman Empire, eventually becoming dominant.

Until Christians became politically powerful, the exclusivist teachings found in Christian scriptures were not a major problem. The primary quest of the early Christians had been for freedom to practice their own convictions and to share them with others. But once Christianity gained political power, its exclusivist claim led it to seek the suppression of competing communities. There is much in the ensuing history of which we can only repent.

New Testament Texts

Let us look now at some of the texts that have seemed to many Christians to justify the denial of religious value to other traditions and communities. Do these texts imply just the meanings that have typically been drawn from them? If so, must we simply reject these biblical teachings or can we understand them better?

Many of the verses that most disturb us today are from the Gospel of John. Here much is placed on the lips of Jesus that is radically different from what he says in the Synoptic Gospels: Matthew, Mark, and Luke. Generations of scholars have argued that few, if any, of these discourses are actually verbatim expressions of Jesus' own teaching.

That does not mean that Christians should take these teachings lightly. They express the convictions of Christian believers of an early generation. Whether these Christians themselves thought that the historical Jesus spoke in this way, we do not know. But they certainly believed that these sayings were of God.

Perhaps the most difficult passage for those who refuse to condemn all who find life and meaning in other communities is John 3:17-21. There we are told that "those who do not believe are condemned already" (18). The belief in question is in the Son whom God sent into the world. "The light has come into the world, and people loved darkness rather than light because their deeds were evil" (19).

This verse certainly points to a sharp separation between those who were drawn to the divine light that shone through Jesus and those who refused to acknowledge that light. The context of this saying is the Jewish community in which Jesus lived. The idea can apply directly only to those who actually encountered Jesus. We may feel that it is unfair to the Jews who rejected him during his ministry, but the point is not meaningless in that context. If we share with the author the belief that the light of God was embodied in Jesus with extraordinary clarity and purity, then we can also share the view that how people responded to him expressed something very fundamental about themselves.

In any case, according to this text, those who fail to respond to Jesus are simply left in the darkness and wickedness in which they were already immersed. No further evil is imposed upon them. If there are those who have escaped from that darkness and wickedness by other means, they too, presumably, would remain in the new condition they have reached. Whatever blessedness they have attained remains theirs, however they have reached it. There is no suggestion that Jesus came to destroy what was good in the world to which he came. Hence, even these seemingly exclusivist verses do not have the meaning the church has too often read into them.

Over the centuries Jesus has been presented to people in more and more diverse forms. In some cases, what it has meant to people to encounter what they understand by "Jesus" has not been good news. If the "Jesus" some encounter is one who demands obedience to the church in order to avoid eternal hellfire, both acceptance and rejection have entirely different meanings from those proffered in the Bible. If other people encounter a "Jesus" who requires them to repudiate a rich tradition of wisdom in order to enter a pietistic and exclusivist community, their refusal does not imply that they "love darkness." On the other side, there are many who are drawn to the Jesus of the Gospels who see no reason to abandon their own communities and join a Christian church. Gandhi is the most famous example, but there have been many others.

One way of reading the Gospel of John is in light of the prologue. There we learn that the true subject of speech and action in the Gospel is actually the word (logos) who became incarnate in Jesus. This word was with God from the beginning and was, indeed, divine.

If we consider in this light the apparently exclusivist statement placed on the lips of Jesus, "I am the way, the truth, and the life" (John 14:6), the implication is far less disturbing. It is the word of God that is the way, the truth, and the life as affirmed in the Psalter (see Psalm 119:105). Certainly Christians believe that that word was incarnate in Jesus and that the word's meaning for us was revealed in him. In the Gospel of John, that meaning is that God loves us and that we should love God and one another. Since the word who is incarnate in Jesus is also the one through whom all things were made and who enlightens everyone (John 1:3-4), we should expect that divine wisdom is to be found also among those who know nothing of Jesus and who find deep meaning in other traditions.

Many find the conclusion of the verse still more troubling: "No one comes to the Father except through me." Again, if we understand that the "me" in question is the word of which we read in the prologue, we need not see this assertion as denying access to God to all who do not relate primarily to the historical Jesus. Since nothing came into being except through the word, and since the word is the light of understanding in all people, it is not surprising that we cannot come to God apart from that word.

The use of the Christian doctrine of the word (or *logos*) to make the gospel credible to nonbelievers and to remind believers of truth and wisdom found outside the Christian sphere is not a recent innovation. It was a major factor in the early church, justifying especially the great appreciation of Plato among Christian theologians. In the scholastic theology that culminated in Saint Thomas, when arguments were assembled for and against a proposed thesis, Greek and Roman thinkers uninfluenced by Christian scriptures were often cited as authorities alongside Christian theologians and biblical passages. In general the church assumed that God's wisdom could be found even apart from her incarnation in Jesus, although its normative embodiment for Christians is always Jesus Christ.

The New Testament Understanding of Salvation

Texts that have led Christians to exclusivist conclusions are found in other parts of the New Testament as well (for example, Acts 4:12). Each requires separate treatment. But it may be even more important to consider broader questions about the salvation that is supposed to be exclusive to Christians.

Many suppose that the standard Christian teaching is that of judgment after death, with the saved going to heaven and the damned going to hell. They then understand that Christians teach that the criterion by which this judgment is made is a particular kind of belief in and about Jesus Christ. Accordingly, many suppose that to accept Christianity is to believe that members of all other religious communities are destined for hell. Such people read the exclusivist tendencies of the verses discussed above, as well as others, from this perspective. The resulting revulsion against Christianity is understandable and even admirable. We might say it is truly Christian.

It is important to recognize that this combination of doctrines is nowhere clearly taught in the New Testament. The passage in the Gospels that speaks most clearly about a final judgment that will divide the saved from the damned is Matthew 25:31-46. Here the criterion for inheriting the kingdom provided by God has to do with feeding the hungry, giving drink to the thirsty, clothing the naked, caring for the sick, and visiting prisoners. Nothing is said of having faith in Jesus Christ. Nothing in the passage implies that Buddhists or Muslims would be excluded from the kingdom if they have cared for their neighbors, or that those who identify themselves as believers in Jesus Christ will be rewarded simply for that belief.

Another of the few Gospel passages that speak of final judgment is Luke 16:19-31. Here again belief in Jesus Christ plays no role in the destinies of Lazarus and the rich man. The rich man is punished because he did not heed the law and the prophets. The story goes on to say that people like him will not heed even one who returns from the dead to warn them of the consequences of their actions.

Far more central to Jesus' teaching as presented in the Synoptic Gospels is the coming of the realm of God. This is the longed-for situation in which God's will is done on earth as it is in heaven. In the community surrounding Jesus there is already a foretaste of that situation. Also, to be a part of that community is to pray for the coming of this New Age and to live by its values as they reverse the values of this world. But in most of the pronouncements, there is no suggestion that those who fail to believe in Jesus Christ are to be excluded or that God cannot work through those who are not believers in bringing the new situation to pass.

Paul also affirms that we are judged in terms of our righteousness. "There will be anguish and distress for everyone who does evil, the Jew first and also the Greek, and honor and peace for everyone who does good, the Jew first and also the Greek" (Rom 2:9). But Paul enriches the picture because of his doubt that when judged by our own righteousness any of us can justify ourselves. Hence he emphasizes the importance of God's grace, a gift that we cannot earn but, instead, receive through faith. Through faith we participate in the righteousness of Jesus Christ. Paul speaks ecstatically about the gifts that come to believers. He does not speak of punishments being meted out to those who do not believe. They are simply left in the sinful and degraded situation into which Paul believes their failure to acknowledge God has brought them.

Obviously, there is no discussion in Paul of how other great spiritual teachers, such as those in India, responded to the human condition. They tended, like Paul, to view it bleakly. Like him, they proposed radical ways of escaping it. To take Paul's enthusiasm for the new way opened up by Jesus Christ as a condemnation of other ways of whose existence he was entirely ignorant is hardly persuasive.

Historical Developments

We must acknowledge that the picture of our ultimate destiny as heaven or hell, with this decided by our beliefs rather than by our relationship to other people, became widespread in the Christian tradition. It led conscientious Christians to engage in strenuous efforts to convert those who did not believe. It often promoted this conversion in some separation from the concern for justice and righteousness. Conscientious Christians have done much evil because of this set of doctrines. Matters have been even worse when conversion has been associated with the expansion of national and imperial rule. The church's role in the European invasion and conquest of Latin America is full of horror stories, beginning with genocide of the natives of the Caribbean islands. In North America the situation was little better. Further, the Christianity to which native peoples were to be converted was identified with the culture of the converters. The leadership of Christian churches in the effort to force Native Americans to assimilate into Euro-American culture is an especially ugly chapter in this history. All too often missions have served, and even now continue to serve, colonial masters, providing justification for their greed.

Since in the modern age Europeans and Euro-Americans carried on most of the missionary work, and since they tended to be patronizing, at best, and contemptuous, at worst, toward persons of other ethnicities or races, modern Christian missions have often been racist. Indeed, some Christians used the Bible to justify the enslavement of other races. Black Africans suffered most from this perversion of Christianity. Even now, when there is universal recognition that the Bible stands against slavery, subtler forms of racism continue to pervade the behavior of predominantly white churches.

Fortunately, there have been other ways of understanding Christianity and other types of missionary activity. None has been perfect, but in an imperfect world, they can be celebrated all the same. For example, one of the great modern Christian missions was to China in the sixteenth and seventeenth centuries. The Jesuits were far from contemptuous of Chinese civilization. They found much in it that they recognized as superior to the European civilization of the time. They thought highly of the Confucian teaching that so richly informed Chinese life. Nevertheless, they believed that they had in Jesus Christ something of great value to offer China. They persuaded many of the leaders of China that this was true. Some converted to Christianity. More were ready to do so if they could be assured that this would not involve abandonment of the Confucian teaching, culture, and way of life on which Chinese governance was based.

The Jesuits agreed with the Chinese that rejection of Confucianism should not be required as a condition of becoming Christian. But they needed the agreement of the papacy. The papacy vacillated over a long period of time, and the Chinese court finally rejected Christianity in disgust.

Even in missions that were much more closely tied to Western imperialism, there were missionaries who did not separate the gospel from justice. Many supported the causes of colonized people against the colonizers or at least undertook to moderate the exploitation the colonizers inflicted. Furthermore, even if unintentionally, they gave to colonized people a Bible that could empower them in their quest for liberation.

The connection between the gospel and meeting the needs of those to whom it was brought was especially prominent in the missionary movement that came to prominence in the late nineteenth century and caught the imagination of the churches in the first decades of the twentieth. Much of this movement was closely related to the Social Gospel. Here the understanding of the gospel did not have to do with rescuing people from hell but with bringing them into participation in God's realm where God's will is done. The missionaries taught the gospel of God's loving concern for each individual and for society as a whole and God's call to believers to share in working for the coming of God's realm. They understood this work to involve education, improving the position of women, health care, agricultural development, democracy, and greater economic justice as well as peace and goodwill among nations. They planted churches that would nurture this whole range of concerns as well as ministering to more personal needs.

Needless to say, there are many valid criticisms of these efforts as well. But they demonstrate that Christians can be motivated by their faith to devote themselves to the overall betterment of others in some independence of whether they accept Christian beliefs. Much of the Christian missionary activity of the old-line American denominations has this character today.

Early in the century, some missionaries developed an appreciative relation to other religious traditions, and in the Second World Missionary Conference, meeting in Jerusalem in 1928, there was talk of a common front of the world's religious communities against the rising power of secularism and atheism. The subsequent rise to dominance of Barthian theology pushed this type of missionary thinking aside for fifty years.

It is, therefore, a mistake to think that past Christian teaching about how we should relate to people belonging to other religious traditions is to be equated with the idea that Christians should rescue the heathen from an eternity in Hell by evoking their belief in Christian teaching. To reject that formula today is not to initiate a new type of Christianity but to side with some emphases in the New Testament and the tradition against others. Nevertheless, it would also be a mistake to suppose that we can find in the tradition ready-made answers to the questions that our new, radically pluralistic situation drives us to ask.

Widespread Contemporary Responses to Religious Diversity: Exclusivism and Pluralism

Christianity has not been alone among the religious traditions in viewing itself as the one way. The tension between such an exclusivist claim and open appreciation of other traditions is felt in a number of communities today. Some resolve the issue by a measure of indifference as to what happens to other traditions as long as they are themselves left alone to pursue their way. Many Jews and Native Americans respond in this way. Others have a keen interest in sharing their insights and wisdom with others. The United States has been a fertile mission field, especially for Hindus and Buddhists. Happily, their missions have not been tainted with connections to imperialism or colonialism or racism. A third response has been a keen interest in coming to fuller mutual understanding and appreciation of one another through dialogue and cooperation.

We Christians have a valid interest in how members of other communities work out their responses to the pluralistic situation in which we are all engulfed. We may profit from learning how they adapt and adjust, and we may develop ideas that are helpful to them. But as Christians, our primary task is to work out our Christian response, leaving to others the freedom to work out theirs.

Among Christians, it seems, there are two responses that come most easily to mind, and these lead to a sharp polarization among us. Many seem, wrongly, to suppose that these are the only possibilities. They are often called (a) "exclusivism" and (b) "pluralism."

Exclusivism and Its Limitations. Exclusivists hold that whatever positive values other religious traditions have, they do not save their adherents. Only

Christian faith is salvific. Similarly, whatever merits other religious leaders or founders may have, they cannot offer the ultimate truth that is given only in Jesus Christ. Exclusivists may affirm that we should be respectful of others and give them religious freedom. They may agree that Christians should repent for much that we have done to others in the past. But they are convinced that this in no way counters the truth that between Christian faith and all other religious activities and attitudes there is a great difference. Only in the former is there ultimate truth and salvation. They believe that to give up the view that Jesus Christ is the one Lord and Savior of all people is to abandon Christian faith itself. The basic stance of Christians toward adherents of other religious traditions, in the exclusivist view, should be to seek their conversion to Christianity. For exclusivists, only this effort adequately expresses Christian love.

Our formulations above express our rejection of this view. We are called to approach other religious communities with full respect for their experience and the affirmations they have been led to make. We should not assume the superiority of our experience and convictions but should be eager to learn from others.

Pluralism and its Limitations. Many of those with whom we share this position call themselves "pluralists." Christian pluralists do not question the truth and saving value to be found in Christianity, but they see no reason to suppose that Christianity is the *only* path to truth and salvation. Instead they believe that there are multiple ways of attaining salvation, and they often use the image of many paths up the same mountain. What other paths there are is to be learned as we encounter other religious communities and see the positive effects their beliefs and practices have on the lives of their members. Pluralists believe that all religious traditions should be judged by their effectiveness in mediating salvation to their members. They may disagree as to exactly what this salvation consists in, but they share the conviction that there is a common goal toward which all religious traditions are directed.

Christian pluralists usually concede to exclusivists that there are strong exclusivist tendencies in both scripture and tradition. But they point out that this is true of other religious traditions as well. Today, pluralists are convinced, we are in a position to view all of the religious traditions with more objectivity and detachment. In this perspective, we appreciate the achievements of all, but we see that most have failed to recognize adequately the diversity of paths to salvation. Pluralists call for all religious traditions to give up their exclusivist claims.

We agree with pluralists that all the great religious traditions deserve not only toleration, but also appreciation and respect. Accordingly, we share many of their views about how Christians should relate to the other traditions. First, we must work for a context in which all can flourish. Second, we will seek dialogue to increase mutual understanding wherever others are willing to engage in it. Third, we will seek relations with each tradition individually that express our appropriate connection with that community. Fourth, we will undertake to cooperate with all who are willing to do so on projects for the common good. Fifth, we will undertake to formulate our own teachings in ways that discourage any sense of our own superiority or negative attitudes toward others.

Although we appreciate the commitment of Christian pluralists to the acceptance of other religious traditions as basically equal with our own, we find their position not "pluralistic" enough. It fails to appreciate the depth of differences among the traditions. These differences are not simply in the way they perceive a common goal but also in their conception of the goal itself. Instead of assuming that they are all different paths up the same mountain, we need to recognize that in some cases they lead up different mountains.

One problem with what we have called "pluralism" above is that it asks each tradition to relativize its affirmations. It rejects the universal claims of all traditions. It supposes that only in this way can believers in one community accept believers in other communities on an equal basis.

The rejection of all universal claims has results that are in deep conflict with our historic beliefs. For example, the relativization of the idea that God loves all people is problematic for Christians. We have always supposed that this is true even for those who do not recognize its truth. To be told that its truth is limited to the Christian community is deeply disturbing and contrary to our understanding of the whole of reality. To think in that way could have quite negative practical consequences.

Furthermore, this rejection of all universal claims is equally disturbing to persons in other religious communities. The relativization of Buddhist teaching, for example, is just as difficult for a Buddhist to accept as the relativization of Christian teaching is for a Christian. Buddhists believe that Buddha-nature characterizes all things whatsoever. They understand that only Buddhists may recognize this, but they do not believe that it is true only for them. To say that Buddha-nature is the true nature of all things only for Buddhists is as troubling to Buddhists as the statement that God's love for all is true only for Christians is troubling for Christians.

A Fuller Pluralism. A deeper appreciation for difference, a more authentic pluralism, is possible. Instead of asking each religious community to relativize its claims, we may find that the universal truth of the claims of one tradition is not in contradiction with the universal truth of the claims of another tradition. Perhaps Buddhists are correct that all creatures are instances of Buddha-nature. This can be explained in language that does not entail the word "Buddha." Indeed, it is often formulated in terms of "emptiness" or "dependent origination." The point is that all things are impermanent and insubstantial. Nothing exists independently. Each thing or event comes into being out of the conjunction of other things and participates in the coming to be of other things. The Buddhist goes on to say that when we recognize this about all things, and especially about ourselves, we experience the world as it truly is and are freed from the illusions that bind us to it. We can live in true freedom, wise and compassionate.

One may agree or disagree with Buddhists about the nature of reality. But there is nothing in these universal claims that conflicts with the Christian claim that God loves all persons. Buddhists may not believe this, but their failure to believe is not caused by their affirmation of the universality of Buddha-nature unless Christians formulate belief in God in a way that contradicts this Buddhist teaching. Christians need not do this. Hence, in principle, the universal claims of both Buddhism and Christianity may be true. Rather than relativizing both, and thereby denying the truth of the deepest convictions of both Buddhists and Christians, one may affirm both. One may do so, not because they are two ways of saying the same thing, or because they point to two ways of attaining the same end, but because they are answers to different questions and suggest different goals for human life.

This way of dealing with the otherness of Buddhism does not work well with Islam. In this relation we must recognize far more similarities. Allah is the Muslim name for the God of the Bible. There are many ways of understanding Allah among Muslims, and there are many ways of understanding God among Christians, but all of these are ways of understanding the God of Israel; and these Muslim and Christian ways of understanding overlap extensively. Muhammad was very much aware of Christianity, and he was, in many ways, respectful toward it. We worship the same God.

In some ways that makes our relations with Islam more difficult than our relations with Buddhism. Muhammad gave high honor to Jesus, affirming, for example, his Virgin Birth. But he rejected the doctrines of incarnation and Trinity. These have often been the points of chief dispute between the two traditions. The "pluralists" we have discussed above can argue that these doctrines work for Christians but have no universal truth, but this is not a satisfactory solution.

Many Christians today, however, would share Muhammad's rejection of the doctrine of the Trinity as he understood it. He thought that the doctrine of the Trinity denied the unity of God, and he shared with Jews a strong commitment to that unity. In fact, however, classic explanations of the Trinity, especially in the West, insist that the unity of the three persons of the Trinity is to be preserved. One may question the success of some of these formulations in adequately preserving the unity, but the intention is not at odds with Islamic concerns. Christians believe in one God, not three Gods. Muslims (like Jews) also recognize that there are many names for God, highlighting different aspects of the way God relates to the world.

In relation to Islam, the great need is for Christians to develop a far more positive appreciation of Muhammad's prophetic role and of the teaching of the Qur'an, as for example its deep concern for the poor and its toleration of Jews and Christians. The Qur'an is generous in its appraisal of Jesus. Christians on the whole have not been generous in our appraisal of Muhammad and the Qur'an. For this we should repent.

Such repentance will not lead to total agreement. For example, there are teachings about the death of Jesus in the Qur'an that Christians cannot accept; and there are Christian teachings about the death and resurrection of Jesus that Muslims reject. But friendly argument in the context of mutual respect is not to be avoided. Many Christians, however, may find more agreement with many Muslims than they do with some fellow Christians. In the context of encounter and conversation, Christians are likely to be deeply impressed by the continuing success of Islam in shaping the whole lives of believers and in resisting features of modernity that are in conflict with the teachings of both traditions.

This is not the place to discuss the stance of Christians toward each of the other religious traditions separately. Enough has been said to indicate that sweeping statements about "other religions" are unlikely to be accurate or helpful. Each religious tradition should be approached on its own distinct terms. The accounts of nine religious communities present in southern California, offered in a later part of this chapter, provide a basis for considering how each is best approached by Christians.

A Third Contemporary Approach: The Transformation of Christian Teaching

Clearly, we must transform our teachings. In their dominant formulation in the past they have been negative toward other religious traditions. They must be reformulated so as to help Christians to understand that, precisely out of the depth of our faith, we are called to love and listen to others with admiration and appreciation for their lives and their insights. Rather than thinking that the acceptance of other traditions as equal partners in our society is a compromise, we must learn to see it as an expression of our faith in Christ.

The most urgent transformation of all is already taking place. Traditional Christian teaching has vilified Jews and Judaism. This has resulted in an appalling history of pogroms and other forms of persecution culminating in the Holocaust. All Christians share in responsibility for this evil, and all Christian teaching must be carefully reformulated so as, at a minimum, to avoid arousing animosity toward Jews. Positively we need to go beyond this to cultivate in Christians a deep appreciation not only for our debt to ancient Jews but also to contemporary Judaism.

In order to make the changes we need not only in our teaching about Judaism but also in our general teaching, we must overcome the Christian tendency to suppose that all the truth we require is already given to us from our Christian past. This idolatry of our heritage is repudiated within that heritage. The New Testament itself points us to the future. Paul writes: "Now we see in a mirror dimly, but then we will see face to face" (1 Cor 13:12). According to John, Jesus promised to send us the spirit of truth who will guide us into all the truth (John 16:12). More fundamentally, Jesus taught us to pray for the coming of the realm of God in which God's purposes will be fulfilled. We live toward that future, not with all the knowledge and understanding that we need, but with openness to learning from others and working with others toward that end.

There is nothing new about learning from others. The Bible itself reflects a long history of the transmission and transformation of traditions. The beliefs expressed in the preexilic period differ from postexilic ones. There is growth toward greater universality. Scholars trace the influence of Sumerian, Egyptian, Canaanite, Babylonian, Persian, and Greek ideas and culture in the history of Israel. This does not mean that the faith of Israel was syncretistic, but it does mean that Israel learned from and was repeatedly transformed by the cultural and religious achievements of other peoples.

This process continued in Christianity. There is profound Hellenistic influence in the New Testament. As Christianity became more and more gentile in its membership, Greek culture played an ever-larger role. The great thinkers of the early church incorporated much of Neoplatonic thought in their formulations of Christian theology. Aristotelian philosophy became a dominant factor in the medieval period. In general, Christians both supported the rise of natural science and also adapted their theology to what they learned from it. In the past two centuries Christians have led in historical study, including study of our own history, and many have adapted our teaching to what has been learned there. Much the same can be said of the social and psychological sciences. In short, much of Christianity has been in a continuous process of transformation through its encounter with new forms of wisdom and knowledge.

Needless to say, this process has often been controversial and has included many mistakes. Christians have needed to discriminate among the many claims for our belief, and sometimes we have failed to do this well. We have sometimes rejected what we should have accepted and accepted what we should have rejected. Later generations have had to purify the faith from cultural accretions that have distorted it. For example, we suffer now from some of the effects of Hellenization, and also from too uncritical an acceptance of the scientific worldview. But openness to learning from Greek philosophy and from the sciences has been crucial to the survival and growth of Christianity.

We now face a great new opportunity. Whereas in the past within the West the privilege of learning from the wisdom of indigenous people and from the traditions of South and East Asia was limited to a few scholars, now it is available to the masses. A Christian faith that, for good and evil, was indigenized primarily in a Hellenistic culture is encountering the religious traditions of India and China and discovering the great wisdom of indigenous people. It can gain in this encounter just as much as it gained earlier from Hellenism and science. If it does so, it will be as deeply transformed.

Our Pluralistic Context

Progressive Christians, while being conscious of the great diversity of religious groups in the United States and the world, as yet have no national consensus on the best policies for living amicably in a religiously pluralistic society. This chapter includes outlines of nine other religious faiths: Judaism, Islam, Bahá'i, Hinduism, Sikhism, Buddhism, Confucianism, Taoism, and Native American religion. How we relate to and understand them is important to our progressive Christian faith.

American History: How Our Religious Diversity Arose

Living with religious pluralism implies acceptance of religious freedom. Turning to history, we find the background of the modern concept of religious freedom in the ideas of religious toleration in seventeenth-century England and eighteenth-century America. The idea that there should be freedom of worship for different sects was at that time by no means generally accepted. Indeed, many people regarded it as an outrageous idea, to be rejected by all right-thinking people. Why should government protect the propagation of false doctrine? Others, like John Milton and John Locke in England and Roger Williams and William Penn in America, believed otherwise. In principle, if not always in practice, they thought most persons could be trusted to come to their own conclusions on political and religious matters. Hence they advocated freedom of speech, of the press, and of religious worship. Of these, Roger Williams was probably the most consistent in matching theory with practice. The fear of a Catholic monarchy affected the limits of Milton's and Locke's principles of toleration. In any case, little thought was given to freedom of religion for African slaves.

In a later generation Thomas Jefferson defended a "wall of separation" between church and state, and James Madison persuaded his fellow Congressmen to adopt the Bill of Rights. The First Amendment states: "Congress shall make no law respecting an establishment of religion, or prohibiting the free exercise thereof; or abridging the freedom of speech, or of the press, or the right of the people peaceably to assemble, and to petition the Government for a redress of grievances." It is important to note that this was originally a restriction on Federal power alone. Several states had established churches. Virginia, for example, used tax monies to support the Anglican Church. The free speech clause of the First Amendment was not applied to the states until the 1920s, and the religion clauses, not until the 1940s. Since then, the fine line between protecting free worship and not "establishing" religion has been trod in many contentious court decisions. For example, some church child-care programs have been held to be exempt from taxation, but some have not. Using Federal funds for busing students to parochial schools is legal, but buying books for them is not.

In 1800 America was a Protestant culture with small minorities of Catholics and Jews. In addition to these groups, there were several hundred thousand Native Americans, some of whom had been touched by Protestant and Catholic missions, but most of whom preserved strong Native American religious traditions. By 1900, white America displayed a three-way religious pluralism of Protestant, Catholic, and Jew. Alongside these, because of segregation, Afro-Americans had established their own churches, which were primarily Protestant but included Catholics as well as Jews of the Ethiopian persuasion.

How did the transformation of white America take place? The answer is found in the waves of immigration, which in the nineteenth century brought to our shores large numbers of both Jews and Catholics. Jewish immigration was stimulated by the reactionary Congress of Vienna (1815) and the failure of the revolutions of 1848. Large numbers of Jews sought the greater freedom of the new world. Initially these immigrants came from Germany, and therefore brought with them distinctive forms of German Reform Judaism, stressing the prophetic emphases of the Bible. Its leader in America was Isaac Mayer Wise (1819–1900), rabbi of congregations in Albany, New York, and Cincinnati, Ohio, and the founder of Hebrew Union College. Later in the nineteenth century some Jewish leaders veered away from what they thought to be the extremes of Reform Judaism and founded, in 1876, Conservative Judaism, which in doctrine lay between the Reform and Orthodox versions. When the source of immigration shifted from Germany to Poland and Russia, Orthodox Judaism made its appearance in America.

Catholics had their own reasons for immigrating to America. As a colony, Maryland had been populated early with Catholics, and the Irish potato famine of the 1850s gave Irish families the harsh alternative of migrating or starving. The Catholic bishops, hoping to maintain a vigorous Catholic presence in Protestant America, favored established religion.

None of these developments took place smoothly or easily. The nativist Know-Nothing movement of the 1850s opposed immigration and pushed virulent anti-Catholic measures. The Ku Klux Klan had as its primary purpose terrorizing blacks so as to keep them in subjection; but in both its nineteenth-century version and its 1920s revival, it judged both Catholics and Jews to be "unAmerican." By World War II, however, America was well established as a country of Protestants, Catholics, and Jews, white and segregated black.

After World War II, another pluralism was beginning to assume its distinctive shape. Like the first pluralism, it was driven by immigration, this time largely from Asia and Latin America, as families saw the United States as the "land of the free" and a source of higher income. But there were deep differences as well. The first pluralism claimed a common biblical source; the second could make no such claim. The first had three parties; the second more than doubled this number.

Among the many religious traditions that are now represented in southern California and the nation, we have selected nine. Of these, the first eight entered primarily through immigration, although in several cases they have also won many converts. These eight are Judaism, Islam, Baha'i, Hinduism, Sikhism, Buddhism, Confucianism, and Taoism. The religious traditions of Native Americans have survived the onslaught of Euro-Americans and are today enjoying a certain revival.

Nine Religious Groups[1]

Judaism. While Judaism is a party to the first and older American pluralism, it also demands inclusion as a part of the current pluralism. Judaism is, along with Christianity and Islam, a monotheistic religion. Unlike them it is not built on one founder but on a long tradition. It claims to go back to Abraham and Moses, through a line that includes the prophets and the sages of Israel. Abraham is sometimes called the "father of the Hebrew people" and Moses the "law-giver," but the sense of being an historical and uniquely chosen people is crucial.

Early Judaism arose out of the ashes of the Solomonic Temple destroyed by the Babylonians in the sixth-century B.C.E., while Rabbinic Judaism arose out of the ashes of the Second or Herodian Temple destroyed by the Romans in 70 of the Common Era.[2] Early Judaism was a highly diverse religion out of which Christianity and Rabbinic Judaism, along with the much smaller Samaritan religion, were the sole survivors.

While Judaism shares belief in one God and also shares extensive parts of the Bible with Christians, it differs from Christianity in two basic respects:

First, whereas Christianity approaches God through faith in Christ, Judaism approaches the same God by practice of Torah, or law, the gift of God to his chosen people. Second, if Christians are asked to explain or interpret faith in Christ, their reply is apt to be in terms of creed and theology. Analogously, asked to explain Torah, Jews reply with Talmud, the body of rabbinical literature that interprets the Bible. The heart of Judaism in all of its forms is Torah, the precious gift of God that distinguished Israel from all other peoples. "Judaism is Torah and Torah is Judaism." Torah includes not the Pentateuch alone, but all of the Hebrew Bible and the whole tradition that arises from it, especially the Talmud. Torah is made up of two major components: *halachah*, or law, and *haggadah*, or story. Though neither excludes the other as unimportant, Christianity as an heir of Early Judaism focuses on Torah as *haggadah*.

Rabbinic Judaism since the Judische Wissenschaft (Jewish Enlightenment) movement in nineteenth-century Germany has three main branches: Reform Judaism, which adapted Judaism to the concepts of the European Enlightenment, with its many secular and pro-scientific elements; Conservative Judaism, which believed this accommodation had gone too far and reacted against the Enlightenment; and Orthodox Judaism, which to varying degrees consciously resisted and resists accommodation.

Islam. The adherents of the religion of Islam consider themselves to be recipients of the self-same stream of divine guidance granted to Jews and Christians. Indeed, the term Mohammedanism is a misnomer, since Muhammad is not an object of worship; only God can be such. Islam means "submission" to God (Allah). Abraham is commended in the Qur'an (the scripture of the Muslims, also spelled Koran) as having been a Muslim—that is, the first to submit to the divine will—and is considered the common progenitor of the Jews, Christians, and Muslims. As the Sufis or mystics of Islam suggest, prophets among humans are like rubies among rocks both are stones, but how much more exalted in the beauty of their inner light are prophets. By their proximity to human experience prophets are best able to communicate knowledge about the divine and give instructions from the divine to humans. Thus, while the Qur'an faults Jews in the days of Moses and Aaron for having lapsed into error from the worship of God, and Christians for elevating Jesus Christ into divine status, it nonetheless promises that heaven will be open to the righteous among them. The divine being alone is to be worshipped and acknowledged as the Merciful and Compassionate Creator, while humans are exhorted to live an ethical and spiritual life mindful of being held accountable for social relations in this world and in preparation for a beatific life in the hereafter.

Historically, Islam as a distinct religion began with the divine revelations communicated to Muhammad in the seventh century of the Common Era, revelations that have been collected in the Qur'an. Conversion to Islam was not, as is commonly supposed, due so much to the threat of the sword as to the persuasiveness of preachers, and, at times, to political or economic pressures. Differences over the question of authority and over how the Qur'an is to be understood and applied led within the first two centuries to two communities: the Sunni, those who followed the "custom" of the Prophet; and the Shiah, those who held that leadership for the community had passed on to Ali, Muhammad's cousin and son-in-law. The Sunni hold the five pillars of Islam to be confession, prayer to Allah, tithing, fasting during Ramadan, and pilgrimage to Mecca. Shiah believe that the first three caliphs (successors to Mohammed) were invalid, the first valid caliph being Ali.

The mystical movement in Islam is the Sufi movement. The Sufis add an attitude of spontaneity to the rigorous historical outlook of the Sunnis. References to Islamic "jihad" have often been misunderstood in the West. The assumption is that it refers to violent activity, as in "holy war," whereas in fact its meaning is closer to the English word "crusade," which can be, but need not be, violent. Sufis seek an inward jihad against selfishness.

In the United States a new Muslim movement originated in 1930 among Afro-Americans, sometimes called the Nation of Islam. Its adherents are often called Black Muslims, and its early teaching demonized whites as a result of the way in which whites dehumanized blacks. Under the influence of the historical Islamic teaching and the impact of Martin Luther King and subsequently Malcolm X, it has deemphasized its racial component and has increasingly become a recognized part of the larger tradition.

Baha'i. The Bahá'i faith was founded in Persia (today's Iran) in the nineteenth century. It is an outgrowth of the Bábi faith and was founded in 1844 by 'Ali Muhammad of Shiraz (1791–1850), who claimed to fulfill the promise of Islam, was persecuted, and put to death. His successor was prophet Husayn 'Ali of Nur (1817–1892), who took the name Bahá'u'lláh in 1863 and died in exile imposed by the Persian and Ottoman governments. His extensive writings form the basis of Bahá'i study, but Bahá'i worship includes prayers and readings from other religions. The name Bahá'i means "follower of glory." The faith emphasizes the oneness of God, the unity of all religions, and the unity of humankind.

Bahá'is believe that God provides messengers at various periods of history to sustain an evolving faith and to serve an ever more complex society. Their faith holds that the ancient and eternal message of God becomes corrupted over time much as a river becomes contaminated as it moves downstream from the source, and the prophets are like filters that remove contamination from the message while adding necessary instruction to cope with changing human circumstances. As mankind evolves and becomes a more mature species, it needs additional guidance appropriate to its development to better understand and apply the eternal truth. Much as teachers instruct a child according to the child's increased understanding as she ages, so do prophets deliver God's message in ways that are appropriate for each age of humankind. Bahá'is hold that among the prophets who perform this function are Abraham, Moses, Zoroaster, Buddha, Jesus, Mohammed, and others. Bahá'u'lláh is the most recent of these prophets.

Bahá'i followers stress a harmony between science and religion, racial and gender equality, the independent search for truth, avoidance of the extremes of wealth and poverty, universal compulsory education, and the aims of social justice and world peace. There are no clergy. There are seven million Bahá'is in the world and about 250,000 in the United States, some of whom are in southern California. The American headquarters are in Wilmette, Illinois, where the Bahá'i Temple, begun in 1912, is located. Being both open and inclusive of other traditions, the religion tends to have a broad range of adherents, from cosmopolitan intellectuals to rural minorities. Most of the Bahá'is are found in developing countries. Europe and America are experiencing a growth in the number of Bahá'is.

Hinduism. The term "Hinduism" is a Western-originated word, derived from the Sanskrit *sindhu* or "river," for the central tradition of Indian religion. To Western observers it appears as infinitely diverse, or multi-verse, the only common trait among its eight hundred million adherents being the caste system and the inspiration of the Vedas, which are the ancient collections of religious writings. Two traditions stand out prominently:

(1) Vedanta, which combines an acceptance of India's polytheism with a belief in Brahman, the Unity or One beyond all variety; and (2) devotional theism of various divinities—notably Krishna, and his holy scripture, the Bhagavad Gita. Krishna and Rama are worshipped as savior deities. They are two of the ten avatars of Vishnu, the god of preservation, who, with Siva, the god of destruction, form the two primary gods of Hinduism. The paths to spiritual liberation (Moksha) are as varied as the psychological types of personality. But, basically, these have been systematized as The Way of the Intellect (Jnana Marga), the Way of the Activist (Karma Marga), and the Way of the Loving Heart (Bhakti Marga). The Way of the Intellect stresses that the ultimate idea is the union of the soul and God, or the surrender of life to Life. The Way of the Loving Heart always retains God as a separate divine Person who can be worshipped.

While Hinduism served its followers well for many centuries, it had to change in order to cope with the altered situation brought about by colonialism, urbanization, and the work of Christian missions. Therefore it experienced a kind of revival in the nineteenth and twentieth centuries, as evinced by such leaders as Vivekananda (1853–1902), Tagore (1861–1941), Aurobindo (1872–1950), and Gandhi (1869–1948).

Today Hinduism shows remarkable vitality. Not only has it gained this vitality in India and among Indian immigrants to the United States, but also it has had extensive influence among Euro-Americans. Yogic disciplines are practiced by millions as a means to an integral health and wholeness of body, mind, and spirit. In addition, Vedantic missionaries have convinced many intellectuals that the deepest insight is common to the mystics of all religious traditions: namely, the identity of one's underlying and truly authentic self (Atman) and the ultimate underlying reality (Brahman). The most advanced Yogic disciplines are the means of spiritually and existentially realizing this identity.

Sikhism. The word "sikh" means "disciple" in the Punjabi language of north India, and Sikhs are considered "seekers of truth." Sikhism was founded by Guru Nanak (1469–1530) at a time when militarily victorious Muslims were aggressively converting Hindus. Nanak, who was originally a Hindu, traveled throughout India and the Near East accompanied by one Muslim and one Hindu musician, singing praise to God. His primary message was that there exists one God, called by many different names. He taught that one should meditate on God and be supportive of others who did likewise, even though their forms of worship might be different. He believed in the equality of all people, and advocated an end to the Indian caste system and interreligious strife.

After Nanak, there was a succession of nine more Gurus. The ten Gurus represent ten divine attributes: humility, obedience, equality, service, self-sacrifice, justice, mercy, purity, tranquility, and royal courage. Some of these men developed a military tradition, and Sikhism came to be known as the Path of the Soldier Saint. (A Sikh has often been India's Minister of Defense). The fifth Guru, Arjun, sent out a call for poetry written by anyone on the topic of divine union with the infinite Lord. He collected verses written by mystics from many different religious traditions and called these scriptures Siri Guru Granth Sahib. The tenth and last Guru, Gobind Singh (1666–1708), stated that the form of Sikhism had been set in these scriptures, that they were a living consciousness of the Guru.

According to these scriptures, all of Sikhism is focused on the direct experience of God. Sikh practice is explained in a fourfold way: Bana, the physical form (for example, leaving hair uncut, as created by God, avoiding meat and intoxicants); Bani, the word of God directly expressed in the scriptures; Seva, selfless service; and Simram, meditation on God. The spiritual brotherhood and sisterhood of Sikhs is called the Khalsa.

In India the approximately twelve million Sikhs have spread from their native Punjab to all parts of the Indian subcontinent, where they are conspicuous by their beards and turbans. Some Sikhs, mainly as professional people, have found their way to Southern California, as well as to other parts of America and to England.

Buddhism. Like Christianity, Buddhism is a personally founded religion. Siddartha Gautama (550–480 B.C.E.) was probably the greatest philosophic mind of classical Indian history. While Jesus has been called Messiah or Christ, Siddartha has been called the Buddha, often translated as "the Enlightened One," but more accurately the "Awakened One." If we ask from what sleep to what awakening state he arose, he and his followers reply that it is from the sleep of samsara, to the awakening of nirvana—roughly translated, from the false belief that the world of appearance is substantial, to the realization that there is no substantial reality whatsoever. This means that, as opposed to Hindu teaching, there is no underlying self

(Atman) or ultimate reality (Brahman). Enlightenment is the blessed peace at which practitioners arrive when they realize the insubstantial nature of all things and therefore let go of all attachments. Buddhism shares with Hinduism the idea that all living things are reborn in new lives, or reincarnation. This idea of causation and rebirth is called karma. Buddhism teaches a simplified practical form of life in which responsibility for life was the chief cornerstone.

Common to different sects of Buddhism are "Four Noble Truths" relating to suffering, and the "Eightfold Path" for overcoming suffering. The central ceremony that unifies Buddhists is relying on or taking refuge in the "Three Jewels": namely, the Buddha, his teaching (Dharma), and the community (Sangha). The teaching and community have endured in two major forms: the Theravada tradition, texts written in Pali which thrives in places like Sri Lanka, Burma, and Thailand; and the Mahayana traditions of China, Korea, Japan, and Tibet that use scriptures written in Chinese and Tibetan. Mahayana added many new scriptures to the basic core surviving in Pali, and embodied many new practices. These new departures were encouraged by the idea that exercising wisdom and compassion required creating skillful methods to help others. A new religious model arose called the bodhisattva to embody wisdom and compassion, and great bodhisattva figures became new objects of worship in Mahayana.

Although Buddhism lacked any central organization except that imposed by state governments, the monastic clergy provided a unifying discipline recognized by both Theravada and Mahayana. In Japan, however, new sects like Pure Land, Nichiren, and Zen allow married clergy; and new lay forms of Buddhism have recently emerged in many Buddhist cultures. In Southern California there are many Buddhists who have come from various Asian countries, and there are also many Euro-American converts.

Confucianism. This system of life and thought is not so much a religious tradition as a distinctive humanism. Its Chinese character (Zen) represents two humans, symbolizing an ethical relationship, but held under heaven (t'ien). Confucius (or Chung Ni, as the Chinese know him) (550–479 B.C.E.) made no claim to divinity or supernatural knowledge. Honor to one's ancestors as a continuing presence in human life has always marked East Asian spirituality. Respect for ancestors and superiors was subsumed into a hierarchy of social and ritual obligations known as ru-jiao, the teachings of the scholar-officials, which became the state religion for East Asia. Since the government adopted Confucius as the model sage embodying these virtues, the system became known in the West as Confucianism. Legitimated by Heaven, and emphasizing group welfare more than the individual, harmony over justice, and loyalty over personal happiness, Confucianism has created social stability and cultural values that challenge Western individualism.

The idea of an afterlife exists in the Confucian code, but it is not clearly defined.

Confucius propounded the Golden rule, offered advice to rulers, and delineated social obligations. The qualities of Confucianism, often in combination with other aspects of Chinese tradition, have influenced East Asian religions, including Christianity.

Taoism. Whereas Confucianism sanctifies the social structure, Taoism represents various alternative sources of empowerment beyond that structure. Among its many forms, Taoism includes a counter-culture tradition flowing from two books, Lao-tzu and Chuang-tzu, that advocate abandoning social conventions as corrupting and instead returning to the way of nature (Tao). Against social sophistication, it emphasized intuition, primitivism, meditation, and simplicity by trusting the natural rhythms of things. On the other hand, beginning in 142 C.E., a Heavenly Masters community arose based on revelations from Lao-tzu to a chosen priesthood who were instructed how to command the gods. The Heavenly Master priesthood offered a superior way to save ancestors through repentance and worship that has endured as a liturgical alternative to the imperial cult.

As a result, Taoism prepared for the coming of Buddhism to East Asia, but in turn adopted Buddhist rituals and ideas of karma and universal salvation, while influencing Buddhism to produce Zen. Taoism is a radical simplification of life, which always tends toward complexity, superficiality, and confusion. It is a way of being open, honest, spontaneous, and in a delicate harmony with the Creative. The name for this is not important. In fact, it could easily be called the Nameless. But this life or energy produces a rich fruit for living and works especially in lowly and humble ways. This is living in harmony with the Tao ("the way"). To be "a person of the Tao" is the highest calling and the greatest fulfillment. But becoming available to the Tao is never easy. It is a lifelong process and goes counter to the spirit of any age and its cultural accretions.

Native American Religions. Despite significant variations among five hundred tribes and difficulties in distinguishing the older traditions from accommodations to European influence, some generalizations about Native American religions are possible: (1) Stories of creation describe the emergence of the people, suggesting where they should live, declaring the seamless unity of all creation, and calling for profound respect for the Earth and all her creatures. Everything is alive. People are a part of the Earth. Although the Creator sets aside land for their use, they are not owners. At their best, they use only what they need. (2) Harmony is a major belief and value of most native people. The creation is harmonious, and all work to maintain, or to restore, harmony with creation and with the community. (3) Most native people have a deep awareness of the spirits of the land and seek to be guided by them in caring for the community. They speak of the Creator as "great Spirit" and "great Mystery," and have no need to explain further. (4) They hold together that which many others separate: spirit/matter, nature/history, cognition/affect, religion/politics/culture, and so forth. They are intuitive, with their interior reflecting the created world. (5) The community is central to the rituals and ceremonies as well as to daily life. Leadership is judged by its ability to serve the people; the economy is organized to feed, shelter, and house all the people. Although the vision quest of the Sioux is solitary, it is in the context of a caring and supportive community. (6) Native peoples are oriented to space rather than to time. They have holy places, not holy weeks or seasons. Nevertheless, while some tribes did not have verb tenses that indicated past or future, they often had a sense of what the Greeks called *kairos*. There were seasons for hunting or farming; there were passages in the life of an individual that marked important transitions.

Practical Implications

The first section of this chapter acknowledged that Christians have often made claims of superiority and even of exclusive possession of the way to salvation that have done great harm. We have blinded ourselves to the wisdom of other communities and have often used political, economic, and military power over them abusively. We have much of which to repent.

The second section described how our nation has become factually pluralistic so that traditions that we once viewed as remote and irrelevant have come alive in our own neighborhoods. This gives us the chance to change both our thinking and our practice in relation to these communities. This section included brief accounts of these traditions that show both their diversity and their respective strengths.

It is time now to consider some practical implications for how we can relate individually and as congregations to these other communities. Few Christians can become richly acquainted with all the other religious communities, even those that are represented in their communities. But most Christians can extend their circles of acquaintance to some degree beyond their Christian neighbors. We can do so with the attitude of respect. We can approach others hoping to learn not only so as to inform ourselves about their beliefs, customs, and practices, but also for the sake of gaining insights and wisdom that can enrich our lives personally and communally.

We Christians are committed, in the words of the World Council of Churches, to peace, justice, and the integrity of creation. As we find others that share these concerns, we can support new interfaith organizations that express and implement our hopes. Whether those should replace our Councils of Churches or supplement them is a practical issue to be considered in each case. But to be genuinely neighborly today must mean establishing positive relations with religious communities other than Christian.

The Presbyterian Church in Claremont has for many years been yoked with a Jewish synagogue. Jews and Presbyterians have come to understand and trust one another through annual weeks of exchange visits. At times they extend practical help to one another. This kind of pairing leads to far deeper relations than do occasional visits.

There are now a good many interfaith discussion groups in local communities as well as at national and international levels. Through participation in such groups, people can come to understand one another and learn from one another. Gradually this affects the congregations from which they come.

This dialogical process does not usually weaken the faith of those who participate. On the contrary, Christians often become more aware of how deeply they are informed by their distinctive faith and come to prize it more. But part of what they come to prize is the encouragement it gives them to open themselves in love to others.

What about evangelism? In relation to vast numbers of people both within and outside the church, communicating the good news of Jesus Christ is of utmost urgency. This is not the question here.

The question is about evangelism in relating to persons of other faiths. Should we share the Good News that is so important to us with them as well? Before we do so we should consider the reality of the situation in which we relate to them. Many of our neighbors in other religious communities have historical, and even personal, memories of aggressive and even oppressive Christians. They are likely to enter into dialogue with us somewhat hesitantly, fearing that this is just another avenue for us to attempt to convert them. If we use the dialogue for that purpose, we will confirm their fears and drive them away. Similarly, if at the same time that we dialogue we also engage in separate evangelistic efforts, they will not trust us.

Given our history, dialogue requires that we create a climate in which there is no manipulation, no effort on anyone's part to convert the others. Christians, especially, need to listen. On the whole, the others know us better than we know them. Much that they know of us renders them distrustful. Our task is to come to understand this distrust, repent of what has engendered it, and work toward a new basis for good relations.

In addition to dialogue, we need to work together on common concerns of community building and social justice. Even when we differ quite markedly in our beliefs, we often find that we share a concern for the relief of human suffering and for maintaining a habitable Earth. Issues of this sort are of such importance that we need to work together with all who are committed to dealing with them.

But none of this means that dialogue precludes honest and open testimony to what we find to be true and important. Quite the contrary. Authentic dialogue requires that we explain our deepest conviction to others even if they are offensive to some of our dialogue partners. We have heard the Good News and been formed by it. We find God in and through Jesus. It is just this that we need to explain to our neighbors of other faiths. With sincerity, conviction, and honesty, our witness to what we believe God has done in Jesus Christ and in the Christian church should be bold and eloquent. In the long run, while we gain wisdom from others, it is our hope that they gain wisdom from us as well.

There are ongoing dialogues in which relationships are established such that people of differing communities are free to try to persuade one another of the truth and value of their beliefs and practices for all. In these dialogues people are free also to criticize one another, pointing out what is offensive to each in the other's tradition. At that point Christians can engage, quite unqualifiedly, in evangelism. By then it is clear that asking others to respond to the Good News of Jesus Christ is not asking them to abandon the wisdom and goodness of their own traditions and cultures.

One urgent issue that few of our churches have addressed is that of interfaith marriage. In an interfaith marriage, a couple has four choices: (1) they can agree to be nonreligious; (2) one spouse can convert; (3) they can celebrate everything and leave the choice to the children at a later date; or (4) they can forge an understanding that binds their religions together while continuing to celebrate both traditions in their distinctiveness. If the couple chooses the first option, it is difficult for the church to help. However, the church should be sensitive to the issues involved in the other three.

The second option is the simplest both for the couple and for the children. It avoids raising the issue of dual faiths within the family. On the other hand, sometimes the one who converts misses what has been left behind and never feels fully at home in the new faith.

The third option provides a more complex spiritual life for the family. However, at some point children are under pressure to choose one faith tradition or the other, and sometimes this wounds the parent whose faith is abandoned.

The fourth option is the one that this position paper tends to support most strongly if the couple is capable of the difficult work involved. Within it, both parents can feel spiritually whole and raise spiritually whole children. To achieve this, both must learn the religious and cultural nuances of the other.

In the case of a Christian-Jewish marriage, one of the most important things to understand is that Judaism is practiced primarily in the home, whereas Christianity is practiced outside the home in a church community. To balance the power of Jewish home traditions, Christians may need to develop Christian rituals for home use. Couples should not try to mix traditions in a way that could infringe on the integrity of either. Instead they need to reflect on how both ceremonies can be appreciated as complementary.

Churches can help by having services in which those of other faiths can participate without feeling marginalized or pressured. They can provide contexts in which couples can discuss their struggles and support them in a variety of solutions.

For Further Reading

Huston Smith. *The World's Religions*. New York: HarperOne, 2009.

Michael Lodahl. *Claiming Abraham: Reading the Bible and the Qur'an Side by Side*. Grand Rapids, MI: Brazos Press, 2010.

Timothy C. Tennent. *Christianity at the Religious Roundtable: Evangelicalism in Conversation with Hinduism, Buddhism, and Islam*. Grand Rapids, MI: Baker Academic, 2002.

Paul Knitter. *Without Buddha I Could Not Be a Christian*. Glasgow: One-world Publications, 2009.

Clara Sue Kidwell, Homer Noley, and George E. Tinker, eds. *A Native American Theology*. Maryknoll: Orbis, 2001.

Questions for Discussion

1. What have you learned about other religious communities that interests you?
2. Does understanding the history of religion affect how you understand your own faith? How?
3. What experiences have you had with persons of other faiths?
4. How does the discussion of exclusivists and pluralists relate to your faith? Do you adopt one of these alternatives or reject both?
5. Does the chapter succeed in making the case for the transformation of Christianity through learning from other traditions?
6. Is Christianity richer and wiser because of the religious diversity of our society?
7. Can we celebrate religious diversity? How?
8. Can our churches find ways of supporting religiously mixed couples?

TWO

Jews and Christians through the Ages

A TROUBLED RELATIONSHIP

Eva Fleischner

In 1979 in Claremont, California, events that were to have unforeseen and long-range consequences occurred.[1] The women's groups of the local Jewish congregation of Temple Beth Israel and the Claremont Presbyterian Church had begun to talk together about each other's festivals. An outbreak of anti-Semitic graffiti around town led to a desire on the part of the Christian members to express and deepen their solidarity with their Jewish neighbors. Under the leadership of Rabbi Mandel and Pastor Jim Angell an interfaith exchange began that, twenty-six years later (at this writing), has become a cherished tradition. It includes today an annual exchange of pulpits, an invitation from the Temple to a Sabbath celebration and from the church to attend Sunday worship, studying the Decalogue together, and joint community service by the women's groups.

This account makes clear that Christian-Jewish relations is not a subject in a long-ago history, but a reality alive today and relevant to our time. The Claremont experience highlights both the ongoing existence of anti-Semitism, and the joint Christian and Jewish efforts to combat it—efforts grounded in a new-found spirit of Christian solidarity with the Jewish people. We shall examine the evolution of Christian anti-Semitism, the new and hopeful rapprochement that has taken place between the two communities, and the challenges—some new, some ancient—that still face us today. We shall seek to explain how we came to be where we are at this time.

Introduction

We begin with a text from the *Baltimore Catechism*, the standard text used in the American Roman Catholic Church until the reforms of the Second Vatican Council in the 1960s:

> Q: Why did the Jewish religion, which up to the death of Christ had been the true religion, cease at that time to be the true religion?
>
> A: The Jewish religion . . . ceased at that time to be the true religion because it was only a promise of the redemption and figure of the Christian religion, and when the redemption was accomplished and the Christian religion established by the death of Christ, the promise and figure were no longer necessary. (391)

No mention is made here of the Jews as Christ-killers, nor as a people rejected and cursed by God—accusations that became staples in Christian preaching and catechesis and that led to centuries of persecution and pogroms. Yet, as we shall see, these deadly accusations grew out of the theological view of Judaism expressed in this text: with the coming of Christianity the Jews are no longer people of God.

In what follows we shall find a frequent interplay between history and theology. Theology does not arise in a vacuum but is profoundly influenced by history. Moreover, without some knowledge of history, there is no possibility of genuine dialogue between Jews and Christians. This presents a problem: Jews are very familiar with a history that has effectively been erased from Christian memory.

The opening page of Father Edward Flannery's book *The Anguish of the Jews* (1965, first edition) eloquently makes the point, "One evening several years ago, I walked north on Park Avenue in New York City in the company of a young Jewish couple. Behind us shone the huge illuminated cross the Grand Central building displays each year at Christmastime. Glancing over her shoulder, the young lady—ordinarily well disposed toward Christians—declared: 'The cross makes me shudder. It is like an evil presence.'" Flannery was shocked. How was it, he asked himself, that the cross, supreme symbol of universal love for Christians, had become a sign of fear, of evil, for this young Jewish woman? In further conversation it became clear to him that the woman's reaction was the result of a knowledge of history he completely lacked: a history of centuries of suffering of her people at the hands of Christians. "The pages Jews have memorized have been torn from our histories of the Christian era." This realization moved Flannery to write what became the first history of Christian anti-Semitism in English by a Roman Catholic priest.

The Christian attitude toward and treatment of Jews over the centuries represents the shadow side of Christianity. Facing up to this dark history is essential for Christian self-knowledge and for a mature, purer Christian faith. This new knowledge will challenge some traditional Christian theological views. It will also enable Christians to understand why, despite the beginnings of a radically new and positive relationship between Jews and Christians over the past forty years, many Jews still approach Christians with unease and suspicion.

There are scholars who maintain that the relationship between Jews and Christians has been one of ever increasing hostility and persecution, inevitably and logically culminating in the *Shoah* (or Holocaust). This is the view of the "Dean" of Jewish historians, Raoul Hilberg, for whom church laws from 306–1434 parallel Nazi legislation from 1935–1942.[2]

We do not believe that this view represents the whole picture. There is no doubt that centuries of Christian preaching and teaching provided a fertile seedbed for the Nazi genocide, and that the church was all too often indifferent to, even complicit in, the Shoah. Yet not all of history between Christians and Jews can be reduced to a story of persecution and hatred. Nor was its culmination in the Shoah inevitable. Several facts that provide a more nuanced picture should be kept in mind:

1. The polemic so evident in the Gospels' anti-Jewish texts was typical of the Judaism of the time, as well as of the Greco-Roman world. This may also apply to some of the sermons of the church fathers, such as those of John Chrysostom.

2. Throughout the Middle Ages we find, in sermons of some popular preachers, certain passages that express respect for, even admiration of, Jews: for example, for their commitment to the Sabbath, high Jewish moral standards, commitment to education and learning, and fidelity to their faith even in the face of death.

3. Even in times of great danger for Jews, such as the first Crusade (1096), there were Christians, often in positions of high authority, who spoke out and tried to protect Jews.

4. While there was indeed frequent enmity and conflict, there were also times and places where Jews and Christians lived side by side in peace. The "Golden Age" in Spain ("Andalusia" at the time) lasted three hundred years; during that time some Jews and Christians occupied high positions in Muslim society (see below).

5. Edicts in favor of Jews from church authorities, even from the pope, did not necessarily affect popular beliefs or prevent pogroms. Thus, accusations of blood libel or ritual murder continued to be made in spite of papal decrees that denounced such charges as groundless.

6. Despite the proliferation of the anti-Jewish literature in patristic and medieval times, the church never issued a theological or dogmatic tract against the Jews. No mention of Jews is made in any of the Christian creeds. (It should be remembered, however, that preaching and teaching generally have a much wider impact than dogmatic definitions.)

7. Although theology was the enduring basis for Christian anti-Judaism (see below, "the teaching of contempt"), economic and social factors also played decisive roles. To take only one example: a severe outbreak of persecution and pogroms occurred during the time when Europe was devastated by the bubonic plague (Black Death) in the fourteenth century. In their desperation the populace needed to find a cause for their suffering, and Jews were a natural scapegoat (as they were to be centuries later, after Germany's defeat in World War I and the Treaty of Versailles). The role of the Jews as moneylenders—a role into which they had been forced because Christians were forbidden to engage in usury—frequently earned them popular hatred.

8. The tragic history of Christian anti-Judaism notwithstanding, it does not by itself account for the Nazi genocide. It took nineteenth-century racism and modern technology to make possible the Shoah. To put it succinctly, Christian anti-Judaism was not the sufficient cause of the Shoah, but it was a

necessary one. Without this foundation Hitler would not have found such a receptive soil for his ideology.

None of the contributing factors just mentioned played as central and constant a role in making the Shoah possible as did the negative Christian teaching about Jews and Judaism. In the words of Rosemary Ruether, "the church must bear a substantial responsibility for a tragic history of the Jew in Christendom which was the foundation upon which political anti-Semitism and the Nazi use of it was erected."[3]

How could this have happened? How could Jesus' teaching of love have been turned into a teaching of hate? We shall attempt to answer this question in what follows, and to trace the calamitous consequences of this teaching. In the last part of the chapter we shall speak of the radical and positive changes that have occurred—and are still occurring—in the relationship of the two peoples over the past forty years.

Terminology

Supersessionism: This is a recent theological term, frequently used today in Jewish-Christian studies and dialogue. It is derived from the Latin *supersedere*—supersede, take the place of, replace—and refers to the ancient Christian claim that Christians have replaced, "superseded," Jews as people of God. Christians are the new people of God, replacing the Jews, who lost this privilege because they failed to recognize Christ as Messiah. Therefore their covenant is null and void, replaced by the New Covenant. Supersessionism is today rejected by most mainline churches.

Shoah: Hebrew for "catastrophe." The word "Holocaust" has been used so widely, for catastrophes of all kinds, that it no longer refers specifically to the Nazi genocide of Jews (for example, "nuclear holocaust"). "Shoah" has been common usage in place of "Holocaust" in France and Germany for some years already and is being used increasingly in the English-speaking world. We shall use it throughout this chapter.

Anti-Judaism and anti-Semitism: Are they two terms for the same phenomenon? The question is still being debated. We believe that a distinction can be made. Anti-Judaism refers to the *religious* or *theological* view—expressed in supersessionism—that the Jewish people failed in their vocation and are no longer people of God. In this view, Judaism represents all that is negative in religion (legalism, hypocrisy, empty ritual, and so on) in contrast to Christianity, which embodies love, grace, and truth. Anti-Judaism is a theological term.

Anti-Semitism is technically a racist term. It appears for the first time in 1879, coined by Wilhelm Marr, a German journalist. It views Jews as a *race*, intrinsically inferior and evil. The distinction between the two is clear if we remember that throughout Christendom Jews who converted were accepted as Christians. Under Nazism this "way out" was no longer an option; conversion no longer saved Jews from the gas chambers.

However, while the distinction seems valid and helpful to us, it is dismissed by some because anti-Judaism so easily, and so often, leads to anti-Semitism. As one reads of the repeated denigration of Jews and the outbreaks of violence against them in the course of Christian history, it becomes increasingly difficult to make the distinction. We shall at times use the two terms interchangeably. The definition by the French historian Jules Isaac may be useful: "Anti-Semitism is used nowadays to refer to anti-Jewish prejudice, to feelings of suspicion, contempt, hostility and hatred toward Jews, both those who follow the religion [of Judaism] and those who are merely of Jewish descent."[4]

Old and New Testaments: These terms suggest that the New Testament has superseded the Old, which is valid no longer. The term "Hebrew Scriptures" is problematic because the Jewish scriptures are not identical with the Christian Old Testament. Some scholars today use the terms "First" and "Second" Testaments—we shall follow this usage.

Pogrom: An organized and often officially encouraged massacre of Jews. There have been literally hundreds of pogroms in the course of Jewish history.

Blood libel/ritual murder/desecration of the host: The "blood libel" charge by Christians against Jews held that Jews kidnapped and ritually murdered Christian children, as their historic role in Jesus' crucifixion had created in them a lust for innocent blood. "The blood libel resembled a virus that then lodged itself in the Christian imagination. . . . Jews were accused of crucifying boys all over Europe, even into the twentieth century."[5] The ritual murder charge appears also in Western literature, from Chaucer to James Joyce. The desecration of the host libel refers to the claim that Jews stole and tortured the elements to be used in the Eucharist and tortured them, just as they had earlier crucified Christ.

Jewish Origins of Christianity: Christianity began as a Jewish sect, one among a number of sects in first-century Palestine (for example, the Pharisees, Sadducees, Essenes, Zealots). Jesus was born, lived, and died as a Jew, faithfully observing the Law (*Torah*). As we know from the Gospels, he was circumcised and presented in the Temple, like any Jew of his time. He extolled respect for Torah (Matt 5:17–7:29). The rhythms of his life were marked by observance of the great pilgrimage festivals, and by attending the synagogue on the Sabbath. His message was addressed only to Jews, as is clear from his insulting words to the Canaanite woman (Matt 15:22-28).

What, then, of the tensions and conflicts between Jesus and the Pharisees that we find in the Gospels—tensions that have made the word "Pharisee" synonymous with "hypocrite" in the minds of many Christians, still today? These tensions must be seen against the background of a complex and diversified movement. In general the Pharisees were among the most devout and respected religious figures of the time—precursors of the rabbis and founders of what came to be known as rabbinic Judaism. Like all devout people in every religion, the Pharisees did not always live up to their high ideals, nor were they immune to the dangers of hypocrisy. Criticism of various types of Pharisees by other Pharisees is equal to and sometimes exceeds any of Jesus' criticism of them. Differences about the interpretation of Torah were typical of first-century Judaism and often led to acrimonious debates within Judaism. Yet it is clear that Jesus in his teaching was closer to the Pharisees than to any other Jewish group of the time.

Initially, Jesus' followers lived peacefully among their fellow Jews, keeping the Jewish times of prayer in the Temple even after the resurrection (see Acts 3). They entertained the hope that their fellow Jews would soon recognize Jesus as the long-awaited Messiah. On the Jewish side, there was the expectation that the new sect would soon disappear, now that the Master was dead.

Neither expectation was to be fulfilled. Not only did Christians not disappear, they soon grew in number, making converts first among their fellow Jews (see Acts 2 and the first Pentecost), and before long among gentiles. As described in Acts, Paul was sent by the Christians of Antioch to Jerusalem to discuss a difficult problem that had arisen for some of the apostles, led by James and Peter, with the gentile Christians. The problem had reached

Antioch through believers who had come from Jerusalem. Paul and Barnabas were to reach agreement with the apostles on the question: Should gentile converts to Christianity before being baptized be obliged to observe the full Jewish law, including food restrictions and the circumcision of males, or did Christ free them from observing the Torah? After a difficult debate, both sides agreed to differ and as a practical matter divided the territory: Paul to the gentiles and Peter to the Jews (Gal 2:7-10). This solved the problem for gentiles outside of Jerusalem.

In Jerusalem the Jewish community was divided over whether Jesus was the Christ, leading to outbreaks like the mob that stoned Stephen, a Hellenistic Jew who followed Jesus as the Christ (Acts 7). Most Jews could not believe that a man who had been shamefully put to death on a cross could be the Messiah; the mainstream of Jewish messianic expectations did not allow for a suffering Messiah. Bitterness increased on both sides, yet prior to the Roman War of 66–70 we can still speak of one people.

The Parting of the Ways

The first Roman war played a pivotal role in the destiny of both Jews and Christians. After fierce fighting for nearly four years and enormous casualties, Jerusalem fell in 70 c.e., the Temple was destroyed, and the people lost what little autonomy they had enjoyed until then. What was left was still more radically destroyed sixty years later, in the rebellion against Rome led by Bar Kochba (132–135). From that time on, until 1948 and the founding of the modern state of Israel, the Jewish people no longer had a land of their own. They were homeless, at the mercy of the goodwill of the peoples among whom they lived in the *diaspora* ("dispersion").

The way in which this catastrophe, the destruction of Jerusalem and the Temple, was interpreted by Jews and Christians differed radically. Jews saw it, as they had the Babylonian captivity, as God's punishment because they had not been sufficiently faithful to the Torah. Yet faith in God's enduring mercy and forgiveness sustained them and enabled them to save what could be saved from the disaster. At Jamnia (Javneh, Jabneh) outside Jerusalem, Rabbi Johanan ben Zakkai established a center of learning, an "Academy," where the work of conservation and adaptation was carried out so successfully that "Judaism not only was tided over the crisis, but entered upon a period of progress which it may well count among the most notable chapters in its history."[6]

Christians, on the other hand, saw the war as the fulfillment of Jesus' prophecy, as God's punishment upon the Jewish people because they had failed in their mission. In 62 c.e.—after the murder of James, the bishop of the Christian believers in Jerusalem, and shortly before the outbreak of the war—Christians fled from their brothers. In spite of the tradition of a move to Pella, for all practical effects the Christians of Jerusalem disappeared. Thus, events on the ground settled what the apostles were not able to settle between James and Paul a generation earlier.

The Second Testament

It was during those critical years that the Christian scriptures took shape in their final form. What we have in the Gospels are not primarily historical documents, but a reflection of the life of the early church. Many of the words attributed to Jesus in the Gospels reflect the way in which the church had come to view Jews by this time: as obstinate and blind, deliberately refusing to recognize God's salvation in Christ. What had been intra-Jewish debates now became debates between "us" (Christians) and "them" (Jews).

There is an unmistakable crescendo in the hostile ways that Jews are portrayed in the Gospels, beginning with the earliest, Mark (ca. 70 C.E.), and attaining a peak in John, written toward the end of the century. The term "Jews" appears sixteen times in Mark and seventy-one times in John. From intra-Jewish controversies in the Synoptics, Jesus' conflict with "the Jews" has become, in John, the story of a cosmic conflict, the battle between the forces of light and the powers of darkness (compare to the prologue of John). And it is "the Jews" who are the symbol of this cosmic evil. Thus, in John 8 Jesus denounces them as the offspring of Satan: "Your father is the devil, and you do your father's will. He was a murderer from the beginning." By implication, his offspring are also murderers. Moreover, by the time John's Gospel was written, the church was composed of more gentiles than Jews, and Christians had been expelled from the synagogue—a fact probably reflected in texts such as John 9:22. Nevertheless, the complexity of the issue is shown by the evangelist John's refusal to blame the Jews for Jesus' execution.

The young church was trying to define itself as separate from the Jewish roots of its birth, while also struggling for survival in the hostile climate of Roman occupation. This accounts for the effort of the writers of the Synoptic Gospels to shift the blame for Jesus' death from the Romans to the Jews.

The Teaching of Contempt

Although the phrase is modern (it was coined by the French Jewish historian Jules Isaac, part of whose family perished in Auschwitz), the phenomenon it describes goes back to the late first century. By the end of the fifth century it was full-blown. What follows is a summary of the main elements of this teaching.

Jews are now portrayed in Christian teaching and preaching as rejected and cast aside by God because they failed to recognize Jesus as Messiah. Therefore their ancient covenant is null and void. The Roman destruction of Jerusalem and its Temple are God's punishment for the crucifixion of Jesus— visible and tangible evidence of God's wrath and rejection of the "old" people of God. A new people of God, the Christian church, has taken its place. This is the "replacement theology," the supplanting of one people by another, which today is often referred to as supersessionism. It was to sink deep roots in Christianity and helped the young church to define itself—which it did in opposition to, and over against, Judaism. Jews now became "the other." As we shall see, the teaching of contempt has been a major source of persecution of Jews and discrimination against them over the centuries.

Late in the second century, Melito of Sardis added a particularly toxic dimension to supersessionism: the accusation of *deicide*. Since, according to Christian faith, Jesus is God, it follows logically that in crucifying him the Jews had killed God. "God has been murdered; the king of Israel is slain by an Israelite hand" (*Homily on the Passover*). Similarly, Justin Martyr said in his *Dialogue with Trypho*: "Tribulations were justly imposed upon you, for you have murdered the Just One." This accusation was leveled not only at Jesus' contemporaries, but at all Jews everywhere, in every age, for all time. It had deadly consequences and was so long-lived that the Second Vatican Council in 1965 found it necessary expressly to repudiate this charge.

The Fourth Century

These second-century beginnings took on a new and far more dangerous dimension in the fourth century, when Christianity emerged from the catacombs and began to be identified with imperial power. Despite the devastation of the Roman wars, Judaism had not only survived but continued to attract converts and was thus seen as a threat to the church. This may explain in part the new and hitherto unprecedented vehemence in anti-Jewish rhetoric that we find in the writings of some of the greatest Christian theologians of the time, the Church Fathers. (These writings are today known as the *adversus Judaeos* literature.) Thus, Chrysostom asserts that Jews worship the devil; their rites are "criminal and impure," their religion is "a disease," their synagogue "an assembly of criminals. . .a den of thieves. . .a cavern of devils, an abyss of perdition."[7] Gregory of Nyssa speaks of Jews as ". . .slayers of the Lord, murderers of the prophets, enemies of God, adversaries of grace, enemies of their father's faith, advocates of the devil, brood of vipers, slanderers, scoffers, men of darkened minds, leaven of the Pharisees, congregation of demons, sinners, wicked men, stoners, and haters of goodness."[8]

The deicide charge is now full-blown. Augustine accuses Jews of:

> guilt for the death of the Savior, for through their fathers they have killed the Christ. The Jews held him, the Jews insulted him, the Jews bound him, they crowned him with thorns, dishonored him by spitting upon him, they scourged him, they heaped abuses upon him, they hung him upon a tree, they pierced him with a lance.[9]

Chrysostom goes further yet: nothing can atone for the Jews' crime, for their "odious assassination of Christ." It lies at the root of their degradation and suffering. For this deicide there is "no expiation possible, no indulgence, no pardon." Vengeance is without end. Hence Jews will always remain without temple or nation. They will live "under the yoke of servitude without end." God hates them and has always hated them. It is a duty of Christians to hate them: "He who can never love Christ enough will never cease fighting against those who hate him."[10]

Given such iniquity, the Jewish people should logically have disappeared. Yet they continued to exist, even to grow—a confusing fact for the church. Augustine finds an explanation for this puzzling fact: he argues that in their homelessness and suffering Jews are a necessary reminder to the world of what happens when human beings reject God. Therefore they must remain alive until the end of time, as "the witness people."[11]

However shocking such views sound to us today (and indeed are!), they had remained relatively harmless during the first three centuries, when both Judaism and Christianity were powerless minority religions. The situation changed drastically, however, when Christianity became the official religion of the empire in the fourth century and took on the trappings of Rome's temporal power. Theological views now began to be translated into legislation, a process that gained momentum and persisted throughout the Middle

Ages. Starting with the Council of Elvira in Spain (a regional council, circa 304) and reaching a climax in 1215 at the Fourth Lateran Council (a general council of the church), a body of anti-Jewish laws developed—ranging from the prohibition of intermarriage to the imposition of special clothing and a badge—that foreshadowed Nazi anti-Semitic legislation.

Indeed, in many respects there was little Hitler needed to invent in the *Nuremberg Laws,* which the German parliament passed in 1935. The main legislative tool for excluding Jews from society, these laws segregated them, prohibited marriage with non-Jews, made Jews ineligible for employment, and ultimately deprived them of all civil rights. Hitler merely completed the process began centuries earlier by the church. He added, however, one unprecedented, critical step that the church had never countenanced: genocide.

Theological Issues

The *Adversus Judaeos* literature of the fourth and fifth centuries must be set within the wider context of the church's efforts to articulate a distinctive Christian theology. Central to this effort was the God-question. That the Christian God was also the God of Israel was not held in doubt (except at an earlier period by Marcion, who was condemned as a heretic.) The question facing Christian theology, however, was this: What was Jesus' relationship to this God? Could the church affirm that Jesus was truly divine and still maintain its monotheism—a belief as central to Christianity as it was to Judaism? Such questions preoccupied not only theologians but also, because they directly affected the language and practice of worship, aroused passionate interest among ordinary people. Gregory of Nyssa reported that if you ask a baker the price of bread, he will tell you that the Father is greater than the Son.[12]

The church's increasing immersion in Greco-Roman culture necessitated a more philosophical interpretation of many Second Testament texts that, while they did not clarify such questions, yet remained the basis for Christian faith. Thus, the ancient hymn in Philippians 2:5-11 exalts Christ above every creature in the universe, while affirming that it is God who has bestowed lordship on Jesus, "to the glory of the Father." While some saw such texts as evidence that the church had cast aside monotheism, others interpreted them as an expanded concept of monotheism. The worship of God, so central to Judaism, now included the risen Christ as well.

This "expanded monotheism" (Boys) found valuable resources in post-exilic Jewish literature, in images such as Sophia—Lady Wisdom—who is God's partner in creation (Prov 8:22-31; Wis 7:25-26). The Greek-speaking Jewish philosopher Philo of Alexandria speaks of *Logos*, the Word, as "first-born," "governor of all things." Paul, in 1 Corinthians 5-6, uses similar language: "Indeed, even though there may be so-called gods in heaven or on earth—as in fact there are many gods and many lords—yet for us there is one God, the Father, from whom are all things and for whom we exist, and one Lord Jesus Christ, through whom are all things and through whom we exist."

Despite frequent references to Father, Son, and Spirit, the Second Testament does not speculate about their relation to one another. Clarification of those texts became necessary once Christianity became a dominant force in the fourth century. The councils, bishops, creeds—especially Nicaea (325), Constantinople (381), and Chalcedon (451)—now emerge as the essential tools by which the church defined and set boundaries to its faith.

In the context of this paper we shall mention only one instance in which this effort to clarify Christian faith impacted directly on the church's relationship to Judaism. The Council of Nicaea was called by the emperor Constantine to deal with the Arian controversy. Arius argued that Jesus was subordinate to God. His major opponent in the years following Nicaea, and leading up to the Council of Constantinople, was Bishop Athanasius. Athanasius used what were by now traditional anti-Jewish themes as his main weapon against "the Arian maniacs." Arians are the "new Jews of the present day"; like the Jews who killed Christ, Arians have become the enemies and slayers of Christ. Athanasius compares them to the Pharisees, who "pretended to study the words of the Law, wishing to deny the expected and present Lord." The Arians' emphasis on the Son's humanity parallels the Jews' failure to see Christ's divinity: "Since this sort of madness is a Jewish thing, and Jewish in the way that Judas the traitor was Jewish, let them profess openly that they are disciples of Caiaphas and Herod and stop disguising Judaism with the name of Christianity."[13]

Although anti-Judaism never made it into any of the Christian creeds, the main themes of the teaching of contempt reappear regularly in the controversies surrounding the articulation of Christian faith, particularly in preaching the Gospels. In this way Christian congregations were fed a steady diet of anti-Judaism, week after week, year after year. Such preaching can still be heard today. [14]

The Medieval Period

"Christendom," the world of medieval Europe, was a society whose every aspect was permeated by Christian faith and culture. In such a world Jews had no integral place; they were inevitably the outsiders. Their fortunes varied, depending on place and circumstance. At times they found friends and protectors among secular rulers, at whose courts they enjoyed influential positions and performed useful services. Bishops and popes also often protected them. The First Crusade, however, marked the beginning of persecutions on a scale not hitherto seen.

The year 1096 remains one of the most tragic dates in all of Jewish history. On their way to the holy land the crusaders passed through France and Germany. With the cry "God wills it" on their lips, they suddenly turned on "the infidels at home." In France (at Rouen) and Germany (at Worms and Mainz) they slaughtered thousands of Jews, in effect exterminating entire Jewish communities. The massacres were largely the work of mobs, whose rage at these "infidels" neither bishops nor popes were able to contain. While some saints (for example, Bernard of Clairvaux) tried to stop the slaughter, others supported it: Jews should be punished because "they defile Christ and Christianity and fleece Christians"; the Crusade should be financed with their money; Jews should not be killed, "but like Cain, the fratricide, they should be made to suffer fearful torments and be prepared for an existence worse than death."[15] There is irony in the fact that medieval church law made discrimination against Jews legal and emphasized their inferiority, while at the same time forbidding their murder. Jews must be kept alive until the end of time, as testimony to and reminder of human sinfulness—the theory of the "witness people" that goes back to Saint Augustine.

The era of the Crusades coincided with far-reaching social and economic changes that profoundly affected the Jews' fortunes. The growth of commerce required large sums of money. Christians were forbidden to engage in usury, yet capital was needed. Jews were the logical solution and were forced into money lending. They now found themselves caught in a vice: protected by the prince as long as he needed their services, abandoned by him when the anger of creditors exploded against them. The Jew as money-lender was hated, yet had become an economic necessity.

Although the underlying factors for the persecution of Jews during the Middle Ages were economic, the reasons articulated were primarily religious. Thus Pope Innocent III, one of the most powerful of all medieval popes, spoke of the perpetual servitude of Jews to Christians because God had rejected the Jewish people. "Their sufferings and homelessness are the just deserts for their crimes." A case could be made that the teaching of contempt, with origins in the second century C.E., bore its full "fruit" only now, centuries later.

In the twelfth century a new accusation was added to traditional anti-Judaism, one that was to prove deadly to Jews again and again: the charge of blood libel. Appearing for the first time in 1141 in Norwich, England, it was to leave a bloody trail through the ensuing centuries. The local veneration of many of the supposed child victims assured the longevity of this accusation, which is still found in twentieth-century Russia. About the same time the accusation of the desecration of the host also made its appearance and frequently led to massacres. Although several emperors and popes exonerated Jews on both counts, they had no influence on popular belief.

Things went from bad to worse during the fourteenth and fifteenth centuries. When the Black Death (bubonic plague) swept across Europe, a desperate populace looked for a rational explanation. Jews provided the answer; they were the natural scapegoats. The rumor that they had poisoned wells with a secret drug first surfaced in southern France. From there it swept like wildfire into northern Spain, Switzerland, Bavaria, Austria, eastern Germany, Belgium, and Poland. Unbeliever and usurer; ritual murderer and poisoner of wells, "stripped of all human features, the Jew assumed a satanic guise."[16]

The traditional theological view of Jews and Judaism at this time is vividly portrayed in two famous statues, which to this day stand on either side of the main portal of the cathedral of Strasbourg. Two tall, stately women face each other. The one—majestic, erect and queenly—represents the church; the other—blindfolded and with bowed head—symbolizes the synagogue.[17]

Medieval Spain

While the situation of Jews in Europe was becoming increasingly precarious, the Iberian peninsula, to the south, presented a very different scene. Cut off from the rest of Europe by high mountains, a rich intermingling of Moorish, Christian, and Jewish cultures had been able to develop under Muslim rule— "what some remember as a kind of paradise."[18] Spanish historians refer to this era as *convivencia* ("living together"), a far richer term than the English "co-existence." Moors, Jews and Christians influenced each other, learned from each other, enriched each other. Jews were taught Arabic by Muslim scholars and in turn taught Christians. Jews became conversant not only with the Koran, but with Plato and Aristotle, who had been rescued from oblivion by Islam during Europe's "Dark Ages." All three religions were undergoing a profound spiritual and material renaissance. Christians and Jews held positions of power and influence under Islamic regimes. In Cordoba, Christians were welcome to worship in the Great Mosque—which they did.

Cordoba became emblematic of the rich intermingling of the three faiths. It was the birthplace of Ibn Rushd, known in the West as Averroes (1126–1198), whose works of Arabic philosophy were mediated to the West by Jewish linguists. The collaboration of Jews, Christians, and Muslims was a natural outcome of *convivencia*. Cordoba was also the city of Maimonides, the greatest of all Jewish philosophers. According to historian Norman Roth, had Maimonides lived in Germany or France he would have become just another obscure rabbi writing commentaries on the Talmud, no matter how great his genius. Because he was nurtured by "the richest diversity of influences in the world, he became the greatest genius ever produced by the Jewish people."[19]

Although *convivencia* was not to last, it represents a moment full of promise of what might have been. Its mere existence shows that the history of Jewish-Christian relations is not monolithic, that it was not fated to lead inexorably to disaster. That Jews, Christians, and Muslims can live together in mutual respect and friendship is no idle dream; for some centuries they did just that.

They did so, however, in an Islamic, not a Christian, world. And even there, *convivencia* was to give way to *reconquista* ("re-conquest") in the thirteenth century, which restored Christian rule to Spain for the first time since the Islamic conquest of that part of the world in the eighth century. Yet for a short time it still survived in Castile, now under Christian rule. Ferdinand III, king of Castile from 1217–1252, called himself "King of the three religions." Castile's capital of Toledo was called the Jerusalem of Spain, and Jews participated actively in its life. Alfonso X, known as the Wise, surrounded himself with Jewish scholars and scientists. When he buried his father, he ordered the tombstone to be inscribed with tributes in Hebrew, Arabic, Castilian, and Latin.

In 1145 a stricter, more militant Muslim sect invaded Spain from Africa, and *convivencia* began to break up. Tolerance toward both Jews and Christians began to decline. In 1159 Maimonides fled with his family from Cordoba to Egypt, where he became famous as the Sultan's physician. Soon after, the crusading spirit of northern Europe invaded Spain, along with the hope of bringing all of Iberia back under Christian control. This goal was achieved in 1212, when Christian armies under Alfonso VII decisively defeated the Almohad rulers of Spain.

With Christian rule the old anti-Judaism reappeared. In Aragon, under the influence of the newly founded Friars (Dominicans and Franciscans), all-out efforts were made to convert Jews. They were forced to attend Christian sermons, and to participate in theological debates where the cards were *a priori* stacked against them and where the outcome was never in doubt. Jewish refusal to convert was now interpreted in a novel way, the ancient deicide charge taking on a new form: by refusing to convert, Jews were accused of crucifying Christ anew. Having murdered him once, it was said, they continued to murder him daily by their refusal to become Christians. The accusations of ritual murder and desecration of the host, already widespread in northern Europe, now reached Spain.

When this theological anti-Judaism coincided with a terrible natural catastrophe, the results can barely be imagined. The Plague, or Black Death, swept across Europe, claiming twenty-five million victims between 1348 and 1351. As we have already seen, Jews were made the scapegoats and accused of having poisoned wells throughout Europe. Pope Clement VI (at Avignon) denounced the accusation as blatantly false, condemned violence against Jews, and ordered bishops to protect them. Other popes, Martin V and Sixtus VI, were to do likewise. But they were unable to stem popular rage and violence. As Rosemary Ruether points out, "the mob merely acted out, in practice, a hatred which the Church taught in theory."[20]

The end of the fourteenth century was particularly tragic for Spanish Jews. In Seville a preacher named Ferrant Martinez preached such vicious anti-Jewish sermons that they led to a massacre in 1391. Pogroms soon spread to other Spanish cities. Faced with the choice of "convert or die," for the first time in their history large numbers of Jews chose baptism. Called *conversos* (or "new Christians," or *Marranos*), they formed a new class that was to subsist in Spain and Portugal into our own time. In some cases conversions were authentic; more often they were a choice for survival. (Some of Spain's most celebrated saints—for example, Teresa of Avila and John of the Cross—were descendants of *conversos*.) Many *conversos* continued to practice their Judaism in secret, which made them heretics in the eyes of the church and, if discovered, victims of the Inquisition.

The existence of these *Marranos* led to the birth of racism within the church. In 1547 the archbishop of Toledo issued a statute that forbade *Marranos*, or their descendants, to hold office in the church, because of "impure blood." This statute of *Limpieza da Sangre*, or "purity of blood," was opposed by Pope Nicholas V but reinstated by Paul IV. Even religious orders—the Jesuits among them—succumbed to what can only be called a "paranoia": fear of the taint of Jewish blood. Not until 1945 did the Jesuits drop their requirement that new recruits must be free of Jewish blood. The distinction we had made earlier, between religious anti-Judaism and racist anti-Semitism, has become moot in the case of Spanish racism within the church itself.

A century after the Seville massacre, in 1492, under "their Catholic Majesties" Ferdinand of Aragon and Isabella of Castile, Jews were expelled from Spain. Expulsion was nothing new in Jewish experience: Jews had been expelled earlier from Germany, England, France, and Austria. But these expulsions had involved relatively small groups and were sometimes revoked not long after. The 1492 expulsion from Spain included tens of thousands and was not rescinded until the twentieth century. Again many Jews converted, thus adding to the *conversos* population. Yet more than 150,000 left their native land. Many settled in the Middle East, in lands under Muslim control; some went to the Netherlands, others to central Europe and the papal territories. The expulsion from Spain is ranked by many Jewish historians as one of four major calamities in all of Jewish history (the other three being the Babylonian Exile in 586 B.C.E., the destruction of the Second Temple in 70 C.E., and the Shoah). The remarkable era of the Jews in Spain had come to a tragic and definitive end.

The Reformation

The Reformation is frequently considered the beginning of modern Europe. It broke the religious monopoly in the West of the Church of Rome, thus effectively putting an end to medieval Christendom. It gave birth to other churches and theologies, and so to the beginnings of religious pluralism. No longer was there one, single Christianity in the West; for the first time Christians could see that society and the Church were not identical. Social changes took place that made it somewhat easier for Jews to live among what still remained, however, a Christian majority.

All this seemed to offer new hope to Jews, promising greater religious freedom and an end to persecution and discrimination. Yet, as far as the religious views of Jews on the part of Christians were concerned, the Reformation represents continuity with, rather than a break from, the medieval world. While the horrors of the fourteenth and fifteenth centuries had abated, and large-scale expulsions, such as that of 1492, had come to an end, the traditional image of Jews as obdurate and rejected by God continued to prevail. In the verbal warfare between Protestants and Catholics, and among some of the Reformers themselves, no accusation was considered more damning than that of "Judaizer."

This applies especially to the initial stage of the Reformation, which is dominated by the powerful figure of Martin Luther.[21] Theologian and biblical scholar, Luther's love of the "Old Testament" might have provided an opening toward a more sympathetic understanding of Judaism. Instead, the antithesis of Law and Gospel so fundamental to his theology brought with it the antithesis between Judaism and Christianity: Judaism stood for the religion of law and legalism, Christianity for gospel and grace. (Luther considered the Epistle of James, the most Jewish of the books of the New Testament, "a right strawy epistle," not worthy of inclusion in the Christian scriptures.)

Already in Luther's earliest writings, his lectures on the Psalms (1514–1515), we find many of the familiar themes we encountered in early and medieval Christian anti-Judaism: God has rejected the Jewish people and their covenant; their place has been taken by Christianity; they remain obdurate in their refusal to recognize Christ, hence cursed by God. Luther's exclusively Christological interpretation of the Hebrew scriptures robs them of any intrinsic value; their sole importance lies in their pointing to Christ.

Luther's 1523 tract *That Jesus was born a Jew* is often cited as evidence that the young Luther was well disposed toward Jews, in contrast to Luther in his old age. In this work Luther chastises his fellow Christians for their brutal and inhumane treatment of Jews. How could Jews be expected to convert to Christianity, when their only image and experience of it was one of inhumanity and brutality? "They have dealt with the Jews as if they were dogs, and not human beings." He calls on Christians to treat Jews with kindness and brotherly love.

It is clear that Luther's motive for urging such a change in behavior is his hope that Jews will be drawn to Christianity and will convert. Luther was no racist. He was ready throughout his life to welcome Jews who were willing to convert to Christianity. But unbaptized Jews—Jews as Jews—were for him part of that "Satanic enemy" against whom he fought all his life: the Church of Rome, Jews, false Christians, and Muslims. Indeed, Jews embodied all other evils. Despite their powerlessness throughout Europe, Jews were for Luther the evil lords of the world.

Luther's theology of Judaism not only reiterated and reinforced the ancient themes of Christian anti-Judaism but had far-reaching negative consequences. Hitler was to make good use of some of Luther's later writings, especially the 1543 tract *Against the Jews and their Lies.* The vitriolic language of this work has rarely been surpassed, nor have the measures Luther advocates in it. They include the following: burn down their synagogues and their schools; destroy their homes, force them to live in barns; take from them their religious writings, including the Talmud; forbid rabbis to teach; deny them safe conduct when traveling; forbid them to lend at interest; force able-bodied men to become manual laborers.

Luther was born on November 10, 1483. Four hundred and fifty-five years later, the Lutheran bishop of Thuringia, Martin Sasse, exulted, "On November 10, 1938, on Luther's birthday, the synagogues are burning in Germany." The bishop was referring to *Kristallnacht.* His joy was expressed in the foreword to his collection of Luther's anti-Jewish writings, which the bishop was publishing in the hope that the German people would take to heart the words, as he put it, of the greatest anti-Semite of his time, the warner of his people against the Jews.[22] At the end of World War II, when Julius Streicher, editor of *Der Stürmer,* the vicious anti-Jewish paper published throughout the Nazi era, was tried at Nuremberg for his crimes against Jews, he said in his defense that, if he stood accused of such charges, Martin Luther should stand beside him.

When we come to John Calvin, the major figure of the second stage of the Reformation, the situation is vastly different. Like Luther, Calvin loved the Hebrew scriptures, but he differed sharply in his approach to them. Unlike

Luther, he was educated from his youth in Renaissance circles. His extraordinary command of Hebrew (Luther also knew Hebrew)—it became his third language, after French and Latin—was at least partly due to his intense and lifelong study of the great medieval Jewish exegetes, whom he considered his "authentic language teachers." (He urged Christian scholars to take language lessons from Jews—"who but Jews can teach the idiom of the Hebrew language?") This unusually deep familiarity with Hebrew enabled Calvin to understand the Hebrew scriptures from within, as it were, in the manner in which Jews understood them. For the first time in Christian history, the "Old" Testament is "old" no longer. Rather, it is "the original testament in which the eternal and lasting covenant is proclaimed to the people of Israel for all time."[23] The distinguished German biblical scholar, Hans-Joachim Kraus, writes that Calvin stands out like "a solitary rock" in the history of Christian interpretation of Judaism. The Hebrew scriptures are the enduring Word of God, first given to the Jewish people who were, and remain, God's first-chosen.

To give but one example, let us cite Calvin's interpretation of Jeremiah 31:31 (the new covenant). Throughout Christian history this text had been seen as proof that God had made a new covenant with the church, which cancelled the old covenant with Israel. Calvin sees in this text *renewal*, not *revocation*: renewal of the covenant God made with Abraham and his descendants.[24] Christians are added to, inserted into, this original people of God (Romans 11).

Ever since the Church Fathers, the "Old Testament" had been considered the key to the New ("the Old Testament bore the New in its loins," Origen). Its relation to the Christian scriptures was that of shadow to light, of promise to fulfillment, and—in Luther and many of his contemporaries—of law to gospel. Calvin does away with this opposition. The Hebrew scriptures are the original, the primary revelation of God to his people, God's free gift, a covenant of grace. Hence, the Torah remains the way of life, also for Christians, today and for all time, within the context of justification by grace alone.

This undercuts one of the main themes of the teaching of contempt: supersessionism. God has not rejected his people; the Jews remain God's people; there is only one people of God. This means that the harsh threats and prophetic critique of Israel in the scriptures are directed to Christians as much as to Jews. There is no cleavage for Calvin between "us and them," a distinction so prominent in Christian theology, beginning with early inter-pretations of the Gospels.

While we find echoes of the traditional anti-Judaism in Calvin—for example, he castigates Jews for their stubbornness in not accepting Christ as Messiah—these are far outweighed by his revolutionary interpretation of scripture, which was to impact history in the centuries to come. Regions where Calvinism predominates seem to have been more hospitable to Jews than other Christian countries. Two examples come to mind. One is the Netherlands, which became a haven for Jews expelled from Spain and Por-tugal, and which has been relatively free of anti-Semitism. It was the first country to grant Jews citizenship.

The other is the French mountain village of Le Chambon sur Lignon. The Calvinists of France, known as Huguenots, suffered long and severe per-secution for their faith at the hands of the Catholic majority. The experi-ence of suffering gave them an innate sympathy for the Jews persecuted by the Nazis. Le Chambon, with its predominantly Calvinist population and under the dynamic leadership of its pastor, Andre Trocmé, became a city of refuge for some 5000 Jews during the Nazi occupation of France.[25] Calvin's own experience of persecution also added to his sympathy for the Jewish people and to his understanding of their scriptures. He and his followers suf-fered severe persecution from 1525–1535. In speaking of Israel's exodus from Egypt, Calvin writes that God "accompanied the children of Israel night and day on their flight, present among them as a fugitive himself."[26] God as fugi-tive is reminiscent of the ancient Jewish mystical belief that the *Shekhinah* (symbol of God) accompanies the people whenever they go into exile.

We can only speculate what suffering, culminating in the Shoah, Jews might have been spared if Calvin's theology of Judaism had become more widespread and deeply rooted throughout Western Christianity. His approach to the scriptures foreshadows themes that we find in the radical reappraisal by post-Shoah Christianity of its attitude toward Judaism. Oberman calls Calvin "the only sixteenth-century Christian interpreter of the Hebrew scriptures who is still relevant as a resource for modern textual studies."[27]

From Reformation to Shoah

Although the Reformation and the Enlightenment spelled the end of medi-eval Christendom, Christianity remained a potent force in Europe. This was true especially of the Church of Rome. Increasingly under attack by liberal political and social forces and, in the nineteenth century, faced with the loss of papal territories, the church held on to what power it still had. One of the last vestiges of its power was the Roman ghetto.

The Roman ghetto had been established in 1555 by Pope Paul IV, by a special papal "bull" (papal decree) that imposed severe restrictions on every aspect of Jewish life. The cramped conditions inside the ghetto led to disease and poverty. Periodically abolished and rebuilt by successive popes, the ghetto was still in existence in 1870 under Pope Pius IX. More than a hundred years later Cardinal Edward Cassidy, head of the Vatican Commission for Religious Relations with Jews, said that "the ghetto, which came into being in 1555 with papal bull, became in Nazi Germany the antechamber of extermination."[28]

While Jews enjoyed a new freedom in much of western Europe, in Rome and the papal states they remained subject to the pope. This is clearly seen in the Mortara Affair—the kidnapping of a Jewish boy, Edgardo Mortara, who had been secretly baptized by a Catholic maid. In 1858 the boy was snatched from his home in Bologna (at that time part of the papal states) and taken to Rome, where he was put under personal protection of Pius IX. Neither his family's desperate efforts nor widespread outrage and protest throughout much of Europe and even the United States succeeded in restoring Edgardo to his family and people. He ended his life as a Catholic priest.[29]

While this event underscores the value that the Roman church gave to baptism, it also proves that by this time the church no longer embraced the "purity of blood" policy it had adhered to in the sixteenth century. Once baptized, a Jew now was considered a full member of the church. This is a welcome sign of the rejection of biological racism within the church. It led, however, to a tragic phenomenon under Hitler: the church's discrimination between baptized and non-baptized Jews. During the Shoah the Vatican regularly interceded on behalf of baptized Jews, whom it considered its "children," while it was largely indifferent to other Jews. Jews as Jews were outside the pale of its concern. We have not yet, however, arrived at the Shoah.

Jewish emancipation was finally achieved as a result of the French Revolution; Jews were granted full citizenship rights. In the nineteenth century Jews were able for the first time to participate fully in modern Western society. They embraced the new opportunities now open to them with enthusiasm—for example, entrance into universities and professions. At the same time, the new freedom gave rise to tensions within the Jewish community that it had not previously experienced. Some Jews now saw assimilation, and even baptism, as "the entrance ticket to society" (Heinrich Heine). Others believed that Judaism had the capacity and vitality to adapt to modern life. Thus was born, in Germany, the Reform movement within Judaism.

Yet there were signs—besides the Mortara Affair—that Christian anti-Judaism was alive and well. Many clergy, both Catholic and Protestant, still saw Jews as alien, linked to anti-clerical and socialist "enemies" of the church. In France, the land that had liberated Jews from the ghetto and that had been the first to grant them full citizenship, reactionary movements against liberalism and secularism were led by conservative Catholics who also, for the most part, were profoundly anti-Semitic. Eduard Drumont, who has been called the "evil genius of French antisemitism" (Flannery) in 1866 published *La France Juive,* in which he blamed the Jews for all the evils that had befallen France since the rise of modernity. The conclusion of his book says: "At the end of this book of history, what do you see? I see one face and it is the only face I want to show you: the face of Christ, insulted, covered with disgrace, lacerated by thorns, crucified. Nothing has changed in the eighteen hundred years. It is the same lie, the same hatred, the same people."[30]

In the late nineteenth century, Christian anti-Judaism found a new ally in the racial myth. Racial anti-Semitism now became widely accepted and respectable. In France, Count Arthur de Gobineau's *Essay on the Inequality of the Human Races* warned against "crossbreeding." Houston Stewart Chamberlain's *Foundation of the Nineteenth Century* quickly became the bible for anti-Semites. A naturalized German citizen of English background, Chamberlain stressed the superiority of the "Teutonic race," and the consequent inferiority of Jews. The word *anti-Semitism* appears for the first time in 1879 in Germany in the writings of Wilhelm Marr, a German anti-Semitic journalist.

It was not in Germany, however, but in France that the most virulent and infamous explosion of anti-Semitism occurred. The Dreyfus Affair bitterly divided France and riveted the world for twelve years. [31] Late in 1894 Captain Alfred Dreyfus, the only Jew on the French general staff, was accused of spying for the Germans. (The Franco-Prussian war of 1870, in which France had been defeated, was still fresh in people's memory.) Dreyfus was tried behind closed doors, found guilty, and sentenced for life to Devil's Island, France's worst penal colony. The only evidence against him was a letter, supposedly in his handwriting, which was eventually proven to be a forgery. Amid passionate controversy for and against Dreyfus, his trial was re-opened; in 1899 Dreyfus was found completely innocent of all charges against him and was pardoned. Throughout the "Affair" anti-Semitism and hatred of Dreyfus were fueled by conservative Roman Catholics, although individuals like Charles Péguy passionately defended him.

Priests throughout France attended anti-Semitic congresses, gave anti-semitic sermons, inflamed Catholic congregations, and invoked the usual stereotypes: the Jew as revolutionary, money lender, traitor, killer of Christ, ritual murderer. The Catholic hierarchy remained silent. This explosion of hatred toward Jews spelled the end of the nineteenth-century hopes for Jew-ish emancipation—although few could have foreseen this at the time. One who did was a Viennese journalist, a Jew by the name of Theodor Herzl. He had been present at the first Dreyfus trial and became convinced that Jews would never be safe except in their own homeland. Thus was born modern Zionism as a political movement.

The Shoah

Whether the Dreyfus Affair is seen as prelude to what was to come one gen-eration later (Hannah Arendt), or as the first act of the Shoah (James Car-roll), nothing had prepared the Jewish people—either in recent history or in the past eighteen hundred years—for the catastrophe. No statistics can even remotely convey the horror of the genocide that murdered one third of the world's Jews, for no other reason than that they were Jews. Millions of other victims were also murdered by the Nazis: those branded racially inferior, for example, Roma (Gypsies) and Poles; the disabled; and the politically unde-sirable (homosexuals, Jehovah's Witnesses, Communists). Only Jews were targeted for genocide as a people, in order to make the world *judenrein* (free of Jews). In the words of Elie Wiesel, "Not every victim was a Jew, but every Jew was a victim." For those of us who were not there, only the testimony of those who experienced the Shoah—whether or not they survived—can begin to convey something of the horror. We cite here one paragraph from Wiesel's memoir of his time in Auschwitz as a teenager:

> Never shall I forget that night, the first night in camp, which has turned my life into one long night. . . . Never shall I forget that smoke. Never shall I forget the little faces of the children, whose bodies I saw turned into

wreaths of smoke beneath a silent blue sky. . . . Never shall I forget these things, even if I am condemned to live as long as God himself. Never.[32]

The overwhelming evil of the Shoah forced the churches at long last to confront the role that their distorted teaching about Jews and Judaism—the teaching of contempt—had played in preparing the soil for Hitler's genocide. Much of the rest of this paper will deal with the results of their soul searching and repentance. Before we come to this hopeful chapter, however, we need briefly to look at the record of the churches during the Shoah itself.

The Churches and the Shoah[33]

"Christianity was not a sufficient condition for the Holocaust, nevertheless it was a necessary condition" for it, writes the Holocaust scholar John Roth. We shall cite three examples that illustrate Roth's point:

1. In 1941 Archbishop Konrad Gröber of Freiburg, Germany, issued a pastoral letter in which he blamed Jews for the death of Christ. He added, "The self-imposed curse of the Jews, 'His blood be upon us and upon our children' (Matt 27:25), "has come terribly true in our time."[34]

2. Also in 1941, Marshal Pétain, head of Vichy government in France, asked Léon Bérard, Vichy's ambassador to the Vatican, to find out the Vatican reaction to the anti-Jewish laws the Vichy regime had enacted. Bérard reported that he had not heard any misgivings in Rome concerning the persecution of Jews. "In principle, there is nothing in these measures which the Holy See finds necessary to criticize."[35]

3. In 1942 Rabbi Michael Dov-Ber Weissmandel (of Slovakia) went to Archbishop Kamerko to plead for his intercession on behalf of Slovakian Jews, who were about to be deported. The rabbi did not know as yet about the gas chambers, but he stressed the dangers of starvation and disease to which the victims would be exposed. The Archbishop of Nietra replied: "It is not just a matter of deportation. You will not die there of hunger and disease. They will slaughter all of you, old and young alike, women and children, at once—it is the punishment that you deserve for the death of our Lord and Redeemer, Jesus Christ—you have only one solution. Come over to our religion and I will work to annul this decree."[36]

The record of the Protestant Church of Germany is no better. The majority of German Protestant Christians (known as "German Christians" under Hitler) supported Hitler, who appointed Bishop Ludwig Muller as their head. As early as 1935, Müller said that Christianity did not grow out of Judaism: "There is no bond between them, rather, the sharpest opposition." Even the "Confessing Church," comprised of Christians who courageously and unambiguously opposed Hitler, did not mention Jews in its statement of opposition to Nazism, the Barmen Confession of 1934.

Before leaving this chapter we need to mention the rescuers. While Jews were abandoned by the institution of the church and of the government (Denmark and Bulgaria are two shining exceptions to this shameful record), thousands of individuals, Christian and non-Christian, risked their lives to help Jews. The story of the rescuers is perhaps the only ray of light that pierces the almost impenetrable darkness of the Shoah. [37] Let us now come to the turning point in the two-thousand-year-old history of the relationship between Christianity and Judaism.

From the Teaching of Contempt to the Teaching of Respect

On September 10, 2000, a remarkable document appeared in *The New York Times*. *Dabru Emet* ("To speak the truth") was the work of four distinguished Jewish scholars and was signed by 275 other scholars. We quote the first paragraph of the introduction, as a summary of what we hope to do in this next part of this chapter:

> In recent years there has been a dramatic and unprecedented shift in Jewish and Christian relations. Throughout the nearly two millennia of Jewish exile, Christians have tended to characterize Judaism as a failed religion or, at best, a religion that prepared the way for, and is completed in, Christianity. In the decades since the Holocaust, however, Christianity has changed dramatically. An increasing number of official Church bodies, both Roman Catholic and Protestant, have made public statements of their remorse about Christian mistreatment of Jews and Judaism. These statements have declared, furthermore, that Christian teaching and preaching can and must be reformed so that they acknowledge God's enduring covenant with the Jewish people and celebrate the contribution of Judaism to world civilization and to Christian faith itself.

What accounts for the "dramatic change" referred to in *Dabru Emet*? The answer is clear: the Holocaust, or Shoah. On the one hand, everything that has been said thus far about Christian anti-Judaism culminated in the until-then unimaginable horror of the Shoah. At the same time, it was precisely this event, once it was acknowledged by the churches, that led to a radical turning point in Christian teaching about Jews and the relations between the two faith communities.

To say that nineteen centuries of the teaching of contempt culminated in the Shoah is not to say that this teaching was by itself solely responsible for the Holocaust. Had it been, the attempted genocide of the Jewish people could or would have happened centuries earlier. It took a combination of other factors to produce the Shoah: modern racial anti-Semitism; Versailles and the crushing defeat and humiliation of Germany in World War I, which eventually propelled Hitler to power; the sophisticated technology of a modern state; and a vast and brilliant propaganda machine, which persuaded millions of people that the Jews were not only responsible for Germany's defeat, but that they were a cancer on society.[38]

Having said this, however, it remains an indisputable fact that Christian anti-Judaism had prepared the soil in which the Shoah could be carried out, with no or only minimal protest from the rest of the Western world, including the churches. It was the gradual awareness of this that eventually led to a deep soul-searching, and to the determination to cleanse Christianity of a teaching that had done incalculable harm to Jews and had disfigured the teaching of Jesus beyond recognition. Certainly, shame and guilt played a major role in the "sea change" we shall now briefly examine. We shall begin with some mainline Protestant churches, and then discuss the changes in the Roman Catholic Church.

The Protestant Churches

The change did not happen quickly, nor all at once. The deep roots that the teaching of contempt had sunk in the Christian psyche could not be eradicated easily. And it took time for the churches (as well as the rest of the world) to confront the full horror and implications of the Shoah. In the two decades following the end of World War II, the World Council of Churches and several individual churches issued statements that decried anti-Semitism. Thus the 1948 WCC Assembly of Amsterdam called upon its member churches "to denounce anti-Semitism as a sin against God and man." But the text reiterated the traditional view that Jews had failed in their mission and reaffirmed Christian responsibility to work for their conversion. The Protestant

Evangelical Church of Germany, in statements issued in 1947, 1948, and 1949, also decried anti-Semitism, but (incomprehensibly!) blamed Jews for the destruction that had come upon them because they had crucified "the Messiah of Israel." Their only hope lay in conversion to Christ. It was a half-hearted beginning at best!

One of the earliest and most promising statements was issued in 1947 at Seelisberg in Switzerland, the work of an international conference of Jews and Christians. Its ten points, or "theses," laid the groundwork for efforts that were to flourish two decades later.

It was only in the 1960s that the churches began to confront fully the implications of their failure during the Shoah. ("Failure" here refers to the churches in general as institutions, not to the often heroic efforts to protect Jews on the part of individual Christians, including some highly placed church officials.) The 1961 New Delhi Assembly of the WCC and the 1967 Bristol Report of its Faith and Order Commission speak of ecumenical dialogue and of a common study based on the Hebrew scriptures. During the next three decades, most mainline Protestant denominations in the U.S. issued significant statements. The United Methodist Church in 1972 adopted "Bridge in Hope: Interreligious Dialogue between Jews and Christians," which it updated in 1996. This statement gives special emphasis to the enduring covenant of the Jewish people, thus reversing one of the most pernicious elements of the teaching of contempt: that God had rejected his people: We believe that just as God is steadfastly faithful to the biblical covenant in Jesus Christ, likewise God is steadfastly faithful to the biblical covenant of the Jewish people. . . . Both Jews and Christians are bound to God in covenant, with no covenantal relationship invalidated by any other."

Statements issued by the Lutheran Church—both the Lutheran World Federation and the Evangelical Lutheran Church in America—are noteworthy for their frank repudiation of Luther's anti-Semitism. Referring to the anti-Jewish writings in his old age, the Evangelical Lutheran Church of America declared: "We reject this violent invective, and yet more do we express our deep and abiding sorrow over the tragic effects on subsequent generations. . . ." Its 1998 "Guidelines for Lutheran-Jewish Relations" offer concrete steps for genuine dialogue and mutual understanding.

The Presbyterian Church's statement published in 1987, "A Theological Understanding of the Relationship between Christians and Jews," makes seven "Affirmations," each of which is followed by a detailed theological explanation aimed at facilitating acceptance by the church's membership of what is essentially perceived to be a new teaching. The affirmations emphasize that Christians and Jews worship the same God. They include repudiation of supersessionism and affirmation of the ongoing validity of the Jewish covenant, and repentance for the teaching of contempt and its contribution to the Shoah. "Jews and Christians are partners in waiting. Christians see in Christ the redemption not yet fully visible in the world, and Jews await the messianic redemption. Christians and Jews together await the final manifestation of God's promise of the peaceable kingdom."[39]

In 2003 the Alliance of Baptists published the following resolutions:

As the Alliance of Baptists, institutionally, and as individual members and churches, we

1. Affirm the teaching of the Christians Scriptures that God has not rejected the community of Israel . . . since the gifts and calling of God are irrevocable (Romans 11:29);
2. Renounce interpretations of Scripture which foster religious stereotyping and prejudice against the Jewish people and their faith;
3. Seek genuine dialogue with the broader Jewish community, a dialogue built on mutual respect and the integrity of each other's faith;
4. Lift our voices quickly and boldly against all expressions of anti-Semitism;
5. Educate ourselves and others on the history of Jewish-Christian relations from the first century to the present, so as to understand our present by learning from our past; and
6. Commit ourselves to rigorous consideration of appropriate forms of Christian witness for our time.

The Second Vatican Council and its Aftermath

The changes in the Roman Catholic Church received their major impetus at the Second Vatican Council (1962–1965). The French Jewish historian Jules Isaac, who had lost part of his family at Auschwitz but had survived in hiding with a Catholic couple in the south of France, had met with Pope John XXIII in 1960 and persuaded the Pope to put the church's relationship to Judaism on the Council's agenda. Thanks to the commitment of the Pope and the capable guidance of Cardinal Augustin Bea, head of the Subcommission of the Secretariat for the Promotion of Christian Unity, a draft on the Roman Church and The Jewish people was prepared for consideration by the Council. It went through many ups and downs, was the object of heated and acrimonious debate by the attending bishops, but was finally passed at the closing session of the Council in October 1965. Known as *Nostra Aetate* ("In Our Time"), the relatively short statement forms part of the larger Council document on the church's relationship to non-Christian religions.

Nostra Aetate rejected all forms of anti-Semitism as sinful; repudiated the accusation of Jewish collective guilt for the death of Jesus, both at the time of Jesus and through the ages; and affirmed God's ongoing love of his people, and the church's unique spiritual bond with Jews. Seen from our perspective of forty years later, *Nostra Aetate* seems rather minimal; even at the time it was promulgated there were many who had hoped for more. One of these was the main architect of *Nostra Aetate*, Cardinal Bea, who had hoped for a far stronger statement. In his book *The Church and the Jewish People,* Bea tried to give as positive an interpretation to the final outcome as possible. His presentation makes it clear, however, that it was not only political pressure from the Arab world (Christian and Muslim) that was responsible for the toning down of the original text. "One reason for the defeat of Bea's intentions. . .was that too many texts from the New Testament were against him. This is the really serious level of Christian anti-Semitism. Can the church admit to the tinge of anti-Jewish elements in its very Scriptures?"[40]

Nonetheless, *Nostra Aetate* may be considered the magna carta of the Roman church's new approach to its relation with the Jewish people. It gave the green light to further theological and biblical studies, which proliferated in the decades that followed, both from the Vatican and from national bodies of bishops, especially those of France and the United States. We can refer here only to the most important of these documents, with special emphasis given to those from the Vatican, because of Rome's authority and wide influence. Taken together they have revolutionized Roman Catholic theology concerning Judaism. They affirm the ongoing validity of God's covenant with the Jews, who remain people of God.

Yet already in 1967 Krister Stendahl of Harvard, later Lutheran bishop of Stockholm, had written: "The question must be asked. . .if the present attempts to purge Christian liturgies, catechism, and hymnals from overt anti-Semitic elements are not only coming too late but are primarily too timid and totally insufficient. The church is not only responsible for its intentions, which may be honorable, but also for what *actually* happens in the minds of its *actual* members and half-members as they have been and are exposed to its Scriptures and message."[41] Despite all the progress in the forty years since these lines were written, the question Stendahl asked then is still relevant today: Are our reforms still too "timid" and "insufficient"?

The Vatican documents frequently built on statements by national hierarchies; the reverse was also true. The American bishops were the first to publish, in 1967, guidelines for the local implementation of *Nostra Aetate*. They pointed out the incompatibility of dialogue and proselytism and urged the involvement of Catholic scholars at all levels of the dialogue. In 1974 the Vatican's newly formed Commission for Religious Relations with Jews issued its own *Guidelines and Suggestions for Implementing Nostra Aetate*. These *Guidelines* are practical in nature, emphasizing the need for educational and liturgical reform.

One important result of this reform was the new and entirely rewritten Good Friday prayer for the Jews. Instead of praying for the conversion "of the faithless Jews"—words that had been used for centuries—the prayer now reads: "Let us pray for the Jewish people, the first to hear the word of God, that they may continue to grow in the love of his Name and in faithfulness to his covenant."

The 1985 *Notes on the Correct Way to Present Jews and Judaism in Preaching and Catechesis* built heavily on two statements by the French bishops (1973) and the American bishops (1975). It raises important theological issues such as Christian worship and problematic passages in the Second Testament.

The 2001 statement of the Pontifical Biblical Commission, *The Jewish People and their Sacred Scriptures in the Christian Bible*, acknowledges the validity and significance *for Christians* of Jewish readings of the Hebrew Bible.

"We Remember: A Reflection on the Shoah," issued in 1998 by the Vatican (accompanied by a personal letter from Pope John Paul II), has been the subject of a good deal of controversy for not going far enough. Nevertheless, it was the first time that the Roman Church acknowledged that its teaching had contributed to the Shoah.

Pope John Paul II did more, during his long reign, to build a new relationship of the Roman Church to Jews than all the popes before him. In addition to his firm support of *Nostra Aetate* and further biblical and theological studies, of statements by the Vatican and national conferences of bishops, and of his recognition of the State of Israel, two "gestures" made by this pope spoke at least as clearly as any written words and have reached a much wider audience. The first was his visit to Rome's Great Synagogue in 1986—the first visit ever to a synagogue by a pope—where he embraced Rome's Chief Rabbi as true equal and as "our beloved brother." The second was his visit to Yad Vashem and the Western Wall in Jerusalem in March 2000. Placing a prayer in the stones of the Wall—an ancient Jewish custom—the Pope begged God's forgiveness and pledged the church's commitment to forging "genuine brotherhood with the people of the covenant." *The New York Times* commented on the latter gesture: "It was a searing image that many Israelis said signaled a new era in Jewish-Christian relations."[42]

Will this "new era" become reality? The documents referred to in the foregoing pages—both Protestant and Roman Catholic—are a sign of extraordinary progress and reason for hope. The highest authorities in many churches have spoken with a new voice. Supersessionism, which is so central to the teaching of contempt, is no longer valid; the first covenant has not been superseded. The challenge the churches still face, however, is how to bring the new teaching to ordinary Christians in the pews. The revision of textbooks, which has been undertaken by several churches, is one step in that direction. Training of clergy in biblical studies and preaching is another, as is reform of texts in Christian worship; much still remains to be done in these areas.

An "Affirmation" published by the United Methodist Church of Claremont, California, in 1993 is a rare example of a local congregation that has embraced and clearly articulated every element of the new teaching. The full text follows:

Affirmation

The Claremont United Methodist Church publicly states its affirmation that Judaism is a continuing bulwark of the faith, that it has not been superseded by Christianity, that God has not rejected the Jewish people, that the Jewish people have never lost their covenant with God, that salvation is available to Jews as a covenant people, that the Jews as an historic nation are not responsible for, and therefore not to be blamed for, the death of Jesus, and that Jews should not be pressured to convert to Christianity. Furthermore, we state that anti-Judaism in all forms should be universally condemned. We ask forgiveness for past sins and persecutions against the Jewish people. We pray that old barriers to communication and understanding will be removed and that the relationships of this church with the congregations of the local Jewish community will be enhanced. (approved by the Administrative Board, 01/19/1993)

Jewish-Christian Relations Today

The "dramatic changes" described in this paper raise a question for us: Can we truly speak of dialogue if all the changes have taken place on one side, the Christian side? It is true that, given the tragic history between us, Christians had to make the first move. It is true that Christianity cannot understand itself without knowledge of its Jewish roots. It is true that there has been much interaction in recent years between Jews and Christians, especially in collaboration on social issues. But can we say that Judaism recognizes Christianity as a faith tradition that is important to Judaism theologically, and from which it has something to learn?

Our response to this implied criticism of Judaism is that the last forty years, or one generation, can hardly undo a tradition that is as old as Christianity. Yes, Christianity has taken "dramatic steps." But given the centuries of suffering that Jews have endured at the hands of Christians, is it realistic to expect Jews to take Christians at their word? Especially when anti-Semitism is on the rise (see below), and when so much work still remains to be done on the Christian side.[43] It may well take generations to build trust on firm foundations. Meanwhile, Christians have every reason to be grateful for *Dabru Emet* and to show by our actions that we really mean what we (or our documents) say.

We return now to *Dabru Emet*. After the initial paragraph, cited above, *Dabru Emet* goes on to speak of theological points that unite Jews and Christians (such as worship of the same God and seeking authority from the same scriptures), as well as those that differentiate the two faiths and will continue to do so. Eight brief statements of *Dabru Emet* unequivocally affirm that it is important for Jews *for their own sake as Jews* to reflect about Christianity as a vital faith. For the first time in history, a group of Jewish scholars has spoken publicly in these terms. *Dabru Emet* is a groundbreaking document, one more sign that Jewish-Christian dialogue has come of age.

Inspired by *Dabru Emet,* a group of Protestant and Catholic scholars called the Christians' Scholars Group (CSG) issued in 2002 a statement of ten points under the title *A Sacred Obligation*. This statement eventually led to the publication of a book, *Seeing Judaism Anew: Christianity's Sacred Obligation*,[44] which expands on and explores the implications of the earlier statement for Christian faith and practice. We quote from the editor's introduction:

> We believe that revising Christian teaching about Judaism and the Jewish people is a central and indispensable obligation of theology in our time. It is essential that Christianity both understand and represent Judaism accurately, not only as a matter of justice for the Jewish people, but also for the integrity of Christian faith, which we cannot proclaim without reference to Judaism.[45]

The essays in this volume build on the work of such theologians as Clark Williamson, who are rethinking Christian theology in light of our new understanding of Judaism and of the Shoah (see suggested reading at the end of this paper).

Can we speak of a corresponding effort on the Jewish side? Are there Jewish scholars who believe that Judaism can be enriched by a thoughtful, serious study of Christianity? *Opening the Covenant* by Michael Kogan attempts to do precisely that.[46] True dialogue, Kogan believes, demands what he calls self-transcendence: I must be willing to let go of my absolutist and exclusivist view that my own faith is the only authentic revelation from God, and open myself to the possibility that other religions are also authentic revelations.

Why should this come as a surprise? After all, every revelation of the divine is of necessity partial and finite, not because God is finite, but because we are. How could the finite ever fully contain or hope to grasp the Infinite? "All of us are finite hearers of the Infinite life of God. We come closer to that Infinite when we realize that we are not alone. Others bear it all with us."[47] Kogan's work builds on decades of a dialogue that had engaged eminent scholars on both sides. His book enables us to take a further step into the authentic mutuality between Jews and Christians.

Challenges

So far, we have described much that is hopeful. Can we conclude that the ancient hostility between Christians and Jews is finally laid to rest? For a brief period, the truly revolutionary changes in the decades that followed Vatican II gave rise to this hope. More recent developments, however, point to a revival of anti-Semitism in general, as well as to a potential resurgence of Christian anti-Judaism. Following is one example of the latter.

In the summer of 2008 two hundred American Catholic bishops voted to delete a reference to the covenant between God and the Jewish people in *The United States Catholic Catechism for Adults*. The sentence to be deleted, pending Vatican approval, is as follows: "Thus the covenant that God made with the Jewish people through Moses remains eternally valid for them." It is to be replaced with a text from Romans 9:4-5: "To the Jewish people, whom God first chose to hear His word, belong the sonship, the glory, the covenants, the giving of the law, the worship, and the promises; to them belong the patriarchs, and of their race, according to the flesh, is the Christ." The reason given for the change is that some bishops feared too many Catholics seemed to misunderstand the sentence, believing that it meant that Jews do not need Jesus to be saved. As one Jewish leader asked, "Why take a very simple sentence and replace it with a very complicated paragraph?"

How are we to interpret the change? Are we to think of Jews as no longer chosen by God? Vatican II and its aftermath represented a giant step away from the centuries-old teaching of contempt. Are some bishops trying to turn back the clock?[48]

As to the danger of a revival of anti-Semitism, events in the Middle East are a major factor in the development of a climate hostile to Jewish-Christian relations. In what follows we examine what appear to us the reasons for this.

In the immediate post-Shoah years, anti-Semitism was taboo. Whether out of a sense of guilt or of genuine horror at what Jews had suffered, there was widespread sympathy for Jews in general and for Holocaust survivors in particular (even though Great Britain refused to admit them to Palestine). The USSR was the first country to cast its vote in the United Nations in favor of an independent state of Israel, on May 14, 1948. The new state was seen by the West as giving Jews—homeless for 2000 years—a land and home of their own. From the Jewish perspective, Israel was the realization of an age-old dream: "Next year in Jerusalem!" had been prayed at every Seder for centuries.

Zionism as a political movement, born in the nineteenth century and spurred on by the unrelenting efforts of Theodor Herzl, was at first rejected by most Western, assimilated Jews, who saw themselves as citizens of their countries of adoption—whether France, England, Germany, or Austria. It was also opposed by ultra-orthodox Jews, for whom only the Messiah could usher in the Jews' return to their ancient homeland.

All this changed dramatically with the Shoah, when it became clear that Jews had nowhere to go. In the words of Chaim Weizmann, "the world seemed to be divided into two parts—those places where Jews could not live, and those where they could not enter."[49]

Arabs had resisted the founding of the state from the first and declared war on Israel one minute after midnight on May 15, 1948. Amos Oz, the Israeli novelist, remembers how his father—who had seen graffiti in Germany, Russia, and the Ukraine: "Jews go home to Palestine!"—years later, as a citizen of Israel, saw new signs: "Jews out of Palestine!" Images of the Shoah, and of centuries of pogroms, lay close to the surface in the memory of every Jew in Israel. Amos Oz tells how he "wanted to be a book, not a man. The house was full of books written by dead men, and I thought a book may survive." Fear was everywhere, even after the Israeli army, vastly outnumbered by Arabs, won an astounding victory.

The early Zionists saw Israel as "a land without people for a people without a land." Only the second part of this phrase was correct. Palestinians had been living for centuries in what was now the State of Israel, and they had not been consulted by the United Nations in the founding of the state. Israel Kantor, a lawyer and old friend of Amos Oz, is quoted as saying, "The original sin of the Israeli Jews is that they thought too much about land and not enough about people."[50]

After the 1967 war, the situation changed dramatically once more. David now came to be seen as Goliath; the victims were no longer Jews, but the Palestinians. The Israeli occupation of the lands conquered in the war became permanent and led to the establishment of hundreds of Jewish settlements on Palestinian land. While the struggle between Israel and Palestine can be seen as the struggle between right and right, the conflict was, and remains, an unequal one. Israel's army has become the most powerful army in the Middle East and is backed by the most powerful nation on earth. Leaving aside Arab hostility toward Israel, Europe's sympathy has shifted more and more to the oppressed Palestinians. The desperate conditions of European Jews prior to the founding of the state have been relegated to history.

Israeli violation of Palestinian human rights has led to strong criticism, by many churches as well as by secular voices. The most visible and extreme example of new tensions that have arisen between Israel and the churches is the issue of divestment. In 2004, at its 216th General Assembly, the

Presbyterian Church (U.S.A.) initiated a process designed to lead to selective, phased divestment from some companies doing business with Israel (special mention was made of Caterpillar, Inc., which builds the bulldozers used to demolish Palestinian homes). Other Protestant churches—the WCC, NCC, and Anglican World Communion—announced that they would study the matter, and a group of American Jews opposed to Israeli policy also recommended divestment. But it was the Presbyterian action that drew the most fire. The Anti-Defamation League (ADL), and Alan Dershowitz of Harvard Law School, accused the church of bigotry and anti-Semitism, of fostering terrorism, and of equating Israel with South Africa under apartheid. Church authorities have been at pains to contain the damage. They pointed out that the study is to be phased and selective. They have reiterated their historic support for Israel's secure existence and their repudiation of Christian anti-Judaism as expressed in the church's "Theological Statement" of 1987. They have renewed their efforts for continuing dialogue and met with a group of Jewish leaders in New York in September 2004. "No one's mind was changed," but concerns were aired and suggestions made for future conversations.[51] Although the controversy shows no signs of abating, both sides at least continue talking.

There are Christians as well as Jews who believe that the criticism of Israel by some mainline churches is part of a deeper, theological problem. One of these is Richard Harries, Bishop of Oxford, who emphasizes the fundamental difference in Christian and Jewish self-understanding. For most Christians, religion is the individual's personal relationship to God, regardless of nationality or ethnic background. For Jews, on the other hand, to be a Jew is to be a member of a particular people. Judaism is inseparable from peoplehood, with a particular people tied to a particular land. In the words of Israeli scholar Geoffrey Wigoder: "The relationship of covenant to land, as of the Jews to Israel, is as much outside the Christian experience as the centrality of Jesus in the mystery of the triune God is outside the Jewish experience."[52]

In this matter, as with regard to criticism of Israel in general, Israelis and many Diaspora Jews complain of a double standard: other nations who commit far greater human rights violations are not criticized. We suggest several explanations for this higher standard:

1. Israel is being judged by Western standards, since it is not a third-world nation.

2. Far from being a victim, Israel today has come to be the strongest military presence in the Middle East, and is supported by billions of dollars annually from the United States, its largest foreign-aid package. We believe that our criticism of Israel's occupation is part of our responsibility as progressive Christians, and that it is, at the same time, also a critique of our government's policies in the Middle East.

3. Jews throughout biblical history have held themselves to higher moral standards than other peoples. This is still so today in many cases (see, for example, the Israeli opposition movement "Peace Now"). Whether consciously or not, we believe that the West has come to judge Israel by the high standards that Jews have set for themselves for thousands of years.

While we understand Israeli fears and support Israel's right to exist and to have secure borders, as progressive Christians we also insist on our right to express criticism where we believe it is called for. Indeed, more than ever today, Israel needs honest criticism from its friends. Many Christians, as well as Jews, are worried that the current Israeli treatment of Palestinians is making those who were oppressed into oppressors.

In this context we express concern about the current alliance between the Israeli government and evangelical Christians. We believe that the all-out and uncritical support for the State of Israel by evangelical Christians conceals, in reality, their hope that the in-gathering of Jews in Israel will facilitate their eventual conversion to Christianity and thereby hasten the final coming of Christ. It is ironic and tragic that Israel, in its search for friends and security, has made an alliance with a group of Christians who, ultimately, desire the end of the Jewish people. Israeli historian Robert Wistrich suggests that many Jews probably take a fairly cynical view: "These guys are nuts, but we want all the voices we can get for Israel, and we can't afford to worry about theological niceties." In his own, more serious words: "From the Jewish point of view, it has not always been easy to balance the advantage of such support against the disadvantage of its linkage with a programme or at least a hope for conversion."[53]

Despite what has been said, it is undeniable that anti-Semitism is on the rise, especially in some European countries where synagogues and cemeteries have been defaced and Jews have been attacked personally. This fuels ancient Jewish fears and intensifies Israeli efforts at security.

As one follows the daily news—the Wall encroaching on Palestinian land, suicide bombers, innocent civilians being killed on both sides—the situation at times seems hopeless. Yet there are both Israelis and Palestinians working for a just political solution: guaranteeing the Palestinians' right to a viable state, and at the same time Israel's legitimacy and right to security. Both peoples are exhausted, tired of the killings, more ready perhaps than their leaders to defeat occupation and displacement. The occupation cannot win. Ultimately, Israel's security cannot be achieved through military might, but only through a just peace in which the Palestinian right to a viable state and Israel's right to security and legitimacy are both recognized.

The current political situation is having repercussions for Jewish-Christian relations. Genuine dialogue must include dialogue about Israel/Palestine, which, given the Jewish tendency to equate any criticism of Israel with anti-Semitism, is often difficult or impossible. It is not always easy to distinguish genuine criticism of Israel from anti-Semitism. Neither theology nor the churches are exempt from history. For the first time in two thousand years, Jews have a land of their own. Along with this come the challenges and temptations of sovereignty and nationalism. Tensions are high, the situation is explosive, and Israel has lost many friends. As long ago as 1967, Krister Stendahl sounded a note of warning as well as of hope. His words seem equally applicable today:

> The present political situation may well unleash a type of Christian attitude that identifies Judaism and Israel with materialism and lack of compassion, devoid of the Christian spirit of love. Even a superficial knowledge of Judaism on its own terms makes it abundantly clear that such is not its nature. And an even more superficial acquaintance with church history suffices to silence such a patronizing attitude. Our hope for Israel should rather be for political wisdom in accordance with the riches of the long and varied tradition of the Jewish faith, a faith rich in compassion, as it always remembers the words, "for you were strangers in the land of Egypt." (Exod. 22:21)

As we look and work toward a new structure for our common trust in the God of Abraham, Isaac, and Jacob—and of Jesus of Nazareth—that trust includes our personal confidence in Judaism as a force for peace and justice.[54]

Whatever the current problems, a return to the often vicious and deadly Christian anti-Judaism of the past is unthinkable. Progress made regarding mutual respect and understanding is solid, with roots deep enough to withstand the current crisis. The Claremont interfaith experience mentioned at the beginning of this paper continues to go forward and to expand, under the leadership of a new and dynamic rabbi. Discussion of the political situation is often difficult, but does not stop the dialogue. To quote Amos Oz once more: "Look at the Europeans. It took them a thousand years to make peace. . . . I will risk a prophecy: It will not take the Middle East as long to make peace. . . . And we'll shed less blood."[55]

Conclusion

Where are we today?

The church as a whole has repented of its anti-Judaism. It acknowledges the profound aberrations and evil consequences of the teaching of contempt, and rejects this teaching. Instead of seeing itself as superseding the Jewish people, it finds its identity in being grafted on to the original people of God (Romans 11). It seeks new ways of understanding and articulating a Christian faith purified of anti-Jewish elements. A promising beginning has been made, but the process is complex and will take time. While official church documents clearly reject the teaching of contempt today, there is evidence that it persists in the minds of many Christians, often unconsciously. To give one example: In everyday speech the word "Pharisee" is synonymous with "hypocrite." Yet the Pharisees were highly respected and devout religious leaders, and most scholars today believe that Jesus was closer to them in his teaching than to any other Jewish group.

Christian liturgy, especially during Holy Week, is an area urgently in need of reform. Much work remains to be done. As progressive Christians we commit ourselves to this ongoing and important task. Therefore, we make the following assertions:

1. We reject supersessionism, the view by which the church has claimed to supersede the Jewish people as people of God. God's covenant with the Jewish people endures forever, because God is faithful (Rom 11:29). "We now live in the new covenant established by and in Jesus Christ, joined in continuity to those who have already been made God's people in the covenant of Sinai."[56]

2. We reject a narrow focus on personal salvation, available to human beings only through conscious acceptance of Jesus as the one and only savior. Our focus, as progressive Christians, is on personal *and* social life *in the here and now.*

3. Finally, we reject an uncritical or literal reading of scripture, uninformed by contemporary biblical scholarship and ignorant of the historical context of the anti-Jewish texts in the Second Testament. Such reading can make the Second Testament into a dangerous book!

Certain aspects of Christian theology that center on the person of Jesus can lead to a negative view of Judaism, for example, (1) neglecting Jesus' humanity and emphasizing only his divinity, or (2) seeing Jesus as the Messiah who fulfilled all Jewish expectations.

With regard to the former, we confess that Jesus was fully human. Like all human beings he was of his time and place, conditioned by the historical and cultural circumstances in which he lived. He was not only a teacher, but a *Jewish* teacher.

With regard to the latter, it is clear that Jesus did not fulfill mainstream Jewish Messianic expectations, which envisioned an earthly restoration of the world as we know it (see Micah 4:3-4) and a king along the lines of David. Jesus' first followers shared this Jewish view—"Lord, will you at this time restore the kingdom to Israel?" (Acts 1:6). They came to look to the future. For some, this future meant the return of Jesus in the *Parousia* (Second Coming); for others, a universal resurrection. After all, Jesus had taught his disciples to pray for the coming of the *basileia theou,* the divine commonwealth or realm, in which God's purpose for the world will be fulfilled. We believe that a different view of Jesus, and of redemption, is imperative for the sake of a more authentic Christian faith and in order to do justice to Judaism. Is it not more accurate to say that the gospel drew gentiles into sharing in Jewish Messianic hope, rather than viewing Jesus as the expected Messiah?

The dominant understanding of redemption in the New Testament is the future transformation of the world, an understanding common to both Jews and Christians. While there are differences in the ways in which both conceive of redemption, the commonalities outweigh the differences between them. As progressive Christians we are committed to social justice. The ancient Jewish concern for the poor and oppressed is a deep bond between us. Speaking of her father's writings, Susannah Heschel quotes Abraham Heschel as saying that, "for the prophets. . .justice is the tool of God, the presence of God, the means of redemption. Justice is the ultimate expression of God."

Differences between us remain with regard to the Messianic future. These may not, however, be as radical as is often thought. Christians have come to believe that in the death and resurrection of Jesus something unique and unprecedented has already happened: the future is mysteriously present in the now. The church sees itself as living in the "between-time" (St. Augustine), in both the "already" and the "not yet." For Jews, the Messianic Age is still to come. And yet, God's presence in history, in particular the saving event of the Exodus, is a pledge that God will one day create "a new heaven and a new earth" (Isaiah). Both Jews and Christians await the fullness of redemption.

Christianity began as a Jewish sect. The "parting of the ways," which for so long has led to hostility, fear, contempt, and persecution, is today changing to a climate of trust and becoming a source of mutual enrichment. As the trust between us deepens, we hope it will enable us to voice criticism where it is needed (for example, of Israeli policy toward Palestinians).

We discover that we have much to learn from each other. The Jewish sense of peoplehood reminds us that, while each of us individually seeks to be a faithful follower of Jesus, fullness of life is possible only as it is universally shared. Salvation is, ultimately, communal: it involves the whole of society and all of creation.

Our emerging dialogue has sometimes been called "a-symmetrical." That is to say, Christianity needs Judaism for its self-understanding in a way that Judaism does not need Christianity; Christians have an interest in theological dialogue which Jews do not share. *Dabru Emet,* Michael Kogan's *Opening the Covenant,* and other recent changes in Jewish attitudes toward Christianity indicate that inequality is giving way to partnership. Given the so often tragic history between us, this is not only astonishing, but deserves to be welcomed by Christians with gratitude.

One of the most fruitful evolutions of the last hundred years has been the rediscovery, the reappropriation, by Jews of Jesus—as one of their own, as a faithful Jew. We recall here Martin Buber's famous words: "From my youth on I saw in Jesus my great brother" (*Two Types of Faith*). Robert Raphael Geis, a German orthodox Jewish theologian, writes: "A Jew can, after two thousand years, understand Jesus' word and deed, life and death, as a piece of himself."[57] Contemporary Jewish scholarship about Jesus is a gift to Christians as well as to Jews. For who can understand Jesus the Jew better than his own people? Such a deepened understanding of Jesus will also, necessarily, change our understanding of the gospel.

None of this means that we seek to turn back the clock of history. Christianity today is no longer the Jewish sect it once was. Nor is contemporary

Judaism the Judaism of the first century. Both traditions have undergone a long historical development. It is precisely in our separateness, our "otherness," that we can learn from and challenge each other. Jews and Christians today live in a world that faces crises of previously unimaginable proportions. As worshippers of the God of Abraham, we hope to be partners—open to God's guidance—in contributing to the healing and redemption of this world that God has created.

For Further Reading

Books

Ronald J. Allen and Clark M. Williamson. *Preaching the Gospels without the Jews*. Louisville: Westminster, 2005.

Mary C. Boys. *Has God Only One Blessing? Judaism as a source of Christian Self-understanding*. Mahwah: Paulist, 2000.

Mary C. Boys, editor. *Seeing Judaism Anew: Christianity's Sacred Obligation*. Lanham: Sheed and Ward, 2005.

James Carroll. *Constantine's Sword: The Church and the Jews*. New York: Oxford, 2001.

Edward Flannery. *The Anguish of the Jews: Twenty-Three Centuries of Anti-Judaism*, 2nd edition. Mahwah: Paulist, 1985.

Franklin H. Littell. *The Crucifixion of the Jews: The Failure of Christians to Understand the Jewish Experience*. New York: Harper and Row, 1975.

Rosemary Radford Ruether. *Faith and Fratricide: The Theological Roots of Anti-Semitism*. New York: Crossroads, 1974.

Paul Van Buren. *A Theology of the Jewish-Christian Reality*. 2 vols. Lanham: University Press of America, 1985.

Clark M. Williamson. *A Guest in the House of Israel: Post-Holocaust Church Theology*. Louisville: Westminister, 1993.

Film and Video

Weapons of the Spirit, Pierre Sauvage.

Walking God's Paths, Produced for the National Council of Synagogues and the Bishops' Committee on Ecumenical and Interreligious Affairs.

Questions for Discussion

1. How might Christians articulate an honored role for other religions while affirming loyalty to their own religious traditions?
2. What might constitute a legitimate Christian witness to Jews? (Keep in mind the continuing validity of God's covenant with the Jewish people, the apostolic nature of the Christian message, and the terrible history of Christian attitudes and behavior toward Jews over the centuries.)
3. In an interview shortly before his death, the great Jewish religious thinker Abraham Joshua Heschel said: "I would rather go through Auschwitz than be the object of conversion." How do you explain this shocking statement?
4. What does it mean to be a chosen people?
5. In what ways is Jesus the promised Messiah for Jews? For Christians?
6. What is going well today in Jewish-Christian relations? Where do you see current difficulties and challenges?
7. What does Zionism mean to Jews? To Christians?
8. In what ways was John Calvin's theology about Judaism four hundred years ahead of his time?

THREE

Islam and Christians

Ward M. McAfee

Man's eternal questions about the meaning of life, suffering, and death, about the highest values and ultimate norms for the individual and society, about where humanity and the cosmos have come from and where they are going, are not simply still with us, but have grown far more urgent in the face of political catastrophes and disenchantment with blind faith in progress. . . . If one wishes to prevent some false god (be it fuehrer, political party, nation, or even science) from being made into humanity's ground for meaning, supreme value, and ultimate norm, then faith in the one true God must replace faith in the false gods of modernity. And so, these days especially, one must confirm together with the Qur'an and the Bible: "There is no god but God." "You shall have no other gods before me." Which means that faith, whether Qur'anic or biblical, in the one true God is capable of demystifying the powers of this world and, insofar as they are idols, of dethroning them.

—Hans Küng[1]

Introduction

Christianity and Islam have much in common and yet are worlds apart. Both proclaim one God. Both religions struggle with both script and tradition in the light of modern insights. Both have emphasized the importance of communal values over selfish individualism. Both have experienced the problems of "state" effectively controlling "church" or "mosque" when attempts are made for religion to inform the state.

Both teach about a common humanity and respect for it. Both still struggle in different ways to make these teachings transform culture. Both incorporate parts of the world that abound in wealth and other parts that know only grinding poverty. Both have emphasized the necessity to give to those who are most needy. Both teach about peace, and throughout history both have subjugated peoples they regarded as disturbing their own concepts of peace. Both emphasize prayer and daily meditative practices. Both have encouraged religious pilgrimages as an essential part of human life. Both are confessing faiths in eagerly proclaiming their perceptions of truth most publicly.

Within Islam, many of these similarities are codified in what are known as the Five Pillars of Islam: (1) faith or belief in the oneness of God, (2) the establishment of a regimen of daily prayers, (3) almsgiving to the needy, (4) an attempt to experience purification through fasting, and (5) religious pilgrimage for those who are able. Christianity has no similar personal five-point catalog of essential practices, but the same teachings are nonetheless present. In the first Muslim pillar, Muhammad is regarded as having the final say concerning the oneness of God, whereas in Christianity the witness of the Christ is regarded as including all that is necessary for human salvation.

Other differences abound. Most strikingly, in the current age many parts of Islamic civilization resist modernity despite its attractions, whereas much of Christendom has readily sought out modernity's benefits despite its detriments. There was a time when both religions may have been said to represent a medieval mindset. For Christianity that day is no more. This difference concerns primarily culture but also religion, because culture has always informed religion and vice versa.

Throughout their long histories, both Christianity and Islam have often unintentionally affected the development of each other, a reality that makes

Islam a participant in authentic Christian teaching and vice versa. In our shrunken world, traditions no longer have the luxury to refuse invitations to dialogue. Each tradition must now accept the challenge posed by the other's existence, to work toward meaningful dialogue and the development of a shared ethic of social justice that is intentionally codetermined. With much wisdom, Hans Küng has written: "Ecumenism should not be limited to the community of the Christian churches; it must include the community of the great religions, if ecumenism—in accordance with the original meaning of *oikumene*—is to refer to the whole 'inhabited world.'" Both Christianity and Islam must "accept a concrete responsibility for world peace."[2]

For this to occur, it is necessary to see beyond the barriers imposed by imagined religious and cultural "iron curtains." We must develop the wisdom to see both what Christianity and Islam share in common and areas where we must agree to disagree. Rather than being separated by barriers made of impenetrable material, the cultural walls separating religious traditions are more like porous layers of skin that take in and give out liquids. This is a good metaphor with which to start. And yet, other metaphors are currently more successful in negatively shaping the thinking of both individuals and nations, thereby discouraging a Christian-Muslim dialogue. In order to proceed, we must first examine these.

A Clash of Civilizations?

In 1989, a State Department functionary by the name of Francis Fukuyama boldly proclaimed that history was over. His logic was peculiarly Hegelian. In his opinion, as the ideological struggle between democratic capitalism and totalitarian communism had apparently ended, there could be no new conflicts great enough to drive Hegel's historical dialectic of "thesis, antithesis, synthesis." Fukuyama's quirky notion, founded on ethnocentric Western philosophical assumptions, produced a temporary intellectual fad. Inherent in it was a celebration of the development of a "true global culture . . . centering around technologically driven economic growth and the capitalist social relations necessary to produce and sustain it." Western economic values stemming from the Enlightenment of the eighteenth century had triumphed and apparently had no more rivals.

In 1993, an influential essay by Samuel P. Huntington, Harvard Professor and Chairman of the Harvard Academy of International and Area

Studies, disagreed that this vision had materialized in the way claimed by Fukuyama. In his mind, history had not ended amidst a supposed new global unity of mind and common economic purpose. Appearing in the summer issue of *Foreign Affairs*, Huntington's essay "The Clash of Civilizations" highlighted enduring differences among key civilizations as guaranteeing competing worldviews well into the foreseeable future. Of the several candidates for cultural conflicts that could shape the twenty-first century, Huntington predicted that differences between Western values and traditional Islam would prove to be uppermost.

Huntington's combative tone was apparent in comments such as this: "Between Muslims, on the one hand, and Orthodox Serbs in the Balkans, Jews in Israel, Hindus in India, Buddhists in Burma and Catholics in the Philippines, . . . Islam has bloody borders."[3] He portrayed Islamic civilization as unreasonably aggressive and hostile toward all of its neighbors and warned that Islam threatened the peace of the world. Even before the events of September 11, 2001, a majority of Americans quietly agreed with this outlook. Since 9/11, this consensus has become noisy and chauvinistic, as American policy makers have favored preemptive action in "bringing on" this clash of civilizations.

The evening news is filled with stories of Muslim suicide bombings, Muslim oppression of women, Muslim hatred of Jews, Muslim beheading of foreign captives, and "Islam's" general support of a terrorist infrastructure that is global in scope. The cumulative effect of these impressions is that Islam per se is indeed a dangerous religion. Other stories of Christian terrorists in the United States blowing up abortion clinics, or Serbian Christians waging genocide against Muslims in Bosnia and Kosovo, or Christian rebels in Uganda routinely kidnapping children for use as sex slaves or as mindless and obedient Christian child soldiers are perceived differently. Rather than involving Christianity per se, such stories are seen as involving extremists who twist Christianity and warp its true meaning to commit unspeakable acts. Likewise, those Christians who endorsed and supported Hitler's hatred of Jews are popularly seen as not true Christians but rather as Germans, Austrians, Ukrainians, or Estonians who strayed from Christian teachings, despite the fact that expressions of contempt and hatred of Jews appear in the Gospels and are prominent in later Christian teaching. When the acts of Christian extremists are involved, the standard American mentality quickly corrects any perception that these acts stem from Christian teachings themselves.

"Christian Identity" is the name of a religious movement uniting many of the white supremacist groups in the United States, but most Americans consider this movement's followers as fundamentally anti-Christian in orientation. However, when Saudi Arabian, Pakistani, Iranian, Indonesian, or Filipino Muslims commit atrocities, their Islamic associations regularly are seen as determinative of these actions. Denunciations of terrorism by Islamic leaders do not satisfy Islam's critics, who seek to expose any telltale verse in the Qur'an that may have been used to inspire such hatred. Such critics are apparently unaware that the Christian Bible is also vulnerable to hostile gleanings of this sort. Muslims are expected to apologize publicly for atrocities carried out by Muslims, whereas the great majority of Christians would find it ridiculous to apologize for the actions of "Christian Identity."

Neither Western civilization nor Islamic civilization is monolithic as Huntington's ideological position suggests. The true conflicts of our age are not between civilizations but rather within civilizations. In the last century, Hitler and Stalin's horrific challenges to Western civilization arose from within Western civilization itself rather than from some outside source. Likewise, a violent, extremist interpretation of Islam today threatens Islamic civilization from within. The true goal of al-Qaida's leaders is not to defeat Western civilization but rather to undermine their own societies, impose their radical views by force, and ultimately change their civilization.[4]

Reza Aslan, author of *No god but God*,[5] argues that the events of 9/11, while immediately directed against the West, were in fact implemented for their potential effect in creating a new paradigm capable of transforming Islam. This horrific display was intended to weaken moderating influences within Islam itself. In producing a predictable reaction from the United States, Osama bin Laden became the effective face of Islam in the West, making instantly irrelevant the work of Islamic reformers over the past century. Against all odds, Aslan and other Muslim progressives intend to revive their movement to accommodate Islam to beneficial realities of modern life, a task made doubly difficult in the face of negative headlines screaming the latest "Islamic" atrocity.[6]

To persuade Americans and Europeans that al-Qaida holds an unwarranted reading of Islam is not an easy task. Historically, the Christian West has demonized Islam with only minor exceptions. This bad habit continues in our current culture. This tendency is based not only on highly selective evidence but also encourages bad policies that serve to transform Huntington's warning of a clash of civilization into a self-fulfilling prophecy. Huntington is correct that religious differences are bound to produce disagreements, but there is no imperative that continuous warfare should come to define our relationship. Wise policy in Washington, D.C., can only result from a better understanding of Islam among our citizenry. For this to occur, we need a theology capable of both encouraging peaceful dialogue and resisting our own assumptions that we should dominate.

We are now engaged in a new global conflict. To some degree, its parameters can be defined as Huntington has suggested. In the process of our struggle, both civilizations involved may well change to incorporate new perceptions and better values. While demanding that Muslims apologize for 9/11, Christians hopefully may become sensitized that they too need to apologize to Muslims for the horrific terrorism against Jews that thrust a new Jewish nation uninvited into their midst. Christians also need to reflect upon how their civilization has encouraged global disorder and cultural upheaval. Muslim criticism of our civilization does not focus on Christianity directly but rather on dysfunctional manifestations of an economic culture that has effectively detached itself from Christianity's moderating influences. A healthy dialogue with Islam will clearly reveal that our own religion has proven too weak to restrain evil tendencies that are now threatening a balanced ecology needed to sustain human life. Hopefully, our engagement with moderate voices within Islamic civilization will lead to new peaceful opportunities as we come to acknowledge the log in our own eye. Unfortunately, our civilization is now tightly focused on the splinter in the eye of Islam.

Early Islamic History

Common Roots of Judaism, Christianity, and Islam

Judaism, Christianity, and Islam arose during a millennium of great religious strife, spanning from the sixth century B.C.E. (when the ancient kingdom of Israel was destroyed) up to the sixth century C.E. (when Muhammad was born). During that time, Macedonia's Alexander the Great conquered the known world and bridged the intellectual and religious worlds of Greece, Egypt, Persia, and India. Next came Roman armies and the expansion of a new empire. The disruption brought about by force of arms changed religions and theological imaginations.

Judaism was born out of the so-called Babylonian Exile, after the disappearance of the states of Israel and Judah. Christianity arose in the century of anti-imperialist conflict against Rome in Palestine in the first century C.E. And Islam developed at a time of shifting caravan routes, emerging opportunities to acquire fortunes quickly, and the cultural disruption that this change wrought on the Arabian Peninsula during the seventh century C.E. Each of these three faith traditions was birthed in a time of great social upheaval.

Babylonian armies destroyed Jerusalem in 586 B.C.E. The victors deported the Hebrew elite, perhaps as many as ten thousand people, to Babylon. The peasantry remained behind in a demoralized condition. It was among the exiled Hebrew priests and nobles that composing the scriptures that became both the Torah and the stories of the Prophets became a serious enterprise. When the Persian defeat of Babylon resulted in the release of the first wave of Hebrew returnees to Jerusalem, Judaism as a religion of the book was born. As a result, Jewish expectations of redemption by a new Davidic ruler arose. This "Messiah" would presumably defeat the demonic powers of the empires, an end-times vision that owed some elements to the Zoroastrian beliefs of their Persian liberators.

When Pompey's invasion of Palestine in 63 B.C.E. inaugurated the period of Roman domination, new expressions of unrest reactivated Jewish theological imaginations. Some Jewish thinkers, such as the Qumran community, read the scriptures as promises of a cataclysmic divine intervention to restore true religion in Jerusalem. Some, such as the Pharisaic teachers, believed that God would bless the people if they faithfully obeyed the laws of Moses. Other groups, collectively known as Zealots, took to the hills with armed resistance. It was in this context that Jesus of Nazareth was born. His message became that God's reign should be seen as an immediate reality to be lived out fulfilling the deepest intentions of the laws attributed to Moses. The fact that he also organized a movement of resisting cultural norms encouraged both the Jewish elite in Jerusalem and the Roman authorities in Caesarea to regard him as a dangerous rebel, a perception that eventually resulted in his arrest and execution.

Meanwhile, turmoil over Roman domination boiled over. A generation after the Crucifixion, Jewish rebels temporarily took possession of Jerusalem. The Romans destroyed the Temple when they regained control in 70 C.E. Two generations later, Jewish rebels again arose in a vain effort to topple Roman authority. As a response intended to be final, the Romans destroyed Jerusalem itself in 135 c.e., expelling all Jews from the city. In the chaos that followed, both Jews and Christians were dispersed, resulting in the formation of both Torah-based Rabbinic Judaism and "gentile" Christianity, whose quintessential missionary was Paul and whose historian was Luke.

Born in 570 c.e., the Prophet Muhammad entered a world wherein Christianity and Judaism had created a religious hothouse with a rich soil capable of breeding strong hybrids. Islam emerged from this fertile environment. Other religions were involved as well. Zoroastrianism, originally of Persia, influenced Judaism, Christianity, and Islam, as did other faiths in the region. And ancient Greek philosophy became part of the mix. This development came after centuries of upheaval. And yet, traditional Christian believers see God as having been at work in all of the turmoil. And Muslims regard that which transpired as part of providential destiny.

In the pages that follow, it will be seen that Muhammad's social context matched the upheaval and collective violence that had earlier given rise to both Judaism and Christianity. The historical origins of these three related faith traditions reveal that resistance to domination systems in each instance provided the catalyst needed for a hearing of God's word. And yet, these various pursuers of divine truth each heard a somewhat different message. The similarity of their intent did not necessarily produce a uniform result. In the end, each would vie with the others in an ongoing environment of cultural strife and religious enmity. Accordingly, Jews came to regard Christianity as a Jewish heresy, and Islam came to be regarded as both a Jewish and a Christian heresy.

Muhammad

Muhammad grew to manhood in Mecca. At that time, the traditional culture of the Arabian Peninsula was tribal, while the "get rich quick" ethos of a burgeoning caravan trade threatened traditional communitarian values in Mecca. Widows and orphans who should have been taken in and nurtured in each tribal community were often abandoned and left to fend for themselves. Muhammad himself had been orphaned at an early age, but a wealthy and powerful uncle adopted him and raised him to manhood. Others were not so lucky. Muhammad's personal brush with the worst kind of destitution made him keenly sensitive to the social inequities in Meccan society.

As a youth, Muhammad traveled to Syria while earning his way on a caravan. Both on the Arabian Peninsula and in Syria, he came into contact with Jews and Christians whose stories and teachings were logged in his memory. Years later, typical of natural mystics, he sought solitude in the many caves in the hills around Mecca. One day, in 610, he felt a strange presence and heard an audible command, "Recite!" Two more times, he heard the command, and then he answered, "What shall I recite?" And this is how it began. The answer promised to reveal to him that which humanity desperately needed. On his way back from this experience, Muhammad saw a figure astride the horizon and feared that he had gone mad. Then his wife Khadija took him to her Christian cousin, Waraqa ibn Nawfal, who declared that Muhammad's encounter was with the angel from God that Christian and Jewish scriptures recorded had once encountered Moses. Islamic tradition considers this angel to be Gabriel, the angel of revelation. Muhammad's mystical experience was repeated many times, and many times Muhammad would fall into a trance from which he eventually emerged with power and began reciting. This was the birth of the Qur'an, which translated literally from Arabic means "Recitation." Khadija became the first convert to Islam. Muhammad also shared his revelations with friends and began making many converts to a new religion. By 615, the established order in Mecca began to worry.

Muhammad's recitations boldly stated that there is only one God. Meccan society at that time housed many stone idols in a building known as the Ka'ba. Each idol was a god of a particular tribe, and each tribe came to Mecca on an annual pilgrimage to pay homage to its particular god. The powerful men of Mecca who made money off of these tribal pilgrimages were threatened by Muhammad's monotheism.

The completed Qur'an was the result of roughly two decades of recitations. Following each recitation, Muhammad's followers memorized the new verses and added them to the growing body of the text. Muhammad was their prophet, equivalent to the Jewish and Christian prophets who had come before. These prior prophets were all mentioned in the Qur'an, from Adam to Abraham to Moses to David and to Jesus. The Qur'an revealed that each of these prophets had received the same message that was given to Muhammad—the unity and power of God, and the oneness of humanity—but that their followers had garbled it to varying degrees. Christ's followers, Muslims believe, garbled this message by worshiping Christ himself as divine, thus necessitating God's communication with another prophet via the revelations of the Qur'an. Muhammad received the message and recorded it unblemished for all time, making him the ultimate "messenger" of God and the "seal of the Prophets." After Muhammad, Muslims believe, there is no further need for prophecy as he recorded the holy message undefiled. Jews and Christians are regarded by Muslims as People of the Book—people whose traditions were originally on the right track but got waylaid because of corrupted transmissions and translations. Therefore, Muslims believe, the Qur'an is unlike either the Hebrew or Christian Bibles in that it is completely accurate and final.

This view of the inerrancy of the Qur'an has had both positive and negative consequences. On the positive side, it encouraged a certainty that helped Muhammad gain converts in a culture that respected nothing but money and material power. He eventually conquered those worldly powers to submit to his message of social justice, human kindness, and the community of all Muslims. The Muslim community in the broadest sense is known as the *ummah*. It is a foundational community, knowing no single bloodline, greater than tribe and nationality, and potentially capable of uniting all of humankind under God. Literally, the Arabic word "Islam" means both "peace" and "submission," and the word "Muslim" means "one who is at peace" or "one who submits" to God. In the act of praying, a Muslim's forehead touches the ground, outwardly symbolizing an inward submission to something higher than self.

In 622 c.e., Muhammad became a civic leader. With his nascent religious community threatened with destruction at the hands of Mecca's hierarchy, he fled under cloak of night and became the political and spiritual leader of Medina, a city several hundred miles to the north. He had been invited to this task as Medina's quarreling tribes discovered in Muhammad's religious teaching a workable common purpose.

As king of Medina, Muhammad ceased to be solely a spiritual leader. In this new role, he became not only high priest, but also chief diplomat and warlord. From Medina, Muhammad and his followers raided Meccan caravans acquiring great booty, in the process attracting independent tribes to join a movement that steadily grew stronger. Muhammad blended the worlds of God and "Caesar" for positive purposes. Wealth taken from the raids went to support the struggling *ummah*, especially meeting the needs of widows and orphans. Hard decisions defined his bold attempt to build a new Islamic theocracy. The designs of his relentless Meccan enemies threatened any weak links in Muhammad's chain of alliances. Facing a rebellion from two Jewish tribes within Medina, he had one expelled from Medina and executed all the adult males of the other, essentially exterminating the tribe. Eventually, Mecca itself was conquered, and Muhammad cleansed the Ka'ba of its idols. Within two centuries, Islam went on to absorb much of the known world, acquiring an empire spanning from Spain to the Indian subcontinent and western China.

Whether one emphasizes religious or secular standards—Muhammad's life is one of the most striking success stories of all time. By worldly standards, Jesus of Nazareth was a failure. Roman authorities regarded Jesus as a threat and eliminated him after a brief ministry. Using the standards of the world, academic historians agree that Jesus' resumé cannot match Muhammad's. In several polls taken in recent decades they have judged Muhammad to be the greatest change agent the world has ever seen.

The Islamic Schism

A greater unity exists within Islam than is the case in Christianity, which is divided between East and West, and in the West, between Roman Catholic and Protestant churches. Protestantism subsequently has splintered into numerous denominations and sects. Islam's schism, which is less complex but no less important, refers to the split between Sunnis and Shi'ites.[7] This split is obvious in current news stories coming out of occupied Iraq. It was also apparent in the late 1970s, when Sunnis castigated the Shi'ite theocracy of Iran's Ayatollah Khomeini in overriding Islamic tradition concerning proper treatment of diplomats. Distrust between the two groups can run high, as evidenced in Saudi Arabia's Shi'ite minority practicing dissimulation (pretending to be Sunnis) so as not to be persecuted by the regime.

The cause of the schism began immediately upon Muhammad's death in 632, with the founding of the first caliphate, or continuation of the religious government established by Muhammad. His closest companions determined that Abu Bakr should become the first Caliph (literally the "successor" to the Prophet). This decision disappointed Ali, the male who was closest to Muhammad in bloodline. Ali claimed that Muhammad had designated him as his future successor while returning from the Prophet's last pilgrimage to Mecca. Muhammad had no surviving sons, but Ali was both his cousin and his son-in-law and had been an early convert and a leader in battles. In the Arabian Peninsula, blood and tribal ties had always been highly important.

However, central to Muhammad's message had been the far different conclusion that all Muslims are equal so far as blood and tribe are concerned. Ali was only a young man at the time of Muhammad's death, so he bided his time, waiting for the proper moment to be elected to the office of Caliph.

The second Caliph was Umar, who served from 634 to 644. The Muslim community's selection of Uthman upon the death of Umar particularly galled Ali, for Uthman showered favors upon his clan, the Umayyads, who had once been part of the Meccan establishment that had persecuted the earliest Muslims. Uthman's behavior angered many and led to his assassination in 656. At that point, Ali stepped forward and claimed the caliphate as his own. But he was not without a challenger. Mu'awiya, a cousin of Uthman and commander of the Arab forces in Syria, mounted an army against him. However, Ali's forces proved stronger. When military victory was all but within Ali's grasp, Mu'awiya caused Ali's forces to withdraw at the sight of pages of the Qur'an hoisted on Mu'awiya's soldiers' spears. Muawiaya then called for arbitration, which Ali accepted as the solution most suitable for intra-Muslim disputes. This outraged some of Ali's more militant followers who thereupon assassinated him as a weak and unfit leader. Ali's eldest son Hasan was then popularly acclaimed Caliph, but he was persuaded by Mu'awiya to abdicate in favor of Mu'awiya, who in turn subsequently poisoned the hapless Hasan to be rid of a potential rival.

Some Christians may regard the fact that several of Islam's early Caliphs were assassinated is strong evidence that this religion is inherently violent. However, these Christians should examine the history of the Popes over the centuries, as well as the behavior of Protestants who sought to supplant their historic authority. Religious warfare sparked by the Reformation constitutes a story of terrible bloodshed.[8] So far as this aspect of Islam is concerned, similarities with the Christian past appear more striking than the differences. Ancient Hebrew Bible stories beloved by Christians also abound with betrayal, murder, and assassination.

Continuing the story of the Islamic schism, Mu'awiya's drunken son Yazid succeeded his father in 680. This new Caliph's tyrannical behavior outraged Muslims residing in Kufa (located in modern-day Iraq). They called upon Hasan's younger brother Hussain to step forward as a more legitimate candidate for the caliphate. Hussain was not only the sole surviving grandson of the Prophet but was also widely regarded as a decent and fair man. Hussain accepted Kufa's call and traveled northward with his entire family from their home in Medina, much as his grandfather had once traveled from Mecca to Medina to rescue Islam.

Approaching Karbala (also located in modern-day Iraq), Hussain's caravan was ambushed by Yazid's forces. Shi'ite legend nurtures what happened next. With his caravan trapped, Hussein anxiously waited for aid to come from nearby Kufa that had received word of the attack but sent no assistance. Death for Hussain and his family could have been swift and merciful, but it was not. The agony was extended over days. Finally, with all but one of his sons dying before his eyes, Hussain was killed in a most gruesome way. His head was cut off as a trophy for Yazid, and then the rest of his body was trampled by Yazid's horsemen. One of Hussain's sons escaped to carry on the bloodline of Muhammad. As the boy's mother was a Persian and as Ali had argued for full equality between Arab and Persian converts, Persia (Iran) became the Shi'ites' official homeland.

Shi'a literally means "a partisan" of Ali. Sunna literally translates as "the beaten path." The meaning here is that the way of tradition is uppermost and that the community rather than bloodline should determine Islamic leadership. Sunnis see their religion as founded on the traditions established by the Seal of the Prophets. Shi'ites, while also revering tradition, place additional emphasis on a secret knowledge (gnosis) and a deeper meaning of Islam transmitted by Ali and his descendents.

Shi'ites have generally practiced a different version of Islam than their Sunni rivals. For example, Shi'ites annually celebrate Hussain's cruel death in an annual festival during the month of Muharran. At that time, Shi'ites recall their own trials in the world, identifying them with Hussain's suffering, yet confident that at the end of time ultimate justice awaits. On the tenth day, known as 'Ashura, Shi'ite men march through the streets, stripped to the waist, beating their bloodied backs with chains, thereby demonstrating that this world holds nothing but unending sorrow and oppression for the pious believer. By the standards of the world, Yazid the tyrant and drunkard and defiler of true Islam succeeded, while Hussain the beloved grandson of the Prophet was ground into the dust. There are some parallels to Christianity here. Whereas Christians like to see their religion as rejecting attitudes of anger and vengeance, Jews, who have long suffered for their supposed historic roles as "Christ killers," can see little difference between Christian attitudes and those of the Shi'ites who thirst for "justice" (vengeance).

Historically, Shi'ites have preferred to wait until the end of time for the arrival of justice, however the rise of Iran's Shi'ite theocracy during the last three decades suggests a different approach. Christians too once relied almost solely upon eschatological expectations, but over time came to seek justice in more immediate ways. Certainly progressive Christianity, with its strong emphasis on social justice in the here and now, reflects this religious tendency. For their part, Sunnis have never postponed the search for good government until the last trumpet. Christian outsiders may regard the differences between Sunnis and Shi'ites as arcane and of little importance. But then, non-Christians often marvel over how Christians have slaughtered each other over which Pope/Patriarch (Roman or Byzantine) should control Christendom or whether there should be any such hierarchical authority over Christian churches. Indeed, the Islamic schism is easier for Christians to understand than is the Christian schism over filioque for Muslims. In Medieval times, the filioque controversy effectively divided Eastern Orthodoxy and Western Christianity. The West taught that the Holy Spirit proceeded from the Father and the Son, whereas the East taught that the Holy Spirit proceeded from the Father through the Son. For both Muslims and Christians, matters of little importance to outsiders are often highly sensitive because they deal with questions of religious legitimacy.

Islamic Expansion

Despite internal divisions, from the outset, Islam rushed to convert the known world. Before Islam, the warring tribes of the Arabian Peninsula had been turned inward, with each tribe the enemy of the others. However, as soon as Muhammad unified them within the Muslim *ummah*, their attentions turned outward in all directions. Muslim conquerors presented pagans only with the choice of conversion or death. People of the Book (Jews and Christians) were treated differently. They were required only to swear allegiance to Muslim suzerainty. As dependent religious communities, they were not allowed to serve in the armed forces, and because they were so exempted, they had to pay an annual tax or tribute. Islam's goal was to conquer the entire earth but force the conversion of only pagans and polytheists. Whereas Christianity sought to bring the salvation of Jesus Christ to the entire world, Islam has sought only to bring all of humankind under a common divine sovereignty.

In 642, Egypt easily fell to expanding Islam. At that time, the Coptic (Egyptian) Christian Church in Alexandria and the Greek Orthodox Church in the Byzantine capital at Constantinople were locked in the monophysite controversy, a theological dispute over the nature of Christ. Byzantium's church at Constantinople held that Christ had two natures and was simultaneously fully man and fully God. The church at Alexandria could not accept this. For Copts, Jesus' divine attributes dominated his nature. Byzantine Christianity pressed the Egyptians to conform. Hating the Greeks, Egyptian Christians initially welcomed the Muslim conquerors who promised to tolerate them as "People of the Book."

Jerusalem was captured, and in 691 Abd al-Malik built the Dome of the Rock on the ruins of the Jewish temple destroyed in 70 C.E. In Muslim belief, this is the spot from which Muhammad ascended through the various levels of heaven during his "night journey"—a mystical experience that the Prophet experienced while residing in Medina.

Spain fell in 711, and had it not been for a Christian victory at the Battle of Tours in 732, all of Europe might have experienced Muslim rule. The Islamic army retreated back across the Pyrenees, which for many centuries became the frontier line between the two faiths. In the east, Constantinople withstood a Muslim siege in 717–718. Further east, Muslim armies conquered the Persian Empire, and by 711, Muslim warriors reached the valley of the Indus. In less than a century after Muhammad's death, Islamic civilization stretched from Spain to India.

The Rise of Sufism

Worldly success breeds hedonistic values and practices. The last two centuries of Western civilization have amply demonstrated this, as did the first several centuries of Islam's existence. Both were periods of extraordinary material success. With an empire stretching from Spain to India, the caliphal court forsook the simple ways of the Prophet and indulged in elaborate displays of luxury. Protesting this drifting away from authentic Islam, a few early Muslims overtly rejected silks and donned clothing of a coarse woolen material, termed *suf* in Arabic. Thereby becoming distinct within the Muslim community, they became known as Sufis.

They did more than simply protest the comforts and luxury of silk garments. They also attacked the emerging pedantry of the *ulema*, the canon lawyers of Islam. They rebelled against Islam being reduced to a set of legal codes and rules demanding outward conformity. Early Sufis tended toward personal asceticism, learned from Christian monks in Syria. Drawing upon Gnostic teachings, which then were being suppressed within Christianity, the Sufis fashioned a religious mysticism surpassing anything in the Western world. Sufism eventually absorbed the additional mystical traditions of Hinduism and Buddhism from the Indian subcontinent. Religious adaptation and inventiveness later made Sufism the most skillful proselytizing branch of Islam.

Sufis preached that religion must be lived rather than studied. They regarded themselves as lions, rather than vultures that eat what they themselves have not searched out. They pronounced aphorisms such as, "He who tastes not, knows not." They sought to live completely in the present moment. Each day, they advised, should be appreciated without the burden of any past agenda or future expectations. The Sufi mystic was completely adjustable to whatever each passing moment might bring. In fact, Sufis viewed every moment as a unique creation of God, perfect in and of itself. *Ibn al-waqt*, or "son of the present moment," was a title adopted by Sufis. "Wisdom descends from heaven," one Sufi wrote, "but does not settle into the heart of any man who pays attention to the next day."

Sufis regularly meditated (and still do) on the Qur'anic notion of *shirk*, or "association" of God with anything that is not God. *Shirk*, often occurring only in one's mental habits, is the worst form of idolatry, the most terrible sin in Islam. *Shirk* is in every selfish thought, for each one effectively makes an idol of "self." Sufi disciples reflect seriously upon this. When they see a flaw in another, they meditate upon the existence of that same fault in themselves much in the spirit of Jesus' metaphor of the splinter in the eye of one's enemy. Sufis tend to seek poverty to break all ego attachment to comfortable existence. In this sense, most Sufis are not highly motivated toward conventional acts of social justice, because instead of trying to improve the material lot of the poor, they seek out living with the poor as a "mercy in disguise" that can drive out materialist cravings.[9] Their version of Islam calls for great self-discipline as well as mental and physical toughness, qualities that they have used through the centuries to preserve their faith against all obstacles—including those erected within the USSR by Josef Stalin during his exceptionally cruel anti-religious regime.

Sufis provided Islam with a new kind of hero—not the warrior but rather the practitioner of the "greater jihad"—the struggle to overcome individual selfishness. Early Sufis looked to the prophet Jesus, a holy man who had no place to lay his head. They termed their movement "the conscience of Islam," and they regarded Jesus as the model for those aspiring to be saints. Sufism might have gone unheralded if it had not been for Abu Hamid Muhammad al-Ghazali, a renowned Islamic scholar who lived in twelfth-century Baghdad. He was widely regarded as the premier Muslim theologian of his day. But he did not find this fame satisfying. He came to realize that his scholastic accomplishments were in fact empty and abruptly left his prestigious position at Baghdad's Nizamiya University. Abandoning respectable society, he went to live with the Sufis. Returning years later, he brought Sufism into the fold of Islamic orthodoxy. Because of his great influence, a community consensus (*ijma*) formed on the authenticity of Sufism. This theological development served further to exalt the model of Jesus within Islam. Unlike the Christian Jesus, who is characteristically regarded as uniquely different from all other mortals, the Sufi Jesus serves as a human model for an authentic "way" and "truth" and "life"—an inspiration for liberation from the misery and prison of self-centeredness.

Theological Similarities and Differences

Religious Pluralism

Christianity has nothing parallel to Islam's notion of "People of the Book"—that is, Jews and Christians who are perceived as within Islam's prophetic religious tradition.[10] Throughout most of its long history, the official church has allowed very little latitude toward anyone not accepting its specific creeds and tenets. By contrast, "People of the Book" living in Muslim countries historically have often known a high degree of toleration, albeit in an inferior status. This relative flexibility produced a golden age of interfaith cooperation and intellectual development between 900 and 1200 in Spain and North Africa. In medieval Egypt, Christians controlled the Muslim government's bureaucracy. Jews and Christians also dominated not only medical fields but also served in banking, foreign trade, and espionage. Specific strictures on their status included a prohibition against marrying Muslim women and a requirement that they wear distinctive clothing and show Muslims deference. At times, this prescribed tolerance has been reduced significantly against the very specific commands of the Qur'an. However, the fact remains that Muslims historically have been far more accepting of people of other Abrahamic traditions than Christians, who have often insisted on faith in Jesus Christ as the only acceptable religious position. On the other hand, in relation to heretical versions of Islam, such as Baha'i, rigorous persecution has been the norm.

Fundamentalist Islam is also an exclusive religion. Only Muslims are regarded as truly submitting to the will of God. Unfortunately, religious exclusivity—starting with the Hebrew notion of the "chosen people," then continuing with those who believe people are saved solely because they accept Jesus Christ as their only Lord and Savior, and concluding with those who claim both that their Qur'an is without error and their Prophet has the last word in prophecy—has throughout history been the source of untold violence and cruelty. Perhaps this is why an anonymous author scrawled the following prayer on a wall in Washington, D.C., shortly after the events of September 11, 2001: "Dear God, please save us from the people who believe in you." In the eighteenth century, Jonathan Swift left a related but more helpful thought: "We have just enough religion to make us hate, but not enough to make us love one another." Hopefully, both progressive Christians and progressive Muslims can move to a deeper level, which evokes love.

Jesus and the Qur'an

Islam's treatment of Jesus of Nazareth reveals another set of similarities and differences. Unlike Judaism, which has no role for this Christian messenger, Islam regards Jesus as one of a long line of Allah's prophets beginning with Adam. This fact is commonly not appreciated by Christians who regard their own faith as far closer to Judaism than to Islam. On the other hand, Islam's acceptance of Jesus is limited. The Qur'an relates Jesus giving the following reply to Allah regarding Christian claims that Jesus is equivalent to God: "Glory be to you! It cannot be that I would say that which is not mine by right" (5:116). The Qur'an describes Jesus as a human, who, accordingly, cannot be God. Still Jesus is not viewed as an ordinary human being. He is said to be one born of a virgin and one who will return at the end of time to usher in the reign of God. Further, Islam accepts all of Jesus' miracles as occurring "with God's permission."

Islam makes no divine claims for Muhammad either. However, he too is no ordinary human being. He is said to be the Seal of the Prophets and is regarded as having been incapable of committing error. The entire practice of revering authentic hadith, or acts performed by Muhammad, is based upon the assumption that his recorded practices reveal the will of Allah as much as do the verses of the Qur'an. In this latter regard, it is interesting to note that one hadith concerning the Prophet is that he prayed in a fashion very similar to the "Lord's Prayer" of Jesus:

> When any one is in suffering, or his brother suffers, then let him pray this prayer: Our Lord God, who is in heaven, hallowed be Thy name. Thy kingdom is in heaven and on earth, and even as Thy mercy is in heaven, so may Thy mercy also be upon earth. Forgive us our debts and our sins, for Thou art the Lord of the good.[11]

Some Gnostic Christian teachings held that Jesus was not crucified but rather was rescued through divine intervention, and Islam accepts this. The Qur'an is sparse and cryptic concerning exactly how Jesus was rescued, but Muslim exegesis later proposed that the one executed in his place was probably Judas. Progressive Christians, some of whom have difficulty with the divinity of the Jesus, might appreciate aspects of the Muslim rendition but nonetheless find strained the Muslim claim that Jesus somehow escaped crucifixion. In any case, both Christian and Muslim narratives of Jesus demand different levels of extraordinary belief.

Christianity regards Jesus as the Christ, God's preexistent word made flesh. The opening verses of the Gospel of John state:

> In the beginning was the Word, and the Word was with God, and the Word was God. He was in the beginning with God; all things were made through him, and without him was not anything made that was made. In him was life, and the life was the light of men. . . . And the Word became flesh and dwelt among us, full of grace and truth; we have beheld his glory, glory as of the only Son from the Father.

This is not the Muslim conception of Jesus. But it is very close to the Muslim conception of the Qur'an, which Muslims regard in much the same way that Christianity defines the Christ. For their respective believers, both Christ and Qur'an constitute the "preexistent word," existing with God before the beginning of time. The Qur'an is viewed as with Allah, just as Christian theology holds that the Christ is with God in Heaven. Christians do not exalt the Bible to this extent. The Bible is a compilation of many writings put together by the church. Many different divinely inspired people composed the books of the Bible over many centuries. The church rejected some candidates for scripture as inauthentic, whereas others were included in the official canon. There are several versions of the Bible within Christianity. The

Catholic Bible contains some books not to be found in Protestant Bibles. By contrast, the Qur'an was revealed to one man in one language within a short time period, and it was transcribed into writing shortly after the Prophet Muhammad's death. Major problems of translation do not burden the Qur'an, which Muslims are urged to read in the original Arabic, the language that the Angel Gabriel used in transmitting the message to Muhammad. Muslims are encouraged to memorize Qur'anic verses in order to invite the will of Allah into their souls.

Muslim tradition holds that Muhammad was not a man of letters, a point meant to emphasize the divine origins of his "recitations," for how could such a person invent a work that is regarded as the finest piece of literature in the Arabic language? Modern scholars have come to roughly the same conclusion. Hans Küng writes: "Muhammad, although hardly illiterate, neither read the Bible himself nor had it read to him. In his time. . .there was no Arabic translation of the Bible in existence; if there had been the passages in the Qur'an relating to the Bible would have been clearer, more precise, and less fragmentary."[12] So the divine mystery of the Qur'an's soaring mastery remains intact.

Free Will and Divine Omnipotence

One last issue deserves emphasis in any review of Christian and Muslim theological similarities and differences. Encouragement for theologies of both free will and predestination occur in both the Bible and the Qur'an, but within Islam predestination has been a far stronger theological tendency than within Christianity. However, at the outset, predestination and free will existed in tension within Islam. The Qur'an states that God alone can change the human heart, which suggests predestination. Yet it also asserts that if one recognizes Allah as the only God, does not steal, does not commit adultery, does not slander neighbors and kill girl babies (an all too common practice in Muhammad's day), one will go to Paradise. These stipulations suggest a theology of free will.

Early in Islamic history, a group of rationalist Muslim theologians inspired by Greek philosophy encouraged a belief in free will. These thinkers, known as Mu'tazilites, taught that God allows evil free play in this life but punishes evil doers in the afterlife. In the tenth century, Abul-Hasan al-Ash'ari disagreed strongly, and his emphasis on predestination has remained uppermost in Muslim theology ever since. In his mind, any agency that allowed God to be restricted (such as human free will) weakened the Almighty, an impossible condition that he saw as false teaching encouraged by human arrogance. Al-Ash'ari regarded God as the immediate and direct author of every occurrence, large and small. As a philosophical atomist, he dismissed all ideas regarding causation in the natural world, including God as first Cause. Instead, he held that God allows repeating natural phenomena out of habit but in fact creates every natural event as a miraculous act. God, he taught, creates every action and every thought. In this way, he dismissed any notion of fixed Natural Law. Al-Ash'ari handled those Qur'anic verses suggesting free will in this way: Allah allows human beings to do what is predestined for them to do, thereby leaving them with the moral consequences of their own actions.

Al-Ash'ari's theology of divine omnipotence taught that Allah creates belief in the believer as well as unbelief in the unbeliever. Under the sway of this theology, the observant Muslim is made to feel dependent upon God for everything. "What reaches you could not possibly have missed you," one well-known Muslim proverb relates, "and what misses you could not possibly have reached you." On a more mundane level, when asked if it is going to rain, an Arab Muslim will typically respond, "*insh'allah*," or "as God wills." Ironically, this tendency of mind does not necessarily breed passivity but often its opposite, for if one believes that God is determining a particular course of action, then backing the cause is sure to result in victory. A similar phenomenon is often observed among Calvinist predestinarians.

From this brief review, it can be seen that similarities and differences between Christians and Muslims are woven into their exclusivist claims, their interpretations of Jesus, their views of the preexistent word of God, and their understanding of the relation of God's will and human will. Differences abound. But both groups use similar philosophical and theological constructs and the emphases of each are reflected in the other tradition as well. Rather than being radically apart in theological approaches, Christianity and Islam appear to be cousins, with some differing customs, practices, and habits of mind.

Social-Ethical Similarities and Differences

Egalitarian Teaching

The message of Muhammad's revelations was one of both divine authority and social justice. Given that today, most American Christians believe that Islam is inherently hostile to women, it is significant that Muhammad's ministry was in part committed to uplifting the status of women. He commanded that the community as a whole assist the downtrodden and that women be respected in marriage and while single, that no man should have more than four wives, and that husbands should not play favorites among their wives. Certainly, he stopped well short of asking for equality of women and men. However, he did challenge Meccan culture regarding its treatment of women.

Modern Christians may take pride that their more abstract religion has proven to be more advantageous toward achieving full equality for women. But the historical record shows that before reforms of the nineteenth century C.E., women in Islam enjoyed a higher legal status than did those in Christendom. Before that time, women in Islam may have had to live with a religious tradition that placed their lives under the rule of men, but in Christianity it was no different. And women in Islam may have received only half the inheritance rights of men, but in Christian lands, no such rights existed at all, even to this partial degree.

Muhammad's message not only attacked the selfish individualism of Mecca's elite regarding the status of women, it also called for ameliorating the condition of slaves. Not all of Mecca's slaves were black, but many were. Throughout all of recorded history, evidence of white racism abounds. The Arabian Peninsula in Muhammad's time was no exception. Muhammad attacked this ugly tradition. He placed blacks in responsible positions in his new religion. A black man named Bilal became the first muezzin, or caller, for Muslim prayers. In Islamic legend, it is recorded that Hagar, the mother of the Arabic peoples, was black. Later in Muhammad's life, he also reportedly married a black woman.

Neither early Christianity nor early Islam forbade slavery, yet both practiced degrees of racial toleration. Long after Muhammad, Muslims and Christians participated in a vicious African slave trade that led to the death of many millions, but these malefactors behaved in contradiction to both Christianity and Islam's best understandings. Those Muslims who sinned in this horrific manner warped the Muslim concept of jihad, or holy resistance, to serve their economic ends. Human greed motivated them, not the egalitarian teachings of Islam. Similarly, Christian participants in the slave trade thoroughly warped their religion to justify their greed-driven practices. In any case, so far as Islam is tainted by this history, it was Christian Europe that created the context for the extremely lucrative African slave trade spanning oceans and continents.

Islamic egalitarianism is underwritten by the Hajj, the annual pilgrimage of Muslims to Mecca. The Qur'an teaches that at least once in a person's life, he or she should go to the Ka'ba in Mecca during the time of annual pilgrimage. There, the Muslim circumambulates the Ka'ba that Muhammad eventually cleansed of false idols and worships the one true God in egalitarian harmony. On this pilgrimage, each Muslim is to be clothed in a simple white garment so as to eradicate any and all distinctions during this holy congregating of the Muslim community. Many new pilgrims have commented with depth of feeling about the egalitarian teaching that is the very texture of the Hajj.

An angry and articulate black American named Malcolm Little, better known as Malcolm X, underwent a second conversion near the end of his life while on his first and only Hajj. He had become a leader of the Black Muslims within the United States. His message of hate had been that all white men are devils. On the Hajj, for the first time, Malcolm X experienced human relations that were truly colorblind. He returned to his homeland with a new understanding of the peace of Islam just before he was assassinated.

Muslim belief that the Qur'an is word-for-word the word of God has a negative consequence for Muhammad's egalitarian message, especially regarding women. During his lifetime, Muhammad definitely improved the status and role of women. Women gained more standing vis-à-vis men than they had ever before known in Arab societies. They gained some inheritance rights as well, and although they did not become fully equal with men, the direction of change was positive. However, because the Qur'an is viewed as inerrant and eternal, its favorable teaching, instead of starting a trajectory toward full equality, discouraged further reform as against God's will.

Today, Muslim progressives regularly argue that the teachings of the Qur'an should be understood within the historical context that existed in Muhammad's day. In Judaism or Christianity, similar approaches to scripture are often helpful in gaining progressive perspectives. But the situation within mainstream Islam is more like that of Christian Fundamentalism. Since its leading scholars hold that the message that Muhammad delivered was eternal and without error, an argument based on historical contexts and cultural relativism is at a tremendous disadvantage.

Progressive Muslims occasionally turn literalism to their advantage. One Qur'anic verse that they commonly use is: "Allah will never change the condition of a people until they change what is in themselves" (13:11). Progressive Muslims interpret this verse as encouraging a reinvention of social consciousness within Islam. They also point out that nothing in the Qur'an mandates that women dress so as to leave only their eyes showing and that the seclusion of women has strong cultural causes independent of Islam. In fact, what the Qur'an does state is that both men and women equally should dress modestly. Most of the treatment of women within Islam results from attributing to traditional practices something of the finality Islam in general attributes to the Qur'an.

Against this tradition, Muslim progressives emphasize that several of Muhammad's wives led active lives that belie any conservative emphasis on secluding women. His first wife, Khadija, was a leading merchant in Mecca, and a subsequent wife, Aisha, led a Muslim army into battle. Muslim progressives argue that it is neither the Qur'an nor the early tradition that oppresses women but a reactionary Islam that scapegoats female independence because of its popular association with Westernizing influences closely identified with colonialism.

The Question of Democracy

Christianity has had a long and diverse history of teaching and practice regarding its proper relation to the state. From the Constantinian establishment until quite recently, the two have been closely related. Today, however, separation of church and state (which is most thoroughly codified in the United States) has come to be viewed as normative throughout most of Western civilization, in order to allow for religious pluralism within each nation.[13]

Those seeking greater pluralism within Islamic civilization are now reinventing Muslim traditions in a similar way—relying upon scriptural reinterpretation to rework ancient concepts in the interests of reform. One example concerns *ijtihad*, "independent thinking" or "independent interpretive judgment." Early in Islam, *ijtihad* came to mean that different religious schools of thought should be tolerated regarding how best to determine Islamic law. In no way was *ijtihad* originally intended to promote the kind of independent individual judgment that is needed in an effective mass democracy. But that goal is approximated if a deeper meaning of *ijtihad* is reimagined to include all Muslims. Muhammad Iqbal (1875–1938), a philosopher and thinker of Kashmiri origin and a leading founder of progressive Islamic thought, crafted the interpretations needed to support this innovative understanding.

The Qur'an teaches that *shura*, or "consultation," should occur regularly in both religious and worldly affairs. Historically in Islam, this has been interpreted as a hierarchical ruler seeking advice from selected subordinates. However, the Qur'anic text does not require this interpretation. Fazlur Rahman (1919–1988), of Pakistani origin and an advocate for democracy within Islamic civilization, emphasized that the literal language used in the Qur'an calls for "mutual advice through mutual discussions on an equal footing." Here Rahman used the strong contemporary Islamic tendency toward literalism to promote a Qur'anic interpretation that virtually requires democracy. Rahman argued that Muslims who negatively claim that democracy leads away from the will of Allah "are willingly or unwittingly guilty of rendering Islam null and void."[14]

Examples from the Christian past encourage hope that an evolution toward democracy can occur within Islam. In the seventeenth century, the English Puritan philosopher John Locke applied Christian egalitarian understandings to develop his idea that all human beings have an inherent right to participate in government, thereby overcoming an earlier Puritan understanding that only God's Elect should have a say in government. The Glorious Revolution of 1688 in England and later the American Revolution were based on his innovative concepts. Similar intellectual transformations are now occurring within Islamic civilization.

Sunni Muslims, constituting roughly 85 percent of all Muslims worldwide, adhere to the doctrine of *ijma*, or "collective judgment of the community," in resolving important disputes. Historically, this has meant that differences among spiritual leaders are ultimately resolved by a consensus developed in the *ulema*, or community of learned scholars. Throughout Sunni history, the *ulema* has emphasized that the legitimacy of state institutions to carry out the will of Allah can only be validated by *ijma*.

The question is then how the collective judgment of the community is expressed. In the West, this gradually moved toward democracy. The potentiality for this development exists in Islam as well.

Indeed, Western Christians should recognize that Western interference has been a major obstacle to the development of democracy in Muslim countries. Over the last half-century, movements toward democracy in Islamic civilizations have been generally quashed by Western powers. American policy in the Middle East has encouraged rulers there to put down any form of dissent that would interfere with those governments' cooperation with

American "strategic interests." It is not that Muslims around the world shun democracy. Rather, it is often the case that rulers have been kept in power precisely because they are willing to suppress democratic movements. The CIA's intervention in Iran when Mosadeq was democratically elected is a case in point.

Consumerism

Progressive Christians are coming to realize that hyper-individualism and selfish capitalist acquisition dominate our culture and drown out the capacity to appreciate and transmit our own religious tradition effectively to the next generation. Today the greatest challenge of Christian teaching and living is consumerism. This functions as the dominant religion of the West, and especially of the United States, and current policies are spreading it abroad.[15]

To date, Islamic civilization, where tradition remains strong, has withstood this modern attack on community values better than many other cultures. We progressives, who have done so much to break the shackles of tradition, must recognize that this force can at times work for good. Tradition clothed in the cause of social justice can be an ally to progressive Christians seeking to recreate a sense of community in a disintegrating age such as ours. If we believe that God is at work in human struggles, we must consider the possibility that that which is best in both Islam and Christianity can be used for transformations that are beyond our current powers of imagination.

Pope John Paul II apparently realized that Islam was outperforming Christianity as an effective bulwark against Western consumerism when in 1985 he arranged for Roman Catholics and Muslims to dialogue concerning living lives of "holiness" in the modern age. The cause of this Muslim superior performance is not difficult to discern, for in Islamic societies human rights are normally not dissociated from religious duties, as they are in the West. As a secular, economic religion currently shapes Western civilization more than any other force, the Pope reached across ancient religious barriers for muscular spiritual allies. With the hope that Christianity itself might be revived into a living force, John Paul II commented upon how devout Christians and Muslims have far more in common than either normally realize:

> In today's world, it is more important than ever that men and women of faith, assisted by God's grace, should strive for true holiness. Self-centered tendencies—such as greed, the lust for power and prestige,

competition, revenge, the lack of forgiveness, and the quest for earthly pleasures—all these threaten to turn mankind from the path to goodness and holiness which God has intended for all of us. The countless numbers of good people around the world—Christians, Muslims, and others who quietly lead lives of authentic obedience, praise, and thanksgiving to God and selfless service of their neighbor—offer humanity a genuine alternative, "God's way," to a world which otherwise would be destroyed in self-seeking, hatred, and struggle.[16]

Our Actual Relationship

Cross Pollination and Conflict

It is obvious from the account of Muhammad and the Sufis above that Christianity, like Judaism, profoundly influenced Islam, especially in its early development. However, for the following thousand years the influence flowed much more in the other direction. Sadly, much of this influence was bound up with warfare, some initiated by Muslims, some by Christians.

Indeed, Christianity and Islam have a long history of military conflict throughout the fourteen centuries that the two religions have coexisted. A root cause of this violent history lies in their theological similarity. Unlike Judaism, both have always been proselytizing religions. From roughly 500 B.C.E. to 500 C.E., Judaism also sought converts, but it gave up this practice when Christianity lured away many of those who initially made a commitment to become Jews. During its proselytizing period, Judaism required that convert families remain in a training status for three generations, after which they were finally accepted as full-fledged members. Christianity's process toward full membership was much quicker, making it a more attractive alternative. Accordingly, Judaism settled for enduring as a minority faith in lands governed by adherents to other religious traditions. When Islam came into existence in the seventh century C.E., Christianity finally had a powerful proselytizing rival.

Linking scientists from Egyptian, Persian, Byzantine, Chinese, and Indian civilizations, Islam established possibilities for tremendous progress. At that juncture, Islamic civilization became the preserver of the knowledge of the ancient Greeks, much of which Europeans of that day had long forgotten. Most importantly, Muslims created a synergistic cultural environment that encouraged intellectual growth and the development of new advances in mathematics and astronomy. Beginning in 1096, when medieval Christendom counterattacked during the Crusades, backward European invaders were introduced to both new and old scientific and philosophical constructs that would change Christendom forever. Indeed, the beginnings of modern European material progress commenced at that time providing the seeds for a European intellectual rebirth that eventually came to be known as the Renaissance.

Today many Americans wonder why Muslim fanatics hate everything Western. The answer can be found in the attitude of the late medieval Florentine poet, Dante Alighieri. On the one hand, he was deeply affected by Muslim insights. For example, his *Inferno* drew heavily upon the Islamic conception of the various layers of hell. Yet, on the other hand, he refused to acknowledge this debt and professed hatred of all things Islamic. He portrayed the Prophet Muhammad deep in hell and suffering the cruelest punishment of all, being cleft from head to crotch. According to Dante, Muhammad's crime was sowing discord within a Christian civilization that still thought it desirable to maintain unity of thought.

It seems that nobody appreciates those who bring about unsought and unwanted change. In receiving this impetus to change through their engagement with a superior civilization in Palestine, Europe was not grateful. Eventually failing in the Crusades after a temporary conquest of the Holy Land, Europe retreated back across the Mediterranean.

Between the Crusades and modern times, the rise of the Ottoman Turks provided Islam with a further opportunity to affect Europe. As the Ottomans conquered the Balkan Peninsula and reached Vienna, they absorbed much of Christendom's attention and created a context in which the Protestant Reformers were able to succeed. The failure of the Crusades and the success of the subsequent Islamic aggression left Europeans deeply resentful.

The history of Christian influence on Islam and of Islam pollinating Christianity is too rich to claim that these two great religious traditions are separated by history. To the contrary, they have long been in a most creative (if often violent) interfaith relationship. Much bloodshed and many cruel atrocities have stained the histories of both, allowing deep hatreds to fester, especially along the frontier territories of the two traditions in regions such as the Balkans. Nevertheless, a Western civilization that now appreciates modern pluralism owes a great debt to Islam, as Western medieval religious and cultural uniformity was the principal casualty resulting from repeated encounters with Islamic civilization.

As Islam once impacted the West, so the West today impacts Islam. The Ottoman Empire declined gradually after being stopped at Vienna and came to be called "the sick man of Europe." It collapsed completely in World War I. Progressive Christians must appreciate the depth of shame that Muslims have felt over the last two centuries in witnessing their once dominant civilization kneeling before a Christian West that carved up their territory into colonies and client states and then facilitated the creation of a Jewish state in their midst.

This Western colonialism and the more recent American desire to attain global hegemony have worked to identify modernity itself with unwanted outside influences. In our own time, the West has unleashed great changes. There have been two types of response. One was the rise of diverse Islamic movements calling upon Muslims to maintain their traditions in order to resist Western imperialism. The other response was the adoption of modernity. Desperately wanting to match Western technological power, Arabs sought to copy Western tendencies toward secularization and modernity, thinking that these were prerequisites for creating powerful Arab nations. In many Arab countries, the seeds of fundamentalist Islam were suppressed after the dismantling of the last caliphate at the close of World War I. Kemal Ataturk, the leader of Turkey after World War I, provided a new model for the Muslim world. Intent upon modernizing Islamic civilization away from its own medieval past, he suppressed what he regarded as a backward religion. New Arab nations followed his lead. Later Gamal Abdul Nasser of Egypt emerged as a hero and model of Arab secular nationalist leadership. Within Egypt, the Muslim Brotherhood that urged a fundamentally religious response to the European threat of colonialism was persecuted and driven underground.

The Six Day War of 1967 was a profound turning point in this regard. Israel blitzed its neighbors after many threatening indications of an imminent Arab attack intent on annihilating the Jewish state. The quick war resulted in a complete Israeli victory that claimed the West Bank and the Sinai Peninsula. The total defeat of the Arab armies showed many Muslims that the nationalist, modernist response was futile. Jews gained access to the Wailing Wall in Jerusalem, and their heartfelt religious devotion was apparent via televised broadcasts to the entire world, including Arab populations.

Thereafter, momentum has been with religious fundamentalism throughout Islamic civilization. Following Israel's smashing victory over Egypt, Syria, and Jordan, Muslim fundamentalists emphasized Allah's obvious displeasure as a divine wake-up call to follow a different path. They reflected on why an almighty Allah had allowed such an outcome. Their preferred answer was deeply disturbing. Allah temporarily favored the Jews because of their greater religious devotion. Seemingly overnight, the mood within Islamic civilization shifted toward fundamentalist Islam intent on producing an even greater religious devotion.

As the Muslim world has shifted away from secularism, Saudi oil wealth has helped fund the spread of fundamentalism, including some of its most violent expressions. If the Six Day War was popularly viewed throughout the Arab world as indicating the direction of Divine Will, so was the fact that the world's largest oil reserves were located in that part of the Islamic world inhabited by the most reactionary expression of Islam in modern times. In the late eighteenth century, 'Abd al-Wahhab revived the theological doctrines of Ibn Taymiyya, creating a movement known as Wahhabism, which found support among the House of Sa'ud, whose men he trained in the use of fire-arms, thereby enabling them eventually to gain control over much of the Arabian peninsula.

Wahhabi doctrine professed a strict monotheism and viewed tomb visi-tations, including visits to the tombs of the Prophet or of Muslim saints, as heresy. Wahhabi theology emphasized God's predestination. Wahhabis fur-ther viewed all Muslims who did not subscribe to their doctrines as heretical, especially the Shi'ites and the Sufis. A Wahhabi warrior community marched northward into Iraq and westward to Mecca destroying all Sufi tombs in its path. The Wahhabi objective was to return Islam to the original "purity" that it had known in the days of the Prophet. Ironically, this effort to go back to the fundamentals of Islam was itself heretical, for ijma (community consen-sus) had long before accepted Sufism into the very body of Islam. Mainstream Muslims crushed Wahhabi military capabilities early in the nineteenth cen-tury, but the Wahhabi fundamentalist ideal lives on today as the state religion of Saudi Arabia. It is understandable that the overwhelming majority of Mus-lims participating in the 9/11 suicide flights hailed from Saudi Arabia.

In 1979, Iran's Westernizing Shah was overthrown. In 2003, the United States ironically furthered the fundamentalist cause by dismantling the cruel but also secular nationalist regime of Saddam Hussein in Iraq, an event that attracted radical Islamic warriors to meet the western infidel in guerrilla com-bat on Arab soil. Inexorably, the region appears drawn into religious warfare.

In our time, religion and politics are no longer separate and distinct realms. Unfortunately, the religion reflected in this gathering storm is characterized by hate. This phenomenon is not restricted to Islam but may be seen within Christianity and Judaism also. This is a most bitter legacy involving the three religious traditions of Abraham.

Progressive Muslims

For progressive Christians a major concern is whether there are progressive Muslims who share our hopes. We do not celebrate all past forms of Christianity, nor are we enthusiastic about much that is done today in the name of Christianity. But we do not reject our tradition because of its past affirmation of religious exclusivism or acceptance of patriarchy, slavery, racism, authoritarian governments, nor for the support that today it gives to imperialism and war. Accordingly, we certainly do not condemn other traditions because they contain much that we deplore. Our question is whether Islam provides support for progressive self-reform. Much has already been said that indicates that it does.

Neither Christianity nor Islam is a static religion. Both are in time, and both may yet be transformed to improve upon that which has been. The purpose here is not to idealize either Christianity or Islam but rather to suggest that both may benefit from entering into a positive interfaith relationship with the other.

Opportunities for reform exist within Islam. Recently, an event occurred in Los Angeles demonstrating how Islam might be changed. In June 2005, the Progressive Muslim Union of North America conducted a town-hall meeting at the USC Religious Center. Both progressive and traditional Muslims were in attendance to observe a debate over whether women should be allowed to lead prayer observances. Examples from the past were used in an attempt to remake the present. The event featured Khaled Abou El Fadl, a professor of Islamic law who argued that Islam requires the most knowledgeable person to lead prayer, regardless of gender. In making his case, Abou El Fadl cited examples of female prayer leaders in Islamic history along with three schools of thought during medieval times that embraced the practice. He emphasized that most Muslims are ignorant of their own vast and diverse heritage and urged those in attendance to become educated to new possibilities that have in fact existed before. In short, one way to reform Islam is through historical interpretation.[17]

The Qur'an, as with Jewish and Christian scriptures, contains many ambiguities and a few seeming contradictions, and is subject to many different interpretations. Within these ambiguities and contradictions are opportunities for new understandings. Hadith, or the compilation of the sayings and deeds of Muhammad himself, is a primary basis for the formation of Muslim understandings of right and wrong, good and evil, and the parameters of legitimate reform. Different Muslim groupings (especially Shi'ites and Sunnis) disagree on what constitutes authentic hadith, opening possibilities for diverse Islamic practices, laws, and teachings. In any case, Muslims typically agree that tradition is a strong primary value within Islam. The Shar'iah, a broad term for the basis of the many different schools of law created through the interpretations of the Qur'an and the hadith, uses analogy and consensus to form rulings applying tradition to changing circumstances.

The message of Jesus was one of radical equality and so was the tendency of Muhammad's reforms in his time and place. Christianity and Islam are two branches of a single tree that obviously includes Judaism as a third branch. Progressives from these three great traditions have enough in common to be in solidarity for the common cause of restoring a revitalized sense of community so desperately needed in our broken world. Global society today is like that of Mecca in Muhammad's time. The ancient witness of Islam's Messenger triumphing over obstructions and obstacles raised by a powerful economic establishment encourages hope. This story, so long excluded within Western religious discourse, should now be added to examples of historic Jewish and Christian religious leaders doing the same thing.

The Judeo-Islamic-Christian Tradition

While we are exploring the relationship between Christianity and Islam, Judaism must not be kept out of the discussion. All three Abrahamic faith traditions stem from common origins. That is not to say that throughout their shared history, there have not been Christian tendencies to equate Judaism and Christianity as closer in form, practice, and mentality than is Islam, which is thereby assigned an inferior status. Typically, Christians have never regarded Islam as a covenantal partner potentially sharing a claim deserving of God's blessing. It is helpful here to consider the Jewish perspective, which sees Christianity as no more closely related to Judaism than is Islam. Effectively, the Christian mentality envisioning a special theological bond with

Judaism is a one-way street as Jews have no theology underwriting Christianity as a covenantal partner.

For his part, Muhammad urged that both Judaism and Christianity be regarded as faiths intimately related to Islam. This teaching was both encouraged and discouraged by actual events. Before he moved his residence to Medina, some of Muhammad's followers bloodied by cruel persecution in Mecca fled to Christian Abyssinia where they found refuge. When Muslims want to remember their Christian coreligionists fondly, memories of this rescue are recalled. After Muhammad removed Islam to Medina, he received a revelation that Muslims should pray toward Jerusalem as Allah's holy city. He experienced a miraculous night journey wherein he instantaneously traveled to Jerusalem ascending through heaven's multiple layers. With two Jewish tribes as part of his Medina constituency, this revelation served to bind Judaism to Islam. However, when these two tribes chafed at this intimate relationship, they were suspected of treason and ultimately exiled or destroyed in order to keep Medina secure in a dangerous time. Later, Muhammad received a new revelation that Muslims should pray toward Mecca, and the Ka'ba came to be regarded as the house of Allah (the geographic focus of Muslim worship).

Upon Muhammad's death, rumors held that a Jewish woman had poisoned the Prophet, adding to some negative memories of Jewish perfidy within Islam. But then, there are also negative Muslim memories of Christians, primarily stemming from the Crusades of late medieval times as well as Western colonialism during the last two centuries. Christians also have their own bad memories, of Ottoman Muslims kidnapping Christian boys in the Balkans and elsewhere to be raised as janissaries, the most disciplined and feared military arm of Ottoman power. Kidnapped Christian girls became harem girls. To this day, the center of anti-Muslim Christian feeling is Christian Serbia that at one time bore the brunt of these kidnappings.

Modern American Christians can also point to the events of 9/11 as justifying negative feelings toward Islam. Despite this, Christian bad feelings for Abrahamic relatives have rarely been primarily directed at Muslims. The genre of Christian passion plays has long fostered hostility toward Jews as Christ-killers. Mel Gibson's *The Passion of the Christ* is a recent and monetarily successful recollection of this particular bad feeling that has long been nurtured and exploited for horrific ends. Jews hold bad memories of both Christian and Muslim atrocities. The systematic extermination of the Jewish people at the hands of Christian-Nazi executioners is linked in the Jewish mind with the violent resolve of Muslim Palestinians to drive Jews from Greater Israel. Hostile theology, forced conversions, expulsions, countless pogroms, colonialism, and negative propaganda have made good feelings and healthy relationships exceptionally difficult among these quarrelling family relatives.

Realities in our world now demand that each faith tradition reduce festering memories that contribute to provincial theologies concerning the greater evil of "the other." The Christian West's nuclear arsenal has the potential to destroy all life on the planet. Israel's reported nuclear weapons have at least the potential to destroy the entire Middle East. Muslim Pakistan is currently the only Islamic nation with nuclear bombs but Iran is not far behind. And just a few bombs would suffice to destroy Israel. The human urge to hate and follow through with acts of cruelty and barbarism must be reduced or our shared future is one of radioactive doom. In light of this, new theologies are called for that encourage respect rather than contempt, cooperation rather than exclusivity, and love rather than hatred. All three Abrahamic faiths need to be engaged in this process of thinking anew.

In recent years it has been commonplace for progressive Christians to think within the confines of a Judeo-Christian tradition—a paradigm that suggests a special, if difficult, relationship between two quarreling senior partners of unequal strength. A negative unspoken corollary of this linguistic and mental habit is that the third Abrahamic faith is more distant and even alien.

Essential in the developing relationship between Christians and Jews since 1945 is an emerging Christian understanding that both Judaism and Christianity share related covenants, the exact relationship of which will be revealed at the end of time. After the horrors of the Shoah, Jews fully appreciate the necessity of improved relations with Christians and so do little to comment negatively upon what they regard as part of Christianity's well-established tendency toward theological inventiveness and invasiveness, so far as Judaism is concerned. This developing Christian-Jewish relationship might be regarded as wholly positive (or at the very least harmless) were it not for the fact that it has no role for Islam other than that of a heretical outsider. Progressive Christians need to raise this theological problem to the level of conscious thinking. With a long history of negativity toward both Judaism and Islam, Christians cannot afford to exaggerate any new supposed "good feelings" toward one of its Abrahamic relatives at the expense of the other. A radical and exclusive theological dividing line between Judaism and

Christianity on one side and Islam on the other has potential for great evil in a nuclear world. The witness of the Shoah should instruct us that our theological and mental habits have serious consequences. No matter how difficult, we must invite Muslims to our family interfaith gatherings. The alternative is unthinkable. Persistent attitudes of exclusiveness and contempt undermine hope for human survival.

As words help shape mentality, the name that we give to our family relationship is theologically important. That is why this section is entitled "The Judeo-Islamic-Christian Tradition." To tack on Islamic at the end of "Judeo-Christian-Islamic Tradition" would appear as an obvious after-thought designed more as a cosmetic than encouraging any real change of heart and mind. Meaningfully to include Islam in the family fold, its place-ment must be more central. In many ways, Islam fits in the middle. Indeed, this is how many Muslims regard their religion in relation to Judaism and Christianity. They clearly see that Islam has greater similarities with either Judaism or Christianity than the other two have with each other. Islam exalts Jesus more than does Judaism. It is oriented to religious law, as is Judaism, which suggests that these two faith traditions should be side by side. Islam and Christianity both have strong proselytizing traditions, which suggest that they should be side-by-side. Most importantly, as Islam is currently the "stranger," it should be given the favored place at the table—or the central place in the grouping. A generous interfaith theology is one that is most likely to bring about a better future.[18]

Theological Conclusions

This survey shows that Christian self-righteousness and contempt for Islam is profoundly inappropriate. However, it indicates that there are real, and quite fundamental, differences between the two traditions. In concluding, we need to explore several theological questions. Beyond fairer and friendlier interpretations, and efforts to work together for peace and justice, what do progressive Christians propose as a theological response to Islam?

God

Christians often ask whether Islam's Allah is the same as their Christian God. This is similar to asking whether the God of progressive Christians is the same as the deity of fundamentalist Christians, just as progressive

Muslims may wonder whether the Allah of Fundamentalist Muslims is identical to their own. The answer to such questions rests in the human inability to define with precision something as unfathomable as "God." Yet, many serious people seek answers to this and similar questions. This can be said with certainty: the word "Allah" in Arabic means "God." It is what Arab Christians call their God. So from a linguistic standpoint, Allah and Christian God are one and the same.

We may stand with Jews who proclaim with certainty, "Hear, O Israel: The Lord our God is one" (Deut 6:4). Despite their shared tendency to place aspects of their faith traditions within an ahistorical realm termed the "Preexistent Word," which easily suggests something equivalent to a second divinity, all of the faiths within the Judeo-Islamic-Christian tradition are truly monotheistic. Jesus Christ is no more a second God for Christians than is the Qur'an for Muslims or the 613 laws of the Torah for Jews. Each of the three related faiths is devoted to the same God, whom they admittedly understand imperfectly. Each faith tradition, and indeed sects within each faith tradition, often describe radically different parts of "the elephant," but they are all attempting to portray the same phenomenon. Theologians, such as the ancient Christian Marcion, who claimed that the God of the Jews was different than the God of the Christians, have rightly ultimately been rejected even within their own traditions, for such commentators undermine the very monotheism that is the bedrock of this shared interfaith tradition.

Is the Muslim understanding of a God who requires submission substantially different than the Christian God of Love and Grace? Perhaps so, but within the Christian Bible is definitely a similar message. Whether or not Christians want to label it "submission" per se is another matter. In answering the Rich Young Ruler who wanted to follow the way of the Master, Jesus required that he first detach himself from the false god to whom the young man had sworn his effective allegiance—the god of his own possessions and wealth. This act was too much for the Rich Young Ruler, who abandoned Jesus as a consequence (Matt 19:16-26; Mark 10:17-27; Luke 18:18-27). The teaching of this story is equivalent to the Muslim conception of Shirk, or the condemnation of associating anything that is not God with God. The God of both Christianity and Islam agree that this kind of idolatry is unacceptable and that believers in both faiths should yearn to adopt a more holy understanding that is "the way, the truth, and the life" (Luke 16:13). And within the theologies of both faith traditions is also the emphasis that God alone can fulfill that yearning as a free gift.

The word "submission" (or "surrender") in Islam is tied to the role of religious law within that tradition.[19] In contrast to Christianity, Islam does indeed emphasize religious law. In this sense, Islam is closer to Judaism than to Christianity. However, there are Jews that do not emphasize religious law, such as Reform Jews, and there are certainly progressive Muslims who do not look to the *ulema* for guidance in their daily lives. Progressive Christians accent freedom rather than submission. Perhaps because progressive Muslims realize the difficulty that Christians have with the word "submission," they commonly emphasize that the deepest meaning of Islam is "peace," as in the peace that one can only know in God. The Gospel of Matthew reports Jesus communicating the same thought: "Take my yoke upon you and learn from me, for I am gentle and lowly in heart and you will find rest for your souls. For my yoke is easy and my burden light" (Matt 11:28-30). While there are definitely differences in emphasis, there is also enough common ground between progressive Christians and likeminded Muslims not to let the word "submission" become an insurmountable stumbling block.

Jesus Christ and the Holy Spirit

Does the Christian understanding of Jesus Christ as a person within whom God and humankind meet irrevocably separate the Muslim understanding of Allah from the Christian understanding of God? On the surface, it may seem so. However, the historic inability to define the Christian understanding of Jesus Christ with rational precision opens other possibilities. The traditional Christian definition of Jesus Christ as both "fully God" and "fully man" constitutes something akin to a Christian *koan*. In Zen Buddhism, a *koan* is a construct intended to frustrate the rational mind beyond artificial categories of human language and philosophical learning. "God" is beyond the powers of our human abilities to corral, limit, and dominate. The Christian claim to Jesus' special status has some parallel in the Muslim claim that Muhammad is the Seal of the Prophets. Christians believe that the fullness of God was revealed in the person of Jesus in a way that makes any subsequent prophecy commentary on that revelation rather than a revision of its truth. In dialoguing with Muslims, Christians need to explain that they do not effectively worship three gods (Father, Son, and Holy Spirit). They need to explain that the mystery of the Christian Trinity was codified in response to a third-century Christian heresy that held that Jesus was an intermediate deity between God and Man. The intent of the Trinitarian concept is to convey the fullness of God as revealed in Jesus' earthly life and ministry and the continuation of that Holy Spirit into the current age.

Muslims have difficulty with the Christian concept of the Risen Christ as well. Muhammad, they say, was just a man. Why do Christians insist that the Prophet Jesus rose from the dead? For the Christian, hearing again the Easter story in a crowded church, the message is clear. Death does not have the final word. Jesus' humiliation and crucifixion did not defeat the meeting of God and Man in Jesus of Nazareth. The Gospel stories present no one rendition of the resurrection story. Indeed the variety of resurrection narratives allows the hearer or reader to hold close the one that best communicates the reality behind the words. A favorite one with progressive Christians is the encounter of several of Jesus' followers with the risen Christ on the Road to Emmaus. They knew him not by his physical presence. Apparently, he looked nothing like the Jesus that they knew. They knew him by the truth that he spoke in intimate communication while breaking bread.

Progressive Christians in dialogue with Muslims may find that the latter also have difficulty with the Christian concept of the Holy Spirit, perhaps the most mysterious aspect of the Christian Trinity. Yet, it is likely that they have much experience with this concept within their own tradition. Islam teaches that Allah is closer to the Muslim than his or her own jugular vein. That could help to communicate the Christian idea of the Holy Spirit. Jesus was a man who was crucified and after his resurrection became sanctified as "The Christ," which is described in concepts and categories that seem removed from the average person. And God the Father likewise seems distant and unfathomable. The Holy Spirit represents God who is most accessible—closer than one's own jugular vein.

Muhammad

Another matter needs to be addressed in communications between Christians and Muslims. Muhammad was a great spiritual as well as temporal leader. In some ways, he is admirable as King David was, adept at leading his people on political and military stages as well as generally setting a religious model for his community. The total witness of Muhammad's life, not just the fact that he was in and of the world, must be weighed.

The Muslim claim that Muhammad is to be understood in the category of "prophet" is somewhat strange to Christian ears. Christians are accustomed to distinguishing the role of prophet from that of priest and king and also lawgiver. All may be appointed by God to perform their proper functions, but prophets do not rule and lead troops into battle as Muhammad did. Islam uses "prophet" inclusively for those who are specially called by God to bring divine truth and guide God's people. For them, for example, Moses and David are great prophets, as are Isaiah and Jesus. For Islam, Muhammad as "prophet" performs all these roles and completes the process the great figures of the Christian Bible began. Hence, his political and military leadership in no way counts against his role as prophet. By some realistic historical judgments it does seem that Muhammad carried the prophetic role furthest and most successfully and that there has been no comparable prophets since his time. In order to facilitate public recognition of a Judeo-Islamic-Christian heritage, if for no other reason, it is time that Christians acknowledge this record.

The Qur'an

Our greatest problem with Muslims, then, is not their monotheism nor their conception of God nor their Prophet. Rather, their doctrines about the Qur'an present the greatest potential theological stumbling block. They tend to deify the Qur'an in ways not unlike the way in which some Christians exalt Jesus as more God than human. We may share the Muslim view that the Qur'an is a truly remarkable document, that its origins are unique, even that in many ways it surpasses the Christian scriptures, for example, in literary style, in internal coherence, and in relative freedom from offensive invective. But Christians in general, and progressive Christians in particular, must deny that it is eternal and inerrant. Progressives must insist that it is historically informed and relative.

The question is, then, whether an ahistorical status for the Qur'an is essential to Islam. That is, of course, for Muslims to say, and many of them will undoubtedly say that it is. Are there progressive Muslims who, with the greatest appreciation of the Qur'an and respect for its remarkable origin and nature, nevertheless are open to consideration of its historical character? There are. And they do not thereby cease to be Muslims any more than progressive Christians cease to be Christians when they emphasize the historical Jesus over the otherworldly images of Christ in the Book of Revelation.

Prospects for Progress

If this is so, then we have all the more reason to deplore the recent radical Islamist success in marginalizing progressive Muslims. The American "war on terror" effectively socializes Americans to view all Muslims as radical extremists. Our task as progressive Christians is to help create a friendly and honest context in which Muslims, instead of being put on the defensive, are appreciated for their many contributions in the past and the present and are encouraged to formulate their beliefs in the most convincing way. Today that requires bringing historical consciousness to bear upon religious issues. progressive Muslim scholars have made a fine beginning. Already it is often the case that progressive Christians and progressive Muslims feel more comfortable with one another than either do with the more rigid and militant members of their own communities.

In the long run there need not always be flat contradictions on basic questions between progressive Muslim teaching and progressive Christian theology. This would not mean that they would cease to differ. Jesus Christ will remain central for Christians, as the Qur'an will for Muslims. We will continue to think out of our Christian history; Muslims, out of theirs. The goal is not unity. Diversity, rather than leading to opposition and antagonism, can be experienced as an enrichment of both parties. Each can challenge the other to grow into God's fullness. The proper goal in any Christian-Muslim dialogue should be that Christians come away from it becoming better Christians, and that Muslims also become better Muslims in the process of free and open interfaith discussion.

One important potential of the interaction between these two communities comes from their different relations to the Western Enlightenment. Progressive Christians have been deeply shaped by this, but today we are trying to overcome destructive consequences deriving from the Enlightenment's overemphasis upon individual liberty at the expense of community well being. In addition to making the individual the measure of all things, the Enlightenment served to exalt scientific methodologies that over time encouraged a compartmentalization of human experience, an approach well suited to rational discourse but falling short of effectively incorporating the whole of personal and social and ecological life, rather than a few of the fragments left to it by an exaggerated scientific rationalism. Despite these negatives, progressive Christians do not seek to undo positive advances made because of the Enlightenment. That which is sought is a better balance between expanding perceived needs of individuals and the overall health of the greater community.

Islam, on the other hand, has not been inwardly informed by this history. However, it has been "outwardly informed." Western-dominated processes such as colonization, colonial education, and most recently globalization have tended to associate these ideas with both Western imperial dominance and Muslim subservience. Nonetheless, individual Muslims have come to appreciate the full range of rights and responsibilities that were encouraged by Enlightenment principles; but Middle Eastern strong-arm rulers receiving financial, political, and military support from the West have thwarted indigenous Muslim democratic expressions. The growth of Islamic fundamentalist ideologies has arisen in part as a meaningful resistance to this unwanted foreign influence over the political life of the Middle East. Accordingly, Muslims are now faced with both internal and external factors that they have to overcome in order to realize their democratic desires as well as their need to acknowledge pluralism within their own societies. It is a difficult bind. Finding a solution to this problem while retaining religious practices and a faith that encompasses and unifies the whole of human life is the growing edge of Islam. In a similar way, overcoming negative results of the Enlightenment provides the growing edge of Christianity.

Each tradition has much to offer the other in a dialogue that recognizes and appreciates differences in an attitude of mutual respect. Christianity has lost much of its past ability to shape Western culture that is now effectively conforming to values having little to do with any meaningful aspect of traditional faith. Muslim practices of self-sacrifice, such as witnessed during the holy month of Ramadan when Muslims go without water, food, and sex during the daylight hours, serves as a reminder of their human frailties and their devotion to a power beyond those frailties. Similar practices need to be recovered by Western Christians where self-denial beyond short waiting periods is commonly regarded as unacceptable. Christians need not convert to Islam to restore these lost practices and virtues, any more than Muslims need to convert to Christianity to grow in the area of individual human rights. All that is necessary is to be inspired by a related religious tradition that perhaps has seen a different side of "the elephant" to grow anew in ways that are pleasing to God/Allah and helpful for the peace, justice, and sustainability of the world.

For Further Reading

Aslam Abdullah and Gasser Hathout. *The American Muslim Identity: Speaking for Ourselves*. Los Angeles: Multimedia Vera International, 2003.

Reza Aslan. *No god but God: The Origins, Evolution, and Future of Islam*. New York: Random, 2005.

Ralph J. D. Braibanti. *The Nature and Structure of the Islamic World*. Oak Brook: International Strategy and Policy Institute, 2000.

Lois Beck and Nikki Keddie, eds. *Women in the Muslim World*. Cambridge: Harvard University Press, 1980.

John Corrigan et al. *Jews, Christians, Muslims: A Comparative Introduction to Monotheistic Religions*. Upper Saddle River: Prentice Hall, 1997.

Bruce Feiler. *Abraham: A Journey to the Heart of Three Faiths*. New York: William Morrow, 2002.

Helmut Gatje. *The Qur'an and Its Exegesis, Selected Texts with Classical and Modern Muslim Interpretations*. Oxford: Oneworld, 1996.

George B. Grose and Benjamin J. Hubbard, eds. *The Abraham Connection: A Jew, Christian and Muslim in Dialogue*. Notre Dame: Cross Cultural, 1994.

Marshall G. S. Hodgson. *The Venture of Islam: Conscience and History in a World Civilization*. 3 vols. Chicago: University of Chicago Press, 1977.

Samuel P. Huntington, et al. *The Clash of Civilizations? The Debate*. New York: Foreign Affairs, 1996.

Nikki R. Keddie, ed. *Scholars, Saints, and Sufis: Muslim Religious Institutions in the Middle East Since 1500*. Berkeley: University of California Press, 1978.

Charles Kimball. *When Religion Becomes Evil: Five Warning Signs*. San Francisco: HarperSanFrancisco, 2003.

Hans Küng et al. *Christianity and World Religions: Paths of Dialogue with Islam, Hinduism, and Buddhism*. New York: Doubleday, 1994.

Oddbjorn Leirvik. *Images of Jesus Christ in Islam*. Uppsala: Swedish Institute of Missionary Research, 1999.

Claire Rudolf Murphy et al. *Daughters of the Desert: Stories of Remarkable Women from Christian, Jewish, and Muslim Traditions*. Woodstock: Skylight Paths, 2005.

F. E. Peters. *Allah's Commonwealth: A History of Islam in the Near East, 600-1100 A.D.* New York: Simon and Schuster, 1973.

Paul Tillich. *A History of Christian Thought.* Clearwater: Touchstone, 1972.

W. Montgomery Watt. *Islam and the Integration of Society.* Evanston: Northwestern University Press, 1961.

W. Montgomery Watt, trans. *The Faith and Practices of al-Ghazali.* Sydney: George Allen and Unwin, 1953.

Paul Winters, ed. *Islam: Opposing Viewpoints.* Farmington Hills: Greenhaven, 1995.

Malcolm X. *The Autobiography of Malcolm X.* New York: Grove, 1965.

Miroslav Volf, et al, eds. *A Common Word: Muslims and Christians on Loving God and Neighbor.* Grand Rapids, MI: Eerdmans, 2009.

Questions for Discussion

1. Is it possible to know Christianity by only knowing Christianity? How can coming to know another religious tradition, such as Islam, possibly make a Christian into a better Christian?

2. How does the authority of scripture differ in Christianity and Islam?

3. Is any religion, including Christianity, unchanging? What evidence is provided in the chapter that demonstrates that both Christianity and Islam have interpreted their scriptures differently at different times? Is there any one theology that has dominated throughout all ages in Christianity? Have divergent theologies likewise existed within Islam?

4. What are the most striking theological similarities and differences in these two faith traditions?

5. Ideally, what should be the roles of religious custom and individual spiritual discernment in the practice of religion? What aspects of Christianity and Islam are today needed in providing a holy balance?

6. As a Christian, do you engage each day with specific religious practices that effectively transform your "lifestyle." Do you recognize that Muslims do focus on such practices that play positive roles in their daily living?

7. Compose a list in which you itemize your own complaints of flaws that currently exist within Islamic civilization. Then compose a list of flaws that exist within your own society. Which one of these two lists is longer? Is your judgment "objective" or conditioned by highly subjective cultural preferences? Which list do you imagine Jesus would regard as being of the greatest concern?

8. Are theocracies that blend religion and state beneficial for either faith or government? Should religion inform politics in other ways? Over the centuries, what role has religion played in the politics of both Western civilization and Islamic civilization? What role should religion play in contemporary American politics?

9. Is God on "our side"? Or is God more subtly at work in the struggles of many different sides? Have you seen the bumper sticker that reads "God Bless the World—No Exceptions?" If you had this bumper sticker, would you put it on your car or would fear of a neighbor's reactions restrain you?

10. Can there be world peace without religious peace? What are you and your church doing to help bring about religious peace?

11. What opportunities exist in your geographic area for a constructive Christian-Muslim dialogue? If such a relationship exists, would you be willing to participate in it? If one does not exist, would you be willing to participate in creating one?

FOUR

Buddha for Christians

Dickson Kazuo Yagi

Introduction

Namu Daishi Henjo Kongo

It is a privilege to grow up in a house of prayer. In the Yagi household in Hilo, Hawaii, during the Second World War, an old man walked quietly into the living room at 6:30 every morning. He burned incense at the altar, rang a small bell three times—ching, ching, ching—and sat cross-legged on the *zabuton* cushion on the floor. He began his morning prayers, "*Namu daishi henjo kongo, namu daishi henjo kongo, namu daishi henjo kongo.*"

Of course, these are not Christian prayers. These prayers are from Shingon Buddhism—esoteric Vajrayana coming to Japan from Tibet, through China. The old man is Seiryu Yagi, my grandfather, patriarch of the Yagi clan in Hawaii, who came from Okinawa in 1907. A few times Grandpa would have me sit on the floor with him below the Buddha altar to chant, "*Namu daishi henjo kongo.*"

Grandpa spoke good Okinawan dialect, passable Japanese, and broken English. I am a third-generation Okinawan American. I spoke perfect Hawaiian pidgin English, and broken Japanese. I said, "Jitchan, what does *Namu daishi henjo kongo* mean?" Grandpa thought of the language gap for a while and said, "Who cares what it means, just say it." Many years later in Japan, I learned what it meant: "I take refuge in the Great Teacher, Kukai, the Diamond Who Lights Up the Entire Universe." This is the slogan chant of Shingon Buddhism.

The Yagi Buddha Altar

My Uncle Ernest died in the Korean War. After basic training when he left for Korea, he told me that he would probably come home in a box. He did come home in a box. That night Reverend Sasai, the head priest of Hoganji, Shingon Buddhist Temple in Hilo, would come to our house to do the wake service.

A zealous Christian in the family phoned the Baptist preacher. She wanted to sneak in something Christian because the wake service and funeral was to be Buddhist. The Baptist missionary pastor knocked on the door.[1] He was relaxed and smiling as he entered the living room. When he saw the Buddha altar, he tensed up. It must have been the first time he was face to face with a Buddha altar. He did a Christian service and left.

We were stunned! The Buddha altar that we cherished and the Baptist missionary pastor whom we loved and respected—we could not put them together in the same room. There were anger, fear, and tears in his eyes. He saw the devil himself inside the Buddha image. I learned that night that we could never expect a Baptist missionary to share our respect for our Buddha altar. Many years later I met a few missionaries who respected Japanese religions, but these were missionaries one generation later.

The Yagi extended family is split between Buddhists and Christians. The Buddhists would be angry if Christian worship were insulted. The Christians would be angry if Buddhist worship were insulted. We are one family, Buddhists and Christians together. Almost all Japanese American families in California and Hawaii are like this—Buddhists and Christians together.

Tear Down the Buddha Altar!

A first-term furloughing Japan missionary came to our church in Hilo. We were third-generation Japanese youth, and we couldn't speak Japanese. The missionary told us the meaning of our Japanese names. We were amazed at a white man speaking our language! Then he asked me if we had a Buddha altar in our house. I said yes, we did. He read to me the Old Testament story about Gideon tearing down the village idol. He said I must tear down the Buddha idol in our living room!

That night after everybody had gone to their rooms, I stood in our living room and looked at the Buddha altar. It centered on the fierce Buddha Protector, Fudo-Myo-O. He was painted black with sharp fangs, holding a sword in one hand and a looped rope in the other. It was Grandpa's greatest treasure. I looked at the Buddha altar for a long time. My head said I should do it. But my heart stopped me. I couldn't tear down Grandpa's Buddha altar. I was a fifth grader, just ten years old.

Many years later when I read the Bible for myself, I saw what the missionary did not see. When Gideon tore down the village idol, he fled the village that night. The Bible says he left that night before the sun came up (Judg 6:25-27). The missionary should have told me that when I tear down Grandpa's Buddha altar, I have to leave home that night before the sun came up and never come home again. When I was ten years old, I learned not to trust American ministers when they trash Japanese religions.

The Japanese Invasion of China

Of all the evils of the twentieth century in Asia, none are as grievous as the horrors unleashed by the Japanese army in the Pacific phase of the Second World War. Images of the Rape of Nanjing, the brutal 1910–1945 occupation of Korea, the forced recruitment of Taiwanese into the Japanese army, the recruitment of unwilling women in the occupied territories of Korea, Taiwan, and the Dutch East Indies as "comfort women" prostitutes for the Japanese army, the sadistic chemical-biological warfare experiments performed on captured Allied prisoners at Kyushu University,[2] and programmed release of dangerous specimens into the atmosphere above Chinese cities—all these atrocities can hardly be forgotten nor forgiven by living victims.

The Japanese invasion of China made it necessary for all Chinese missionaries to leave. When the United States entered the war after the attack on Pearl Harbor, most Japan missionaries also were forced to leave. Those left behind were sent to internment camps in Japan, some temporarily and others for the duration of the war.

Instead of waiting out the war in the American homeland, many Southern Baptist missionaries forced out of China and Japan came to Hawaii to work until the war ended. A tall veteran missionary from inland China, Dr.

Charles Leonard, came to Hilo to start a mission. He was joined by a brilliant young scholar missionary, Dr. Tucker Callaway. I was baptized by Dr. Callaway on Easter morning, April 1946. So the massive evil of the Japanese army's Pacific invasion resulted in a little good in bringing thousands of Hawaii residents to faith in Jesus Christ. That is why I could become a Christian to say, "I believe in Jesus Christ as my Savior and Lord," instead of saying, "*Namu daishi henjo kongo.*"

Make Me a Zafu

God called me to become a missionary to Japan. I was accepted for admission to four American seminaries. I turned down Princeton Seminary. I turned down Fuller Seminary. I turned down Southern Baptist Seminary. I turned down Southwestern Baptist Seminary. I took a ship from Honolulu to Yokohama. I went to Tokyo Union Theological Seminary partly because I didn't want to hear American theologians trash Japanese religions.

In 1972 I joined the faculty of a university in Fukuoka. There was a tour of Zen Buddhist monasteries for foreign scholars. We first went to Hosshinji, a small monastery in a fishing village called Obama on the Japan Sea. The small monastery has some kind of celebrity status today because Obama is the same name as the first black President of the United States. We imitated the daily life of monks in training. We woke up to the loud racket of a monk running down the hall, banging a metal pot with a wooden spoon.

The next day we traveled to Eiheiji, which was close by. Eiheiji was famous as one of the two headquarter monasteries for Soto Zen. We woke up at 4:30 a.m. We sat on our meditation cushions by 5 a.m., joining hundreds of pilgrims in a large hall. When I came home to Fukuoka, I asked my wife, Ellen, to make me a *zafu* meditation cushion. That was my start in Zen meditations about thirty years ago.

Basic Teaching

Four Noble Truths

1. Life is suffering (*dukkha*: suffering, affliction, unsatisfactory).
2. Suffering comes from desire (*tanha*: craving), attachments to survival, wealth, possessions, power, youth, sex, food.
3. Cutting desires ends suffering (renunciation, non-attachment).
4. Cut desires through the Eight-Fold Path.

Eight-Fold Path

Mind: 1. Right Views, 2. Right Thought
Action: 3. Right Speech, 4. Right Action, 5. Right Job
Meditation: 6. Right Effort, 7. Right Mindfulness, 8. Right Concentration

Three Marks of Existence

Anicca: Impermanence (nothing is permanent, not even your soul nor God's)

Anatta: No self (non-substantiality of all things)

Dukkha: Suffering (insufficient, unsatisfactory). Life is suffering, not fulfillment, adventure, or pleasure. Old age, sickness, and death begins the list of eight basic sufferings. Of course, the varieties of suffering are countless.[3]

Early Buddhism

The Hindu Background

Just as Christianity came out of Judaism and cannot be understood without its background in the Hebrew scriptures, so Buddhism came out of Hinduism and cannot be understood without its Hindu background. Brahmanism and its later development, Hinduism, are the cumulative result of the religion of Aryan invaders from the Northwest. They imposed their Vedic religion on the conquered Dravidian tribes as they won control over the sub-continent over the centuries. Tight-fisted control over the priesthood and the sacrificial system by the Brahmin caste slowly created a backlash. Beside Islam, the religion of a foreign conquering dynasty, three native heretical religions rose up to defy Brahmin controlled religion: Jainism, Sikhism, and Buddhism. Their heresy is defined by their open rejection of caste and the sacred Scriptures of Hinduism—the *Vedas*.

The cultural influence of Brahmanism and the later Hinduism on Buddhism were many: karma, countless cycles of rebirth, non-attachment, homeless holy men, inward Vedanta meditation, and liberating *moksha* enlightenment experience. The nonviolence in the backbone of Buddhist ethics points to the Jain foundation principle of *ahimsa* that informs all Indian culture and religions. Against popular views of simplistic, legalistic karma, the Buddha's teaching was more an ethical principle. Karma was complex, encompassing a comprehensive mix of individual, family, and tribal responsibility. Accounting for intention and repentance, the total effect of any one action was beyond human calculation. No one could predict when in the future the fruit of any specific action would appear.[4]

Gautama Buddha

The lifetime of Gautama Buddha was eighty years. There is some debate over when this was: Western scholars think 566–486 B.C.E.; Sri Lanka and Southeast Asian scholars, 624–544 B.C.E.; and other scholars, 448-368 B.C.E.[5] The ancient traditional Chinese dates are about 900 B.C.E. The idealized traditional story reads like an extremely reworked script in a drama. Siddhartha was born in Lumbini, near the capital city of Kapilavastu, in the region now divided between India and Nepal in the foothills of the Himalayas. Siddhartha belonged to the Gautama family of the Sakya tribe. Sakyamuni is his title of honor, Sage of the Sakya tribe.

The traditional texts pictured Siddhartha as a prince coddled in royal luxury, brought up to inherit the kingdom.[6] By chance he met an old man, a sick man, a dead man, and a holy man. Deeply troubled by the inevitable suffering in human life, he bade farewell to his sleeping wife, Yasodhara, and their infant son, Rahula. He fled the privileges and powers of the throne to overcome the problem of human suffering. The story is embellished with numerous miracles that allowed him to escape the castle at age twenty-nine for the ascetic life of a begging holy man in the forest.

For six years he trained in spiritual disciplines. His first teacher, Alara Kalama, taught him meditative absorption into a state of "no-thing-ness." His second teacher, Udakra Ramaputra, led him to a meditative trance of "neither perception nor non-perception." He then gave himself to severe asceticism, testing his limits in holding his breath and in extreme fasting. Finding asceticism to be a dead end, he ate some food and recovered his strength. At Bodh Gaya he sat under a large tree and passed through several stages of advanced yogic absorption. Finally reaching the highest level of enlightenment, he became at age thirty-five a Buddha—one who wakes up to his true self. His five companion seekers became his first disciples.

As many others subjected themselves to Gautama's path, the Sangha community of monks was born. They were wandering holy men who at first came together only in the few months of the rainy season. Gautama taught and trained disciples for forty-five years, traveling back and forth across north

India, to the cities and towns of the central Ganges basin. He continued teaching his Sangha monks until he died at age eighty.[7]

Over the years the Sangha of celibate monks formed settled communities near villages. They made regular visits with their begging bowls to gather food from sympathetic villagers. The material dependence of the monastery on the village was reciprocated on the spiritual level. That is, the villagers in giving food were piling up good merit for a better rebirth. Families whose sons became monks were honored by both monastery and village. This living bond between monastery and village is what guaranteed the survival of the monks through hard times.

Theravada and Mahayana

In time, Mahayana, a new branch of Buddhism, arose with distinctive social and theological developments. The earlier Theravada is a two-tiered system of monks and villagers. The monks trained through temple chores, meditation, and scripture studies aimed at a three-pronged deliverance: psychologically at non-attachment, chronologically at breaking out of the cycles of rebirth, and spiritually at a transforming mystical enlightenment experience. The villagers were excluded from any hope of deliverance. Their highest hope was to earn good merits through good deeds and through generosity in putting food into the monks' bowls on their regular begging schedule. A good accumulation of merits at death would propel the villager to a good rebirth as a man worthy of becoming a monk. By the traditional model no woman could gain non-attachment and enlightenment to become a "never-returner." But if she earned enough good merit, she could be reborn as a man, become a monk, and then train for nirvana.[8] Many monks would not reach enlightenment in a lifetime of training, and may need to try again next time around or for several lifetimes—so difficult is it to reach enlightenment. So it was fantastic good news for villagers that Mahayana offered liberation even to those outside the monastery.

Several doctrinal developments gave birth to Mahayana. First is savior Bodhisattvas. A Bodhisattva is simply a person on the last stage before becoming a Buddha. In Mahayana as the "Great Raft," however, the Bodhisattva became a principle of absolute compassion. The Bodhisattva refused to enter Nirvana as a Buddha, until he could save all beings.[9] Of course, since Buddhist cosmic history is thought of as endless cycles with no beginning and no end, there is no conceivable time when all will be saved. The temporary Bodhisattva status, then, became a permanent icon of absolute compassion—the description of a Buddha. Super-hero Bodhisattvas, then, are revered and worshipped equally with Buddhas.

There are Bodhisattvas whose extreme compassion has won the adoration of millions, and whose cultic fame rivals that of any Buddha. Avalokiteshvara, the Bodhisattva of Compassion, is known as Kuan Yin in China and as Kannon[10] in Japan. Although a male in India, he was transformed into a female mother figure in China, Korea, and Japan. She often stands, cradling an infant in her arms.[11]

Manjusri, the Bodhisattva of Wisdom, is the focus of veneration along with Avalokiteshvara in most Zen circles. By tradition Zen practitioners prostrate themselves completely on the floor three times at every zazen session—not before any Buddha, but before these two Bodhisattvas. Ksitigarbha Bodhisattva (*Jizo*) with a staff in his right hand and a pearl in his left hand is greatly beloved for leading deceased children through the long journey to heaven. Maitreya Bodhisattva, the Buddha to come, is invoked by Tibetan Buddhists in the Red Crown Ceremony to appear before his time to bless us now with the powerful blessings of the New Age still to come. The ability of Bodhisattvas to bless us comes from the infinite surplus of merits they earned through countless lifetimes of self-sacrifice. In contrast to the severe path of Theravada monks, Mahayana showers blessings of grace on both monks and villagers from a multitude of savior Bodhisattvas.

A second doctrinal development is savior Bibles. The Perfection of Wisdom Sutras claim guaranteed power to deliver the believer safely to the other shore.[12] By far the most celebrated savior Bible in East Asia is the Lotus Sutra. The first and second largest religions in Japan, Soka Gakkai and Rissho Kosei Kai, are both Lotus Sutra religions. It is salvation by grace in chanting the holy slogan, "I take refuge in the wonderful law of the Lotus Sutra—*Namu myoho renge-kyo.*" The collective power of the countless Buddhas in the macrocosm is concentrated in the microcosm of the seven syllables of this powerful mantra invoking the title of the Lotus Sutra.[13]

A third development is Pure Land Buddhism. The Pure Land religion of grace stands on the foundation of the three Pure Land Sutras available in Pali and Chinese translations. The story is about Dharmakara Bodhisattva. He made forty-eight vows refusing to become a Buddha unless forty-eight miraculous conditions were guaranteed in his Buddha Land of Bliss and

Purity to be built in the West. Since Dharmakara Bodhisattva did become Amida Buddha, all forty-eight qualities are now guaranteed realities. By the Foundational Vow, the Eighteenth Vow, all creatures who call on his name would be welcomed to this Pure land to be purified. The purification is by overwhelming their bad karma by the infinite surplus of merits earned by Dharmakara through countless lifetimes.

By chanting the slogan, "I take Refuge in Amida Buddha," *Namo Omi-tofo* (Chinese) or *Namu Amida Butsu* (Japanese), not only does Amida's store of merit flow into the believer's account, but also, the absolute faith of Amida replaces the wavering faith of the believer. The Protestant principles of "grace alone" and "faith alone," stressed by Martin Luther, and the "once saved, always saved"[14] perseverance doctrine of Calvin are amazingly preached in Pure Land Buddhism, especially in the Shin Buddhism of Shinran in Japan. Mahayana grace of savior Bodhisattvas, savior Bibles, savior Buddhas, and savior mudras, mantras, and mandalas all effectively short circuit the tortuous route of multiple rebirths to immediate salvation now—in this lifetime. That is, multiple cycles of rebirth are no longer an effective psychological model in Japan.[15]

A fourth development is the Madhyamaka "Middle Path" School of Nagarjuna (second century C.E.). Whereas Gautama taught the psychological middle path between hedonism and asceticism, Nagarjuna taught the philosophical middle path between eternalism and nihilism. The everyday world does not exist as ultimate truth (*paramartha-satya*) or inherent existence, but it does exist as conventional truth, though radically impermanent. It is in this realm of conventional reality that the Buddha's path was meant to be applied. Besides the middle path, Nagarjuna's slogan was *sunya*, emptiness. Everything is empty in lacking *svabhava*, inherent existence.

A fifth development is the Yogachara "Mind Only" School of Asanga (c. 310–390 C.E.) and Vasubandhu (c. 320–400 C.E.). The Yogachara School, of course, is based on the experiences of yoga meditations. They saw Nagarjuna's claim that the everyday world does not exist as ultimate truth as leaning too far toward nihilism. Against Madhyamaka's claim that nothing has inherent existence, the Yogachara insisted that mind has inherent existence. Whereas Madhyamaka defined emptiness as devoid of *svabhava*, inherent existence, Yogachara redefined emptiness as devoid of subject-object duality.[16]

Consciousness was analyzed into eight levels. The lower levels involved physical awareness through our six senses of eye, ear, nose, tongue, body, and mind. The eighth and highest level is the *alaya-vijnana*, storehouse consciousness. The Himalaya is the *alaya* (storehouse) of the *hima* white [snow]. The specific mixture of good and bad karma accumulated over multiple lifetimes determines the quality of consciousness that is ours in this lifetime. The quality changes for our next lifetime according the mix of good and bad karma we contribute in this lifetime. The Buddha denied the natural immortality of the soul. How can there be cycles of rebirth if there is no soul to be reborn? The Yogachara answer was that the *alaya-vijnana*, the ever-changing "repository of consciousness," is what is transmitted from rebirth to rebirth.

A sixth development is the *tathagata-garbha* doctrine. *Tathagata* is a euphemism for the Buddha. *Garbha* means womb. *Tathagata-garbha* teaches that the womb containing the Buddha is already present in all living beings. The womb-buddha is Buddha as an embryo or seed. In the early teaching all beings were said to have the potential of becoming Buddhas. But later the womb-buddha began to be spoken of as some definite thing with substance. Whereas Madhyamaka claimed that all things were empty of *svabhava*, inherent reality, this new teaching claimed that the *tathagata-garbha* was an indestructible, permanent core to all beings.[17]

It has become a presupposition of Tibetan Buddhism and Japanese Buddhism that we all are guaranteed to become Buddhas in some lifetime because we are already Buddhas at our core. The Lankavatara Sutra and the Awakening of Faith in the Mahayana Sutra connected the dots in stating that the *alaya-vijnana* (storehouse consciousness) was identical to the *tathagata-garbha* (womb-buddha).[18] This doctrine in Japan has been called *hon-gaku*, "Original Enlightenment," in contrast to the "original sin" of traditional Christianity. Mahayana displays this radical optimism of guaranteed buddhahood lacking in Theravada.

Vajrayana

A new type of Buddhist literature appeared from the third to eleventh century C.E., called *tantras*, meaning "thread." Although the new movement related to this literature holds essentially to Mahayana doctrine and is often classified as such, it is also given a distinct name, Vajrayana, because of radically distinct practices. *Vajra* means diamond and thunderbolt. Vajrayana is esoteric, hiding its secrets from all except monks initiated into their ranks. All esoteric religions, of course, protect mystical practices heavy with magical overtones. Central is what may be called "the three m's" in English, *mudras, mantras,* and *mandalas.*

Mudras are secret hand gestures formed while both hands are hidden under a piece of cloth during funerals. In monthly fire ceremonies monks use mudras to built invisible walls around the worshippers at the start of a service to protect them from evil spirits and various forms of curses. They use other mudras to call the Buddhas to attend the service. They use mudras in conducting the service. At the end of a service they use mudras to bid the Buddhas to depart. Then they use the mudras to dissolve the invisible protective walls they created at the start of the service. At my uncle's wake service I asked the tantric head priest, Rev. Sasai, how many mudras there were in all. He said about four hundred.

My friend, an esoteric Tendai monk, said that if he made a mistake in his mudra during a funeral, the dead would not "go to heaven." The head priest of a Shingon temple made three beautiful mudras, one flowing into another, to show my students upon my request. The next year he would not show us any, even at my request. He had remembered that they were secret. Dale Saunders has published a book called *Mudras*, with hundreds of photographs of mudras.[19] How could he publish it, since everybody knows they are esoteric secrets! All Buddha images hold their fingers in mudra positions.

Mantras are secret word formulas. A former Jesuit priest became an apprentice to a high ranking Tantric Taoist priest on Taiwan. In the class on Taoism, which he taught at the University of Hawaii, a student asked that he teach us some mantras for protection against evil spirits, spells, and curses. He said it might be more effective for us to say our "Hail Marys" than to try to manipulate powerful mantras that we did not believe or understand. When my students went into the sacred waterfall of a Shingon temple in Japan, rugged veteran mountain adepts screamed mantras from the creek bank to protect them from demons, spells, and curses.

Mandalas are geometric pictures crammed full of powerful Buddhas and Bodhisattvas. Unlike secret mudras and mantras, mandalas, as magnificent religious art, are impossible to keep secret today. They are readily available in bookstores as photo collections. Vajyarana temples openly display their main mandalas prominently on the wall for all to see. The central Diamond and Womb Mandala of Shingon and Tendai are displayed as giant ceiling-to-floor hanging rug mandalas in the two-story Toji museum of Shingon esoteric art in Kyoto. Poster copies of mandalas are sold in art shops everywhere in Buddhist countries. In Tibet mandalas are called *thangkas*. Any tourist can buy them. Carl Jung studied mandalas as archetypal images of the racial subconscious. Jung claimed that religious adepts sank into trances in which they descended into the depths of their psyche. After returning to normal consciousness, they drew as mandalas what they saw in their trances.

The main Vajrayana worship service is the fire ceremony. They build a fire in a special fire altar in the temple enclosed on three sides with a sacred rope. Small dishes of many varieties of seeds and plant oils sit on the altar. Preparation is made with the prostration of priests and a succession of mudras. A fire is built in the midst of loud chanting, banging of drums, and cymbals. The small metal dishes of seeds and oils are poured into the fire throughout the ceremony. Pieces of firewood the size and shape of twelve-inch rulers are collected in three or four participating temples. Each stick has been chosen by a temple member for a specific prayer written on it for secular benefits: safety from fire, painless childbirth, passing university exams, a raise in salary, safety from traffic accidents, protection from disease, and others. These sticks are collected for that month, tied in huge bundles. These sticks are tossed into the fire throughout the service. Often the believer thinks his prayer will be granted, while the priest is praying the opposite—that his prayer greed will be consumed in the fire.

Any explanation of Vajrayana would be incomplete without mentioning sexual yoga—the use of sex between a monk and his consort for intensifying spiritual energy. I asked a senior Vajrayana theologian from Nepal about prescribed sexual activity in the training of monks. He said that the master monk would consider the spiritual condition of all monks under his care. He would select only those monks who would benefit by sexual practice. All other monks would know nothing, he said. He would be naïve, of course, if he thought the monks would not gossip.[20] A professor at the University of Hawaii went to the airport to greet eminent Vajrayana monks from Nepal. Several women dressed as nuns followed them off the plane. He asked the monks who the women were. They did not give him an answer.[21]

Theism or Atheism?

Transpersonal

In India, Hinduism has three kinds of gods. First are personal gods like Kali, Shiva, Varuna, Agni, Krishna, Rama, and 330 million other gods. You worship the gods with *puja* offerings of water, flowers, buttered honey, music, and bloody sacrifices of chickens and goats. If you praise the gods enough to make them happy, they will take care of you.

Alongside this popular religion, thoughtful Hindus have sought to find the underlying divine unity. The Upanishads, the last section in the Vedas, moved toward a monistic paradigm. The many gods are no more than masks of the One. This was systematized in the Vedanta school of philosophy formulated most influentially by Shankara. The slogan of his followers is *Brahman equals Atman* (God equals Self). Brahman is the ultimate reality or ground of all things, very much like what in the West is called Being Itself. Atman is the ultimate reality or ground of the human person. The formula means that my ultimate ground is identical with the ultimate ground of the universe. There are not two things, therefore, the self and Brahman or Being Itself. Instead what each person ultimately is, like everything else, is an instance of Brahman or Being Itself.

All the characteristics that differentiate us and other things are appearances rather than reality in the fullest sense. Thus Brahman is not a person or any kind of being alongside other beings or person alongside other persons. Brahman is transpersonal. You do not talk to this God or seek to please this God. Rather you seek through spiritual exercises and meditation to become aware of your identity with God. By realizing existentially that this God is also you, or that you always already are this God, you transcend your illusory, ephemeral self and make real the divine Self that is God.

However, not all those who sought the unity of the divine underlying the myriads of gods moved in this transpersonal direction. The clearest expression of the monotheistic tendencies in India is found in the work of Ramanuja. His philosophy offers a version of panentheism, that is, the idea that all things are in God, thus contributing to the divine reality. This divine reality is distinct from and more than the sum of other beings. It is personal in a way the Brahman or Being Itself is not.

Impermanence

Buddhism arose in the context of popular polytheism. It opposed any sort of worship of these gods or seeking their favor. Whatever gods there may be are caught up in the same cycles of birth, death, and rebirth as are we. Individuals must liberate themselves by personal disciplines. Like the Vedantists, Buddhists oriented themselves to the transpersonal reality equally present in all things. But whereas Vedantists thought of this reality as enduring through all change endlessly and unchangingly, Buddhists taught that it, too, was characterized by impermanence. For Buddhists nothing is permanent. Everything is in flux.

In place of Brahman and Atman, Buddhists speak of Buddha nature. This is often defined as "dependent origination." That is, all things are instances of dependent origination, and this means that they are nothing in themselves but rather products of other things, which are, of course, themselves products of other things. Each of these things is transitory. None has being in itself. Buddhist meditation is, then, not designed to realize within ourselves the being that is at the same time the being of all things. It is designed instead to enable us to realize that we have no self in the sense of something permanent underlying the flux of experience. We are empty of any such being and therefore open to everything. Hinduism and Buddhism both teach nonattachment. For Vedantists, attachment to anything impermanent prevents us from realizing the permanent being that is truly what we are. For Buddhists, attachment to anything blocks our disinterested openness to whatever is as it is.

On the other hand, the negative melting of the false self into no-self is synonymous with the dynamic action of "riding the tiger" or "going with the flow" in popular Zen vocabulary. Manjusri is often portrayed as riding a tiger. Tibetan Buddhists speak of the "Wind Horse," which charges the disciple for action. Just as Jesus appears as a Spirit-charged being in the Gospel of Luke-Acts, the seeming Buddhist quietism of no-self is only the preliminary condition to the adventure of riding the tiger in hot pursuit of Manjusri and Kannon, the Bodhisattvas of Wisdom and Compassion. They beckon the disciple forward with vision, direction, and energy. Buddhists see divinity in verbs, and not in nouns. This basic dynamism is what we see in the "engaged Buddhism" of the last section of this essay.

Are Buddhists Atheists?

Jesus was God-centered; Gautama was not. That is, Jesus prayed to God as to a divine person. Gautama sought to realize his true nature. He meditated intensively, but he did not pray for help. Although the doctrine of impermanence easily leads to atheism, Gautama was not interested in drawing out its metaphysical implications. As his famous parable of the poisoned arrow[22] indicates, he viewed theoretical questions of this kind as a distraction from the urgent work of enlightenment or liberation.

The primary issues for early Buddhists were the relation to polytheism and the understanding of what is ultimate and universal. They dealt with polytheism by asserting the irrelevance of these gods to the urgent task of liberation from false consciousness. Buddhists as Buddhists neither affirm nor deny the existence of polytheistic deities, but they do oppose paying attention to them.

Buddhists have also opposed the Vedantist tendency to treat the trans-personal as having its own substantial reality, but they have affirmed the transpersonal reality as of ultimate spiritual importance, calling it Buddha nature. In many forms of Buddhism the Buddhas, or Enlightened Ones, are divine realities. Buddhism in general is not theistic, but since its understanding of reality was shaped in a quite different context, not in opposition to Abrahamic theism, it is quite misleading to call it atheistic.

The possibility that Buddhists should be considered atheistic is hardly considered in Asia. Even Christian theologians there do not raise it. It is a question that arises only as Westerners impose their categories on a spirituality that arose and developed in a different context facing different questions. Just as it would be unreasonable for Buddhists to demand that Christians believe in Buddhas, it is unreasonable for Christians to demand that Buddhists believe in God. Is there a naïve assumption that God is a religiously neutral word of absolute value in evaluating religions? God is a Christian word with Christian content and Christian philosophical frameworks. We cannot ignore controversies among Christians today concerning omnipotence, impassibility, predestination, and determinism within God-talk. At the center of popular Christianity is the Father God. Too often male chauvinism is expressed through the Father God in the patriarchal hierarchies of church institutions and priesthood.[23] For all these reasons, Ken Tanaka, a Japanese American Buddhist theologian, wrote that Buddhists can answer positively or negatively about God only after Christians have defined what they mean by God.[24]

The Trinity as a thought structure allows for the transcendence of God the Father to be balanced with the immanence of the Holy Spirit. But the history of Christian doctrine and popular Christianity see God the Father and Jesus the Son overwhelming the role of the Holy Spirit. The dominant posture of Christian spirituality is talking to God the Father, instead of merging with the Holy Spirit. Many of the Christians who now practice Zen silent meditations are bold to claim authenticity for their practice through the Holy Spirit within the Trinity.

Buddhist and Christian Idolatry

Jews, Christians, and Muslims share the Bible's abhorrence of idols. Buddhism, on the other hand, has charmed the human spirit through the creative imagination of religious art in the brilliant colors, intricate patterns, and multiplicity of images—Buddhas, Bodhisattvas, and *devas*. The missionary knows that as Christian hymns have been the effective weapon of Christian evangelism, so Buddhist images have been the awesome weapon of Buddhist evangelism. The ferocious power and subtle beauty of Buddhist and Hindu images have overwhelmed Asian aesthetic and mystic consciousness. So it is a big surprise to Westerners to hear that Buddhism has little interest in gods! A multitude of idols but no dependence on gods? The Jewish-Christian-Muslim taboo of idolatry has especially targeted Hinduism and Buddhism.

When Moses climbed Mount Sinai and met God for the first time in the burning bush, he asked God what was his name. To lead a crushed slave people out of Egypt, Moses needed to know God's name. God's answer was "*I am who I am.*" That can mean, "I refuse to reduce myself down to something humans can understand." Of course, in the rest of the Bible God does exactly what he refused to do for Moses at the burning bush. To save human beings, God lowered himself into earthly forms as *El, Elohim* (God), *El-Elyon* (God Most High), *El-'Olam* (Everlasting God), *Shaddai* (Almighty), *Abir* (Mighty One), *Adonai* (Lord), *Sebaoth* (Hosts), *Pahad* (Fear), and *El Roi* (God Who Sees Me). For Jesus, God was especially *Abba*, Father.

The original hesitancy of God to be revealed in a human way was reinforced in Judaism with the prohibition of representing God by idols. This taboo of idolatry was to be the high wall to forever remind the Jews that God was beyond anything in their world. The symbol of God as wind, breath, and spirit in the Hebrew *ruah* and the Greek *pneuma* reinforced this mystery about God. Though we benefit from wind, breath, and spirit, we cannot define or control them. They are invisible.

The need to protect the transcendence and mystery of God and at the same time to satisfy the craving of the people for earthly models of God was brought to a head in the Iconoclastic Controversies (787–794 C.E.). Was it permissible to use three dimensional images of Christ and the saints in worship (salutation, reverence, adoration, and homage)? These intense disputes promoted by Charlemagne, Empress Irene of Constantinople, and Pope Hadrian I were complicated by problems in Greek-Latin translations. Today, three dimensional images are prohibited in worship by Protestants, but allowed by Roman Catholics. Eastern Orthodox icons are two dimensional. Describing the character of God through earthly models, while protecting God's formless mystery, has been a never-ending problem for both Christianity and Buddhism.

Mahayana Trinity

In dealing with the Western word "God," Mahayana Buddhists should describe what they mean by *Tri-Kaya*, Three Bodies of the Buddha, 三身. This threefold thought framework corresponds well with the Christian Trinity. First is *Dharmakaya*, the formless form of absolute Truth. Second is *Sambhogakaya*, the relative forms taken by absolute Truth to save all beings. Here live the countless Buddhas and Bodhisattvas who never descend into human history. Third is *Nirmanakaya*, the Buddhas of form who enter our world of history. This list is headed by Gautama Buddha, and includes Nagarjuna, Vasubandhu, and the founders of Buddhist denominations. Taking to heart this Mahayana parallel to the Christian Trinity, can anyone accuse Buddhists of being atheists?

Yin Yang: Redemptive Defeat

The God of the Jews had become a Man of War, Exodus 15:3.[25] Their religion had become triumphalist—a winning army under a winning God with a winning strategy under a winning commander, Joshua. It was win, win, win; kill, kill, kill! The Canaanite inhabitants of the land were being punished, the Book of Joshua claimed, for polluting the land with their evil. Evil cannot be rehabilitated. Evil must be destroyed. Take no prisoners. Every Canaanite must be killed, even women and children.[26] Defeat was impossible under a God of victory.

Then the unthinkable happened. Assyria defeated with finality the Northern Kingdom, Samaria, in 722 B.C.E. Babylon defeated the Southern Kingdom, Judah, in 586 B.C.E. The leading classes were taken into exile and lived in the land of their conquerors. A religion of victory is not worth five cents when you lose. The defeated Israelites buried their dead, bound their wounds, and sank into despair. Then their prophets heard something. They heard a voice that turned their religion upside down. They heard God crying with the losers instead of celebrating with the winners. If God was crying with the losers instead of celebrating with the winners, then the winners are losers and the losers are winners. It was just a matter of time. So time became a key to New Testament religion—that the Kingdom was near, that it was already here but still coming. They looked for the time when losers will become winners, and winners will become losers. [27]

The new Judaism, the Judaism of the exile, was the opposite of the Good and Evil triumphalism of the Book of Joshua. The new icon of exile Judaism greets us in Isaiah 53. The hero is so ugly that people turn away their eyes. They pity him and despise him for being so brutally punished by God and abandoned by all. The big surprise is that he was punished for our sins—by his wounds we are healed. The old Judaism was about winning. The new Judaism is about losing—redemptive suffering. The God of losers claimed all losers as his own. Their badge of membership was their suffering. So Jesus chose all losers of society as his friends. The new message was that evil can and must be redeemed. No revenge. Love your enemies, forgive your enemies, pray for your enemies. Jesus died for his enemies. Return good for evil, so evil might be transformed into good. Contradicting the good and evil theme of the book of Joshua, the gospel of Jesus was Yin Yang.

It is regrettable that the book of the Revelation of Saint John ignored or rejected the message of Jesus and returned to the Good and Evil theme of the Book of Joshua. Evil cannot be redeemed. Win, win, win; kill, kill, kill! No returning good for evil. No loving enemies, no forgiving enemies, no praying for enemies. No turning enemies into friends. The Christianity that promotes the good and evil theme against the Yin Yang of Buddhism is a Christianity that ignores or rejects the Yin Yang gospel of Jesus.[28] Can we reject the violence of triumphalism in the book of Joshua and the book of Revelation to choose the revolutionary peace of Jesus, the wounded healer? Walter Wink said it well, "When Jesus said, 'Those who try to make their life secure will lose it, but those who lose their life will keep it' (Luke 17:33), he drew a line in the sand and asked if we would step across—step out of one entire world, where violence is always the ultimate solution, into another world, where the spiral of violence is finally broken by those willing to absorb its impact with their own flesh. That new approach to living is nonviolence, Jesus' 'third way.'"[29]

No Self and the Christian Faith

Dogen Zenji, founder of Soto Zen in Japan, said: "To study the Buddha is to study the self. To study the self is to forget the self. To forget the self is to be awakened by all beings."[30]

Jesus Christ Is a Buddha

Daisetsu Teitaro Suzuki was the primary advocate of Zen Buddhism to the West. After his death, Zen Buddhism has been promoted in Western universities by another giant, Masao Abe. Abe lectured that the Buddhist slogan of emptiness is fulfilled in the self-emptying of Christ in the second chapter of Philippians. The Buddhist word for emptiness in Sanskrit is *Sunyata*. The word for emptying in New Testament Greek is *kenosis*. So Masao Abe wrote a book with the title *Kenotic God and Dynamic Sunyata*.[31] Abe lectured from Philippians 2:5-8: "Let the same mind be in you that was in Christ Jesus, who, though he was in the form of God, did not regard equality with God as something to be exploited, but emptied himself, taking the form of a slave, being born in human likeness. And being found in human form, he humbled himself and became obedient to the point of death—even death on a cross."

Because Christ made himself nothing, God made him everything (at the name of Jesus, all bend the knee and confess that Jesus is Lord [vss. 10-11]). All Christians are instructed to imitate Christ's self-emptying (have this same mind in you that you have in Christ Jesus [v. 5]). Christ is the model Buddha for all Christians for no-self. This was an issue in the series of debates between Masao Abe and John Cobb Jr., known in Buddhist Christians circles as the Cobb-Abe debates, which continued for years. John Cobb Jr. and Christopher Ives edited *The Emptying God,* essays in response to Abe's multiple challenges to Christian theology.[32] Buddhist scholars see Philippians 2:5-8 as a Buddhist passage in the Christian Bible.

The Apostle Paul Is a Buddha

Koshiro Tamaki, renowned Emeritus Professor of Tokyo University, had immersed himself in Buddhism in a lifetime of studies in Theravada and Mahayana sacred texts. Now he vowed to meet the Christian God. He traveled to Europe. In interviews with Tamaki, theologians and pastors explained the amazing grace in the message of Christ as what was so special. Tamaki was disappointed. All Japanese as children learn exactly this same logic of radical grace from Shin Buddhism. The Christian God must be great, but Christian theologians did not know where the power was. So when he returned to Japan, he took his Bible up to a mountain hut and vowed never to come back down until he met the Christian God. Of course, being a Buddhist scholar of religious texts, he brought his Greek Bible to the mountain hut as well as his Japanese Bible.

Tamaki lectured to Buddhist and Christian scholars about where he found the power in the Bible. Paul wrote in Galatians 2:20, "I have been crucified with Christ; and it is no longer I who live, but it is Christ who lives in me. And the life I now live in the flesh I live by faith in the Son of God, who loved me and gave himself for me." Paul died while he was still alive. He became no-self. That is, Paul died to his trivial, puny, false self who lives for me, myself, and I. He now lives by his True Self—"Christ lives in me." Paul experienced a personality shift. Paul had become a Buddha, one who wakes up to his true Self.

Tamaki asked the Christian theologians how many Japanese they had converted so far. Less than 1 percent of the population! He said, "You Christians don't know where the power is in your Bible. You Christians don't know what happened to Paul." Pointing to the monks, he said, "These Zen Buddhist monks know what happened to Paul. The same thing that happened to Paul happened to them. When the same thing happens to you, you will convert the whole Japanese nation!"

Ryomin Akizuki, brilliant editor of a Japan Zen journal, often gave lectures to Christians and Buddhists from Galatians 2:20. He did exegesis from the Greek text. He had an extraordinary grasp of Christian thought and Christian feeling because he was a Congregational Christian until his sophomore year in college. Like Tamaki, Akizuki found the Apostle Paul's crucifixion with Christ an unmistakable sign of no-self and buddhahood. Paul had become a Buddha in finding his true self. Both Akizuki and Tamaki were prominent members of the Japan Branch of the Society of Buddhist Christian Studies. I heard their lectures at their annual three-day-conferences at the Palace Hotel in Kyoto.

Saint Francis of Assisi Is a Buddha

Celebrated Zen scholar Shinichi Hisamatsu published in Japanese an essay on Francis. He identified five events in the life of Francis that show genuine enlightenment—that Francis had become a Buddha. One event was the red-hot blade. Francis was wounded. The wound festered. They brought in a red-hot blade to cauterize the wound. Francis chased everybody out of the room, saying they would not want to hear a grown man yell, scream, and cry. Alone, Francis talked to the blade about how he was a coward, feared pain, and hated heat. He talked to the red-hot blade until he became one with the blade. Then he said, "Welcome, Sister Fire." Nobody heard that grown man yell, scream, or cry.

Monks on Mount Athos

Mount Athos is famous for its string of Eastern Orthodox monasteries. Monks practicing prolonged meditation sessions are often startled when they experience overwhelming flashes. They sought older veteran monks for counseling. The veteran monks calmed them by saying, "You have seen the light of Tabor!" Mount Tabor by tradition, of course, is the New Testament Mountain of Transfiguration.[33]

No-self, shift in personal identity, transforming flashes of enlightenment, becoming True Self—these are universal experiences found at all times throughout the world in most religions. They are not the exclusive property of Buddhists. They are especially common in Buddhists, Taoists, Neo-Confucians, Sufi Muslims, Christian mystics, and Romanticists in British literature—all nature mystics. The Sufis even major on the theme of "no-self." The Christian group whose worship is centered on silent meditation is Quakers. The Quakers' move away from the Father God toward the "inner light" places them close to the world of Zen Buddhists.

Islam means to submit; to submit to the will of God. When you submit your will to the will of God, you become no-self. A Muslim Imam told a Methodist congregation that all Christians who submit to the will of God are actually Muslims, because Islam means "to submit." No-self, then, is not exclusively a Buddhist theme. Jesus said in the Garden of Gethsemane, "Not my will but thine be done." Jesus Christ was no-self.

Disappointing Developments

Ancestor Worship

By the themes of "no-self" and "impermanence," Buddhism taught that when we die, we disappear. But the first ethic of the Chinese was filial piety with its foundation in ancestor worship. "No self" was subversive to ancestor worship—you cannot worship ancestors if they simply disappeared at death. So the waves of Buddhism entering China through the silk routes caused spasms. Sons took vows of celibacy and entered monasteries, abandoning their parents. Sons were expected to care for parents in their old age, maintain the family land for posterity, marry and produce the line of descendents who were the necessary worshippers in ancestor worship. Buddhist monks even defended their betrayal of filial piety by claiming that in the countless cycles of rebirth all beings were their parents in some lifetime. Why show preference only for their parents of this lifetime? Although the direct causes of the three persecutions of Buddhism in China were complex, this sabotage of the ancestor worship system was a contributing factor each time. After the third persecution, they compromised with ancestor worship by adopting the doctrine of the forty-nine days.[34]

Some people have earned so much bad karma that when they die, they are already destined for a bad rebirth. Some people earned so much good karma that they are already destined for a good rebirth. Most people, however, are not that good and not that bad. When they die, the quality of their rebirth is suspended for forty-nine days—seven weeks of seven days. During this period, the family can create good karma for the deceased by proxy to guarantee a good rebirth. The good karma is created by the family through Buddhist memorial services during the forty-nine days. Through this concept of forty-nine days, ancestor worship effectively entered Buddhism in China, Korea, and Japan. In many countries, as in Japan, ancestor worship has become the tail that wags the dog. The man in the street has come to see Buddhism as ancestor worship, a practice that contradicts the foundations of Buddhism.[35]

Japanese Persecution of Christianity

In 1549 Francisco Xavier, Cosme de Torres, and John Fernandes arrived in Kagoshima, Southern Kyushu Island, to begin Roman Catholic mission work. Feudal Japan was ruled by *daimyo*, feudal lords, who schemed to lure the lucrative Portuguese trade into their ports, to steal the technology of canons, and to stock saltpeter for gunpowder. Understandably, many daimyo became Christians. The daimyo of Oomura, Arima, Tsushima Island, Bungo, Kameoka, and Ooshu all became Christians. Two outstanding Christian daimyo were Takayama Ukon and Konishi Yukinaga. Between 1553 and 1620, eighty-six daimyo were officially baptized. It seemed for a while that Japan might become a Christian nation.

But everything slowly unraveled. Spanish trade arrived through Manila, bringing Franciscan and Dominican missionaries. They challenged the Portuguese trade and the Portuguese Jesuits. Then the Protestant English and Dutch traders arrived, bringing not only friction in trade, but also in religion. Things came to a head in the shipwreck of the San Felipe in 1596. The Spanish crew took out a world map and showed the Japanese soldiers the conquered colonies of Philippines, Mexico, and Peru. This confirmed rumors through Protestant traders of the alleged Roman Catholic agenda of trade, missionaries, converts, then conquest.

The reaction of the Shogun Toyotomi Hideyoshi was immediate. In 1597, twenty-six Christian clergy and laymen were arrested in Kyoto and Osaka, forced to march four hundred miles to the southern edge of Honshu Island, put on a ship to Kyushu Island, and were crucified on Nishizaka Hill just outside Nagasaki Harbor. In 1638 there was a major revolt of Christian peasants of the Amakusa Islands in Kyushu. They defeated the local armies. The Shogun had to send in government troops. The peasants crossed Nagasaki Bay in boats and defended themselves in Hara Castle in Shimabara near Nagasaki. After a siege, all rebels were killed, a number between seventeen and thirty-seven thousand.[36]

The persecution begun in 1597 with the twenty-six Martyrs of Nagasaki reached its peak after the Shimabara Revolt of 1638. More than 650 missionaries and thousands of lay Christians were beheaded, burned at the stake, and executed in imaginative ways of torture.[37] To be a Christian became a capital offense. Christianity virtually disappeared until 1855, marking 258 years of persecution, annihilation, and prohibition of Christianity.[38]

Buddhist Certificates (Tera-uke)

The method by which Christians were weeded out was the *danka* (temple-householder system) or *tera-uke* (Buddhist Certificate System) established by the shogunate in 1635.[39] All Japanese were required on the pain of death to register at Buddhist temples as believers, even families of Shinto priests. The temple would give out certificates vouching that that person was not a Christian. Anyone without a certificate would be arrested and executed. A daimyo was appointed *jisha bugyou*, the secular government official to oversee the *tera-uke* system in all temples nationwide. The government did not trust Buddhist priests to police Buddhist priests.

Secret Christians who sneaked into the registration lines were weeded out by a clever method of *fumie*. "To step on" is *fumu*. "Picture" is *e*. Everybody in the registration lines was forced to step on a stone image or wooden picture of Jesus or Mary. This was *fumie*. People who could not bring themselves to step on such sacred images were then identified as Christians. They were given a chance to recant. Some did, but most were tortured and executed.

The *tera-uke* system was devastating to Christians, of course. But it had debilitating results on Buddhism also. Evangelism is unnecessary when everybody must register as believers by government decree. To this day, many Buddhist priests in Japan do little evangelism, confident that the masses will come for funerals and post-mortuary rituals. The intimate trust and respect between families and priest disappeared as the priest became a government agent with powers to criminalize anyone at will. The priest was overcome with administrative work as a registrar. There was little time for counseling or pastoral care. Many temples in rural areas became local land-lords, and many temples in urban areas became money lenders.[40] Changing your family registration temple to another Buddhist temple was not allowed throughout the Tokugawa era. Children were tied to registration temples of their parents. That is, just as the priesthood was a closed caste, the believers also were a closed community. The believers were set free by the Meiji regime, which at first favored Shinto, and later proclaimed freedom of religion.

Funeral Business

It was predictable that Buddhism would take over funerals from Shinto. The Shinto concept of clean-unclean centered on "red pollution" and "black pollution." Red pollution was blood. Black pollution was death. If a corpse were brought into the sacred area of worship, the whole Shinto complex would be unclean. So funerals naturally gravitated to Buddhism, the new continental religion that invaded Japan in the sixth century. The *tera-uke* system decreed that all Japanese must register as believers at the Buddhist temple on pain of death, and all who registered must have their funerals done by the Buddhist priest. Where people had related to Buddhism and Shinto out of personal faith and family heritage, now everybody was ordered by law to have a Buddhist funeral! So in Japan today, generally speaking, all weddings are Shinto and all funerals are Buddhist.[41]

Funerals are lucrative. The priest must be paid to officiate. There are hefty fees for use of the temple buildings. There are fees for cremation. There are fees for burial plots. There are fees for the forty-nine-day services. There are fees for services on death anniversaries up to the thirty-third or fifti-eth anniversary. There are fees for maintenance of ancestral ashes if kept in temple storage in Buddha altars.

The most notorious fee is for posthumous names given to the dead. Our birth names are useful only during this life on earth. Upon death the priest gave new Buddhist names, *kaimyo*, written in Chinese for use in the next world. The war dead were heroes who sacrificed their lives for the nation. It became a custom during the Second World War for the war dead to receive elaborately exalted Buddhist names. After the war, business companies, political parties, elite blue-blood families, and rich people began to demand these elaborate names at funerals as a matter of status. Being that these were powerful groups and families making special requests from vanity, Buddhist priests felt no guilt in charging exorbitant fees for these names. After a while it became common knowledge in the neighborhood that the fee was for adding each new Chinese ideograph for the death name. This was scandalous! It was obvious to all that Buddhist temples had become a funeral business. The common people often ridicule Buddhist temples as *soshiki bukkyo*, "funeral Buddhism."[42]

Temples as Family Dynasties

The urgent need for permanent priests in each temple to administer the *tera-uke* system was a contributing cause in transforming the Japanese Buddhist priesthood from celibate monks in monasteries to married priests in hereditary family temple dynasties. Historically Shinran, the founder of Shin Buddhism, is credited with the break with celibacy. He, a celibate monk, officially married. Shinran's example and pressure from the Meiji government are usually the acknowledged causes of the cloudy subject of how and when monks started breaking their vows of celibacy and officially married in public. Eldest sons in Japan are pressured to take over the temple even if they have little religious interest. That is, the priesthood by rejecting celibacy has become a closed caste of hereditary priests. As a strict rule, only sons of priests are allowed to matriculate in Buddhist seminaries.[43] An elitism of priests has become a wall separating the common people from the treasures of the faith.

Laymen in esoteric Shingon and Tendai are not initiated into the mysteries of the mudra, mantra, and mandala. Most Japan Zen temples offer no meditation classes for laymen. "If you are serious about meditation, why don't you become a priest?"—seems to be their attitude.[44] Commoners can become priests only by marrying daughters of priests with no sons. They are then adopted into the priest's family, taking the family name. The impression in Japan is that laypeople are not supposed to be really interested in religion, the hierarchy being a closed caste of priestly families. Once I telephoned the head priest of a Shingon temple, my good friend, to ask how my American,

Caucasian, male friend could enter a Shingon seminary. He laughed in surprise at the thought and grew silent. He never gave me an answer for the next decade.

As a backlash, the so-called "new religions" that emerged in the twentieth century completely rejected the priesthood, claiming the equality of laypersons (priesthood of all believers). Soka Gakkai and Rissho Kosei Kai, two of the largest religions in Japan, are both Buddhist "new religions" with no priesthood. Laypersons flock to Zen Centers in the West run by laypersons for laypersons—not to Japanese Zen temples. Two Buddhist denominations are exceptions. Sanbo Kyodan, Soto members doing Rinzai practice, is a Zen movement with an iconoclastic bent and a definite lay focus.[45] Shin Buddhism, whose founder Shinran was the first monk to officially marry, also has a strong lay emphasis.

Japanese Buddhist temples in Hawaii and the West Coast, lacking the powerful and lucrative *danka/tera-uke* system, have been forced to rely on evangelism, pastoral counseling, and rites of passage. Besides teaching religion, they, for good or for ill, have become Japanese culture centers to promote Japanese psychosocial values, Japanese festivals, Japanese dance, Japanese music (especially taiko drum corps), judo, Japanese language, Japanese calligraphy, and Japanese flower arranging (ikebana). Because Shinto is so anchored on the physical Japanese archipelago and on the political rule of the divine imperial family, Shinto has shown little enthusiasm for transplanting its faith and institutions overseas.[46] In the absence of Shinto weddings, Japanese Buddhism in the West not only does funerals, but does weddings as well. So the accusation of Buddhism degenerating into "funeral Buddhism" does not hold true for Buddhism in the West. Freed from the *danka/ tera-uke* system, the social demand for ancestor worship, the closed caste system of family temple dynasties, and the Japanese government's manipulation of religion until the close of the Second World War, Japanese Buddhism in the West has some aspects of a purer Buddhism.[47]

There is another advantage to Buddhism in the West. The Tendai Bishop Ara, a highly revered Japan missionary to Honolulu for many decades, wrote that Buddhism in Japan is "unconscious Buddhism," while Buddhism in the West is "conscious Buddhism." That is, Buddhism in Japan that has not yet confronted Christianity is "unconscious Buddhism," while Buddhism in the West that has confronted Christianity is "conscious Buddhism."

Encouraging Developments

There are internal and external sources for the breadth of Buddhist social action of the last half century. We see a modern social, economic, psychological, and political analysis adopted from the West. There is the deep inspiration from Gandhi. There are the apocalyptic crises of genocide in Cambodia, nuclear bombing in Japan, war in Vietnam, civil war in Sri Lanka, invasion and cultural genocide in Tibet, repressive regimes in Myanmar and Thailand, and ecological disasters in Southeast Asia. Chronic issues have come to a head—social inequality, bigotry, and poverty, especially for the outcaste Buddhist converts in India.[48] For Westerners the myth of Buddhist quietism was shattered in 2007 by the nonviolent revolt of monks in Myanmar, who rose up to march in the streets in open defiance of their government. Furthermore, who can forget the courageous decades-long struggles of Aung San Suu Kyi against the military dictators in Myanmar.

Sri Lanka: Sarvodaya Shramadana

A Buddhist organization, Sarvodaya Shramadana,[49] emerged in Sri Lanka for village reform out of rural poverty. Founded by A. T. Ariyaratne,[50] Sarvodaya is perhaps the best example of Buddhist environmental action in Asia. It linked economic development with spiritual development. It rejected Western development models for promoting consumerism—the nurture of greed and the growth of debt. The Middle Path of Gautama taught the meeting of needs, not insatiable greeds. Theravada taught self-reliance. The monks of Sarvodaya may provide assistance and guidance, but they may not make decisions or actually execute programs. They may help organize and inspire, but the villagers themselves must decide the priorities in projects—a school building, sanitation system, a road, or a day care center. They do not wait for government initiatives or funding. Foreign contributions are accepted, but the villagers themselves essentially raise the project funds by countless small donations.

> Basic needs pertaining to a healthy environment, clean water, adequate clothing, optimum food requirements, sanitation and health, energy needs, communication, education, and cultural as well as spiritual needs have to be satisfied first. Without looking to governments or other external agencies, the Sarvodaya Movement assists people to organize

themselves with their own self-reliance and community participation to satisfy as many of these needs as possible.[51]

The labor is donated by the villagers themselves. Each village family that joins a work camp must donate at least a matchbox of rice in order to eat at the communal meal. All feel they are contributors and none feel diminished by the generosity of others. This heals the sense of worthlessness that accompanies the poverty syndrome.[52] Going beyond the boundaries of any one religion or village, Sarvodaya's vision includes all people of the world as one family:

> The idea behind the term "family gathering" is that the whole world is one family, and all of them represent humanity in microcosm. All religious, caste, race, linguistic, class, national, or political differences are of no importance in these family gatherings. Instead, meditations on loving kindness for all beings, songs, dances, and other cultural items that promote the concept of "one world, one people," occur.[53]

Thailand: Abbott Nan Sutasilo and Sulak Sivaraksa

Throughout Theravada countries, villagers give to the monks and temples. This forms the economic base for the monasteries, and the villagers also earn merits for a better rebirth. Today most temples are financially stable in land and buildings. Abbot Nan Sutasilo has courageously initiated creative practices in his temple, proclaiming that the temple money is the people's money. He began transferring money out of his temple and depositing it into his village projects, such as a Fertilizer Bank and a Village Rice Bank. He promoted Buddhist vows for lay people to resist consumerism, to reduce spending so the money saved could be donated to a village savings system. The funds were used to set up a medical cooperative and to pay off villagers' loans before bank foreclosure and the seizure of land. Abbott Nan transformed the annual three-day robe presentation ceremony, the main festival for giving to the temple. He turned it into a fund-raising drive for village development projects.[54]

Acharn Sulak Sivaraksa was born in Thailand and educated in England and Wales. Returning home in 1961, he taught at Thammasat and Chulanlongkorn Universities. For six years he edited the *Social Science Review*, which he had founded in 1963. By these writings, he awakened student awareness that escalated to the overthrow of the military government in 1973.

Beginning in the late 1960s he worked with several service-oriented, rural development projects with Buddhist monks and student activists. During the 1970s Sulak became the central figure in the Komol Keemthong Foundation, the Pridi Banomyong Institute, the Slum Childcare Foundation, the Coordinating Group for Religion and Society, the Thai Interreligious Commission for Development, and Santi Pracha Dhamma Institute. Through his involvement with these nongovernmental organizations, Sulak aimed for indigenous, sustainable, and spiritual models for change. He has cofounded the Asian Cultural Forum on Development and the International Network of Engaged Buddhists.

In the 1976 bloody coup, hundreds of students were killed and thousands were jailed. The soldiers burnt everything in Sulak's bookstore and ordered his arrest. He spent the next two years in exile, lecturing in American, Canadian, and European universities. In 1984 he was arrested in Bangkok for criticizing the King, but was released after a storm of international protest. In 1991 a warrant for his arrest sent him into forced exile once more. He returned in 1992 and won the court case in 1995. Sulak gains insight through Buddhism by questioning everything and questioning himself. By this insight, he moves into action. His themes include democracy, human rights, and accountable government.[55] He is among a handful of Buddhist activists promoting socially-engaged Buddhism. His passion for social change is expressed forcefully in his writings:

> Spiritual considerations and social change cannot be separated. Forces in our social environment, such as consumerism, with its emphasis on craving and dissatisfaction, can hinder our spiritual development. People seeking to live spiritually must be concerned with their social and physical environment. To be truly religious is not to reject society but to work for social justice and change. Religion is at the heart of social change, and social change is the essence of religion.[56]

Vietnam: Thich Nhat Hanh

In 1963 the South Vietnamese government of President Ngo Dinh Diem oppressed Buddhism. Eighty percent of the people were Buddhist, while Diem was Catholic. In May his troops fired on a crowd of protesters, who rose up in indignation to his shutting down public celebrations of Buddha's birthday. There were strikes, marches, protests, fasts, and self-immolation of several monks. In August Diem's forces raided Buddhist temples throughout the country, arresting many monks. Protests and arrests continued into October. In November Diem and his brother Nhu were executed in a coup.

A series of governments followed, some affirming the Buddhist anti-war stance. Other governments supported by the United States–backed military tried to marshal the society to battle the Ho Chi Minh threat from the North. In 1966 the Thieu-Ky regime crushed military factions that had withdrawn support from the government and arrested virtually all the Buddhist activist leadership in the Buddhist Struggle Movement for peace. Besides the anti-war struggle, Buddhists at this time developed a new social work program. In 1964 the monk Thich Nhat Hanh started the School of Youth for Social Service. Through social work of this kind, monks and nuns erected public buildings, cared for the needy, and helped promote agriculture, sanitation, and roads.

The Buddhist Struggle Movement was nonviolent. There was determined effort to protect deserters and draft resisters. The few monks who burned themselves to death consciously accepted the bad karma of violence against themselves for the greater good of ending the war for the many. The Buddhist Struggle Movement refused to take sides between the communist North and the capitalist South. In the Buddhist analysis, the karma of this war was a gigantic tangle of interconnected interests of national groups, political ideologies, Russia, and the United States. Instead of dividing everybody into "them and us," the monks saw their role in reconciling and healing all factions.

The reunification of Vietnam under Ho Chi Minh has been bad for the monks. The communist government has exerted tight control over the Buddhist leadership and many monks are under house arrest.[57] They refused a return visa for Thich Nhat Hanh, who lives in exile in France. During the boat people crisis, Nhat Hanh rented boats to rescue floundering boat people. His group continues to find ways to send money to Vietnam for war orphans and poor war victims. He has established many Buddhist sangha groups in the West, including France and Southern California.[58] He is a prolific author. He is also an immensely popular conference speaker in Europe and the United States.

Tibet: Dalai Lama

Tibet was invaded by China in 1949 and fell completely under Chinese control in 1959. The Dalai Lama escaped to India in that year. He lives there today with about one hundred thousand Tibetan refugees. The Cultural Revolution was an especially horrible time for Tibet. Over one million people are estimated to have died from torture, inhumane prison conditions, execution, and famine. This was one-fifth of the population of Tibet.

The damage since the Cultural Revolution includes the massive transfer of Han Chinese into Tibet, threatening to make Tibetans a minority population within their own country. Over six thousand monasteries, temples, and historic buildings have been destroyed. A huge number of monks and nuns have been forcibly returned to lay life. Many call this "cultural genocide." The Dalai Lama, in his government-in-exile in Dharamsala, has responded with the deepest principles of his religion. He consistently held to nonviolence in all relations with the Chinese government. He has also instituted fundamental reform of the Tibetan government-in-exile, reforming top-down patriarchal religious institutions to representative rule by democratic process. He is intent on preserving Tibetan culture and religion.

The Dalai Lama consistently calls for the demilitarization of Tibet, the restoration of human rights to their people, the end of the population transfer, the protection of the natural environment (land, vegetation, and animals), and a negotiated settlement of Tibetan-Chinese relations. The Chinese had virtually wiped out all wildlife through organized hunts using machine guns on entire herds. They wreaked havoc on the environment by clear-cutting 70 percent of the forests. He warns his people against anger and violence, calling for peaceful third-party mediation. He pleads for his people to be as forbearing as they can be. Anger is no solution, he claims. Love takes longer, but in the end love is the only real alternative.[59] The Dalai Lama was awarded the Nobel Peace Prize in 1989.

India: Ambedkarite Buddhists

Although Dr. Bhimrao Ramji Ambedkar was an outcaste in India, a sponsor financed his graduate studies in Great Britain, Germany, and America. Returning to India, he became the Father of the Constitution of modern India. Even with such fame, he was still subject to humiliation and insults as an untouchable. Gifted in organizational skills, he organized mass rallies of Dalits, as untouchables call themselves today (broken, smashed people). In his major address, Ambedkar said it was not his fault that he was born a Hindu. But he would be a fool if he died a Hindu. Hinduism was the religion that had relegated Dalits to nonhuman status. He would convert to the religion that welcomed Dalits most warmly. Five hundred thousand Dalits joined him to convert to Buddhism[60] at the Diksha Bhumi in Nagpur in 1956.[61] Instead of turning to the violent revolution of communism, Ambedkar sought to build a society of liberty, equality, and fraternity— principles he claimed were not from the French Revolution, but from Buddhism. That is, he sought to build a Dhammaraja, a society born of the Buddhist Dhamma. Against the traditional Theravada two-tier hierarchy of monks dominating village laypeople, Ambedkar sought to democratize the communities of new outcaste converts. He claimed a new sangha that raised laypeople to equality with monks. He, a layman, led the mass conversion service, instead of relying on monks.

This new breed of Ambedkarite Buddhists has been a challenge to Buddhism. They have had a primary social and economic focus. Meditation, renunciation, and no-self had only a secondary appeal. They demanded social justice in this life, not in the next rebirth or in a nirvana several lifetimes away. They rejected the "blame the victim" rationale within the karma concept. They demanded social and institutional reasons for their sufferings. In 1978 Sangharakshita established the Trailokya Bauddha Mahasangha, which today has more than twenty centers spreading much-needed Buddhist teaching and social activities among the Ambedkarite communities. These communities have now grown to several million. Under the name Bahujan Hitay, they operate nineteen dormitories where poor village children can live while attending school. The uplifting Buddhist teachings and the teamwork of village communities have done much to alleviate the feelings of worthlessness, helplessness, inertia, and passivity that have accompanied the untouchable castes for centuries.[62] Some Ambedkarites have begun to gain an interest in traditional Buddhist spiritual practices.[63]

Thailand: Ordaining Trees

Thailand was a country 80 percent covered with trees. Within only forty years, only 20 percent of the land had trees. The consequences were reduced harvest, loss of topsoil, flooding, aridity, loss of water sources, and ruined farmers. After exhausting other methods of protest and appeal, the Buddhist leadership decided to ordain trees. It is a serious evil in Theravada to harm a monk. So they began clothing trees in monk's robes and conducting ordination ceremonies. Thus transforming trees into monks, it would be a rare logger with the courage to cut down one of these trees.

Japan: Nihonzan Myohoji and Soka Gakkai

August is the season in Japan for two gigantic ceremonies that shake the hearts of the people—the commemoration of the tragic atomic bombing of Hiroshima and Nagasaki. The Nihonzan Myohoji sect of Nichiren Buddhism was founded by Nichidatsu Fujii. It has chapters in several countries. Even before World War II, Fujii was an active anti-war activist. He was moved by meeting Mahatma Gandhi. Today the sect is known for its peace poles erected everywhere in Japan. The peace poles are about four feet high and written in about five different languages saying, "May peace prevail on earth." A peace pole movement has begun in America among Christian churches with no indication of its Buddhist origins. On the peace pole website, however, the basic literature offered is written by Japanese. Nihonzan Myohoji is also known for its peace marches by monks beating on small hand drums and chanting, "*Namu Myoho Rengekyo*" (I take refuge in the Wonderful Gospel of the Lotus Sutra). They lead long lines of Buddhist and non-Buddhist followers. Their monks often sit beating their hand drums and chanting in protest at armament shipment sites and exhibitions of new weapons. They believe that war and the making of weapons are criminal activities. They aim to raise public awareness of the need for global nuclear disarmament.[64]

Soka Gakkai has major long-standing anti-war projects. Soka Gakkai is a Lotus Sutra religion of Nichiren Buddhism. They are known for exhibitions of the evils of war, especially about victims of nuclear war. Some Soka Gakkai exhibitions are periodic and others are permanent at local headquarters. They are conscious of the urgent need to display graphic photos of war victims so the post-war youth may also become anti-war and anti-nuclear advocates.[65] Soka Gakkai has its American national headquarters in Santa Monica in Los Angeles. Soka Gakkai has an unquestionable pacifist heritage. It is easy to be pacifist in times of peace, but it can be dangerous to be pacifist in times of war. The founder of Soka Gakkai, Tsunesaburo Makiguchi (1871–1944), his successor, Josei Toda, and close associates were imprisoned (1943–1945) for preaching peace while the militarist government was heading for war.[66]

Stories

Two Waves

Two ocean waves were racing from Hawaii across the Pacific. They were having a hilarious time, seeing who could jump the highest, who could dash the fastest. Then they came to the shores of Japan. One wave was horrified: "Did you see what happened to the waves? They rushed in to shore, got smashed on the rocks, and disappeared!"
The other wave said, "No sweat."

"What do you mean, 'No Sweat?' Don't you see the waves rushing in to shore, getting smashed on the rocks and disappearing? 'No Sweat!' What do you mean, 'No Sweat?' Don't you know that's what's going to happen to us? We're going to rush into shore, get smashed on the rocks, and disappear."

"No sweat! We are the ocean."

Two waves racing across the Pacific. They look exactly alike. But one wave was just a wave. The other wave had already become ocean while he was still a wave. How? By insight into his true nature. What do I want to do before I die? I want to become ocean while I am still a wave—by insight into my true nature.

After the Parrot Left the Cage

A man had a parrot in a cage. He put the parrot on his shoulder while he read the newspaper. He petted the parrot before putting him back in the cage. In the morning he made sure there was enough seed in the cage before he left for work. The first thing he did when he came home was to take the parrot out and play with it.

But when he came home from work one day, the parrot was not in the cage. The door of the cage was open. He got in a panic, running from room to room, but no parrot. He ran downstairs. Still no parrot. And then he saw that the window was open. He ran outside down the street. He saw trees, clouds, dogs, children at play. He was so surprised. He had never looked down the street before. He ran to the next street and was surprised at what he saw. There were mothers pushing babies in their carriages. Boys playing baseball. Bright colored flowers. He never noticed them before. As he looked to find his parrot, he paid attention and saw the whole world for the first time. He would never have noticed the whole world, if he had not lost his parrot.

I sit facing the wall with my feet folded on my thighs. My mind can be ruled by fantasy. My mind can be slanted by anger or frustration. My mind at times is depressed by worry and panic. There might not seem to be any signs of progress in thirty years of sitting. But a mentor once said that our minds are like the many layers of onions. Regardless of the storms of thoughts and feelings on the outer layers, the inner layers of the mind are always being nourished toward the still point. Often meditation does seem to be a waste of time. Yet meditation creates a soul environment that nurtures insight into our true nature. For some, insight is unexpectedly sudden (Rinzai and Obaku Zen). Insight for most of us duller people is a day-by-day affair (Soto Zen). Not waiting for an overwhelming mystical experience, we practice insight day-by-day. We focus on enlightened thoughts, enlightened feelings, and enlightened decisions—refusing to wait for a mystical experience before we start.

Is the parrot leaving the cage? Am I slowly disappearing? As I lose myself, I look everywhere to find myself. Where did I go? As I look everywhere, I find myself in the dog, in the tree, in the flower, in the sun, in the moon, and in the ocean waves. I find myself in the goldfish, the toddler, and in my companions at the dinner table. Is my counterfeit self getting lighter and thinner? Dig deep enough in your backyard, and you end up in China! Dig deep enough into your belly, and you end up in God!

No Self: Liberation from Guilt

I was the interim pastor of a church in Hawaii. One day there was a knock at our parsonage door. There stood a girl from a hippie community. She said she had just been released from a detox facility. She wanted a place to sleep. Her eyes looked dazed and her feet unstable. My mind immediately turned negative. Once she was asleep in our parsonage, we would not be able to get her out until she had recovered her health. I said, "No," that we would need church approval. I pointed out to her the city health service offices just down the street. She was desperate and pleaded that we let her sleep just for an hour. But she seemed ready for a twenty-hour-sleep. So I would not let her in our door and pointed her down the street. And she left.

Within the hour, I felt so terrible. I should have immediately opened our home to her, glad to retrieve a wayward Baptist youth. We should have been ready to die with her and die for her. My heart condemned me for many months. I could not believe that I had turned her away. When I shared this story with a small group of ministers, they reminded me of the strongest Protestant medicine for guilt: "God has forgiven you; therefore, you must forgive yourself." I did believe that God had forgiven me. But for some reason I could not manage to forgive myself.

Then a strange thing happened. I had been doing Zen meditations for decades. No-self came to me both from Zen and from the witness of Paul in Galatians 2:20. Paul had been crucified with Christ and was, therefore, no-self. There was a personality shift—Christ living through Paul. There was no longer any Paul to be praised or blamed! For whatever reason, I felt liberation from guilt. There was no longer any Dickson Yagi to be praised or blamed! Someone protested that this was total irresponsibility. But it was liberation for me and for the Apostle Paul. No-self is liberating Good News!

Living under Vows

Buddhists do not have the equivalent of creeds and confessions of faith that demand assent to religious doctrines, although Theravada monks in monasteries have hundreds of *vinaya* rules by which they are examined monthly for confession, repentance, and rededication. Instead of creeds, Mahayana Buddhism has the Four Bodhisattva Vows. They are unattainable ethical principles that inspire committed disciples all the days of their life.[67]

衆生無辺誓願渡	Living beings are numberless, I vow to save them. (environment)
煩悩無尽誓願断	Desires are inexhaustible, I vow to cut them off. (consumerism)
法門無量誓願学	Gates to truth are countless, I vow to open them. (truth seeking)
佛道無上誓願成	The awakened path is unsurpassable, I vow to embody it. (insight/compassion)

For Further Reading

Karen Armstrong. *Buddha*. New York: Penguin Books, 2004.
Robert Aitken and David Steindl-Rast. *The Ground We Share: Everyday Practice, Buddhist and Christian*. Boston: Shambala, 1994.
Charlotte Joko Beck. *Nothing Special: Living Zen*. New York: HarperOne, 1994.

David Chappell. *Buddhist Peacework: Creating Cultures of Peace.* Somerville, MA: Wisdom Publications, 1999.

Rita Gross and Terry C. Muck, eds. *Buddhists Talk about Jesus; Christians Talk about the Buddha.* New York: Continuum, 2000.

Rita Gross and Terry C. Muck, eds. *Christians Talk about Buddhist Meditation; Buddhists Talk about Christian Prayer.* New York: Continuum, 2003.

Ruben L. F. Habito. *Living Zen, Loving God.* Somerville, MA: Wisdom Publications, 2004.

Thich Nhat Hanh. *Living Buddha, Living Christ.* New York: Riverhead Books, 1995.

Steven Heine and Charles S. Prebish, eds. *Buddhism in the Modern World: Adaptations of an Ancient Tradition.* New York: Oxford University Press, 2003.

Dennis Hirota, ed. *Toward A Contemporary Understanding of Pure Land Buddhism: Creating a Shin Buddhist Theology in a Religiously Plural World.* Albany, NY: SUNY Press, 2000.

David J. Kalupahana. *Buddhist Philosophy: A Historical Analysis.* Honolulu: University of Hawaii Press, 1975.

Phillip Kapleau, ed. *The Three Pillars of Zen.* Boston: Beacon Press, 1971.

Damien Keown, ed. *Contemporary Buddhist Ethics.* Richmond, Surrey: Curzon Press, 2000.

Paul Knitter. *Without Buddha I Could Not Be a Christian.* Oxford, England: Oneworld Publications, 2009.

Jack Kornfield. *A Path with Heart: A Guide through the Perils and Promises of Spiritual Life.* New York: Bantam Books, 1993.

Hans Küng, et al. *Christianity and the World Religions.* Garden City, NY: Doubleday, 1986.

Julia Ching and Hans Küng. *Christianity and Chinese Religions.* Garden City, NY: Doubleday, 1989.

Chwen Jiuan Lee and Thomas G. Hand. *A Taste of Water: Christianity through Taoist-Buddhist Eyes.* New York: Paulist Press, 1981.

Leo D. Lefebure. *The Buddha & The Christ: Explorations in Buddhist and Christian Dialogue.* Maryknoll, New York: Orbis Books, 1997.

Bhante Walpoola Piyananda. *Saffron Days in L. A.: Tales of a Buddhist Monk in America.* Boston: Shambala, 2001.

Charles S. Prebish and Kenneth K. Tanaka. *The Faces of Buddhism in America*. Berkeley: University of California Press, 1998.

Richard H. Seager. *Buddhism in America*. New York: Columbia University Press, 1999.

Taitetsu Unno. *River of Fire, River of Water*. New York: Doubleday, 1998.

Taitetsu Unno. *Shin Buddhism: Bits of Rubble Turn into Gold*. New York: Doubleday, 2002.

Questions for Discussion

1. In Buddhism, there are two apparently contradictory concepts that exist side by side—the belief in reincarnation and the belief that nothing is of lasting substance. How do Buddhists reconcile this apparent contradiction?

2. Is it possible to become non-attached to life's basic cravings without being attached to a personal godhead? Do any versions of Buddhism offer something akin to worshipping a personal godhead?

3. Do you find that an understanding of Buddhism helps you be a better Christian, or does it offend your own sense of what Christianity is?

4. Is nirvana in Buddhism in any way similar to salvation within Christianity? Are both Buddhism and Christianity solely focused on the individual, or do they both offer communal salvation? Is Christ solely interested in individuals? Are bodhisattvas?

5. In Christianity, there is a tension between grace and works. Is there anything similar within Buddhism in general and in Mahayana Buddhism in particular?

6. Can one overcome craving by craving enlightenment? If not, then how can one achieve enlightenment?

7. What are the essential differences between Theravada, Mahayana Buddhism and Tibetan Buddhism?

8. What is the purpose of a koan within Zen Buddhism? Is the Christian concept of the Trinity a Christian koan?

FIVE

Indigenous American Religious Advice for Our Troubled Age

Ward M. McAfee

Nature, the First People and the spirit of our ancestors are giving you loud warnings. Today, December 10, 1992, you see increasing floods, more damaging hurricanes, hailstorms, climate changes and earthquakes, as our prophecies said would come. Even animals and birds are warning us with strange change in their behavior such as the beaching of whales. Why do animals act like they know about the earth's problems and most humans act like they know nothing? If we humans do not wake up to the warnings, the great purification will come to destroy this world just as the previous worlds were destroyed.

—Address by Thomas Banyacya, Hopi Spiritual Spokesman,
before the United Nations General Assembly, December 10, 1992

Introduction

Chief Seattle and Chief Joseph, both of the nineteenth century, warned their conquerors in words similar to those of Thomas Banyacya in 1992. This prophecy has been persistent over the past several centuries. Now, as the realities of climate change and species extinction are widely recognized, this message is being heard by the majority society.

The centuries-long genocide of Indigenous Americans at the hands of those whom they term "invaders" is familiar. The details of this encounter are horrific, involving not only physical violence but also many ongoing unwholesome developments that always accompany the attempt of one culture to eradicate another. But contemporary times have produced another perspective. Today, it is clear that the earth is in crisis. Modernity, once seen as providing unending progress, is running amok. Climate change and species extinction are the most obvious long-term problems. Descendants of the "invaders" are aware that they have been poor stewards of God's created order. They are open to learning from many sources, including Indigenous Americans who have much to say that goes beyond their harsh treatment at the hands of European colonizers.

First and foremost, Indian theologians relate that authentic religion capable of nurturing a reverential attitude toward the ongoing creative processes of the Earth must be rooted in definite locations. They tell us that human beings in a meaningful relationship with Creation must largely stay put and be committed to the particular circumstances of one region. In past ages, Indian tribes ranged far and wide in trading expeditions and even moved when circumstances demanded it, but characteristically Indigenous peoples maintained a mythological understanding of stability in their timeless and sacred locations. While at certain times and places Christian groups have similarly tried to maintain that their religious norms were unchanging, by and large the story and style of Christianity is one of historical development whereas Indian religions value maintaining stasis or equilibrium within particular ecosystems. In short, the Indian mentality is "spatial" more than "historical." In Western civilization, the dominant paradigm of historical development allowed modernity to take root and eventually flourish.

Indigenous people tell us that their ancestors considered human beings as co-inhabitants with the other creatures sharing their sacred locations rather than as a master species commissioned to reshape the natural order. Each tribe knew the particular rhythms of their unique place and lived accordingly. California Indians farmed oak trees by various methods that included both irrigation and intentional burning of brush for a predictable supply of nutritious acorns. The Sioux knew when and where to hunt the buffalo. But in all cases, Indigenous tribes never surrendered their mental rootedness to a particular place. They knew their limits and boundaries and thought of maintaining their place in a balanced existence in which they were not the only creatures that mattered. Other animals, the trees and even rocks were regarded with reverence. These kinds of sensibilities, Indigenous prophets emphasize, have been forgotten in the modern world.

Some recent Euro-Americans, such as Bill McKibben and Wendell Berry, have called for Americans to reorient their living patterns to specific places for both a more efficient use of natural resources and a restoration of a reverence for the land that is only possible in a specific locality. Amish Americans have long practiced a close attachment to location and community that is in harmony with Indigenous ways. With each passing year, a growing minority of Americans are open to changing living patterns in order to be more "Earth-friendly." In 2007, in preparing a new edition of *New Oxford American Dictionary*, Oxford University Press selected "locavore" as the 2007 Word of the Year. The invention of four San Francisco women, "locavore" is defined as a person who eats "only food grown or produced within a hundred-mile radius." Once made, this choice encourages a human identity with a specific location, a consciousness that pervades the writings of McKibben and Berry. This new sensibility is unfriendly to the workings of a global economy.

Overall, these examples of resistance are spotty at best. Modern and modernizing people everywhere generally hold a global economic consciousness. For a century, California oranges have been shipped to Florida, and Florida oranges to California. Now we fly Chilean wines to wine-producing California. Our living patterns bear almost no attachment to a particular place. Native American prophets warn that this must change if our species is to achieve a sustainable existence. Yet how can we turn away from an economic system that has become familiar, comfortable and profitable to large numbers of people? Where should we begin? Where should we look for our salvation?

Indigenous prophets urge us to rethink Christianity, the bedrock of Western civilization. The Earth Crisis has revealed its anthropocentrism as extremely dysfunctional. Mary Evelyn Tucker, who with her husband John Grim is a codirector of the Forum on Religion and Ecology, applauds the Native American critique of Christian human-centeredness: "In reexamining history we are less inclined to exalt the human in light of a continuing inhumanity to persons and of an assault on the Earth. More than ever before, we question our purpose, our function, and indeed our very being."[2] To some, this might sound as self-hatred, but it is more a rejection of human excess and a willingness to hear Indigenous advice. Before the coming of the Whites, Indigenous peoples regarded themselves as part of nature, not separated as a master species. This earthly and holistic consciousness, Indigenous prophets tell us, has to become universal.

These prophets warn that focusing too tightly upon a monotheistic God is part of the problem. It is not that Indian religions are hostile to monotheism. Most varieties of Indigenous American religion refer to something akin to a "Great Spirit." But this unifying force has always been regarded as highly mysterious and not the sole spiritual property of any particular group. Indian religions are not exclusive in orientation. They have always recognized that many tribes have their own unique relationship to the Great Spirit in their respective sacred places. Being spatially oriented, tribal religions always have focused on the specific, knowable, and familiar. As such, Indian religion is "down-to-earth" and readily engages common people toward earthly concerns while maintaining what some have termed a "cosmic consciousness." This mentality is experiential rather than word-oriented and intellectual.[3]

Vine Deloria Jr.

In modern times, Vine Deloria Jr. stands out as an Indigenous prophet. His *God Is Red: A Native View of Religion* is a thought-provoking analysis that has appeared in many editions. Deloria hailed from a Sioux family long devoted to the Christian faith. Both his father and grandfather had been Episcopal priests. He himself served on the National Executive Council of the Episcopal Church in the late 1960s. Shortly thereafter, he underwent a significant life change and rejected Christianity in favor of restoring ancient tribal religious traditions. His personal experiences and educational pursuits convinced him that Christianity was incapable of being reformed to meet the needs of our troubled age. He emphasized that in Native Indian religions, as practiced in their complete fullness long ago, a deep awareness was nurtured that the individual is part and parcel of the ongoing processes of creation. Most importantly, this awareness was common among all in the tribe, not just a select few.[4]

Deloria criticized not just Christianity but all of the religions shaping modern civilization. To a greater or lesser degree, all of them are exclusive in their foundational principles, a bad tendency that he claims leads to dreams of manifest destiny, war, conquest, and domination of others. Specifically, both Christianity and Islam seek to proselytize all of humankind. By contrast, Indigenous American religions are by their intrinsic nature tied to particular localities. As such, they are not universal, although they are harmonious with much that appears in the Christian scriptures. Above all, each tribe is respectful of other Indigenous stories that are rooted in places far removed from their own unique space. While specific Indian tribes certainly engaged in wars of conquest, they generally remained respectful of the spiritual stories of those whom they conquered. As such, Indian religion embodies a non-exclusive attitude quite uncommon among the religions of the West.[5]

A tone of bitterness colors the writings of Deloria. In explaining the Indigenous perspective to readers who are from the majority culture, Deloria cannot avoid expressing the pain accumulated during many centuries of European cultural domination. Christianity is held out for especial condemnation, as much of this oppression was done in its name. The first foreword to his book, written by Leslie Marmon Silko of the Laguna Pueblo, explains Vine Deloria's attitude this way: "In *God Is Red*, Vine explains how Christianity is at the root cause of the great weakness of the United States—the inability to respect or tolerate those who are different."[6] It is clear that Deloria developed his own intolerance toward Christianity as a result of what he perceived as Christianity's original sin of intolerance for any other religion. *God Is Red* considers the Christian style as an unwillingness to hear any religious insight that appears foreign or alien—and much in Indigenous religion can easily appear alien. In this regard, Deloria cites Walking Buffalo, a Stoney Indian from Canada, who long ago articulated the Whites' inability to listen to Indigenous perspectives:

> Did you know that trees talk? Well they do. They talk to each other, and they'll talk to you if you listen. Trouble is, white people don't listen. They never learned to listen to Indians, so I don't suppose they'll listen to other voices in nature. But I have learned a lot from trees; sometimes about the weather, sometimes about animals, sometimes about the Great Spirit.[7]

Deloria also blasts what he regards as Christianity's bad habit of framing its teaching in the form of "abstract religious principles." He compares this unfavorably to the Indigenous religious identity that is "virtually indistinguishable from the earth itself." Throughout his book, Deloria repeatedly shows that he is familiar with Western philosophical constructs that he criticizes. One suspects that this familiarity derives from that period in his life when he valued and seriously studied Christian philosophical thought.

The second foreword to *God Is Red* explains that Deloria challenges "the presumed inherent hegemony of the western intellectual tradition" so that "many bright Indian youth—a future generation of Indian scholars"—may come to realize the greater validity of their own native traditions. Describing the better way of Indian religion, Deloria writes: "Religion for them [Indigenous peoples] is an experience and they have no reason to reduce it to systematic thought and the elaboration of concepts." He blames the Earth Crisis on a mentality that conceives of this world "as a testing ground of abstract morality" and calls for "a more mature view of the universe as a comprehensive matrix of life forms." "Religious experiences," he writes, "are not nearly as important to Westerners as their creeds, theologies, and speculations—all products of the intellect and not necessarily based on experiences." His attack is unrelenting.

> It is the non-philosophical quality of tribal religions that makes them important for this day and age. . . . Modern society has foreclosed the possibility of experiencing life in favor of explaining it. Even in explaining the world, however, Western people have misunderstood it.

His message is clear: if one focuses on words and ideas, one will never hear the trees talking.[8]

Among the Christian "abstractions" that Deloria questions is the idea of "God" itself. Indian religions, he reports, do reference the "Great Spirit" or the "Great Mystery," but their ceremonial songs are not about any such indefinable entity. Instead, "they are directed to plants, birds, animals, and the earth asking for assistance in performing rather mundane tasks." The "Sacred Energy" or "Great Mystery" is too amorphous and general for such specific matters. Being immediately oriented to identifiable earthly concerns, Indian religion does not focus on an afterlife. Death—death of animals or humans or insects—is viewed as part of the rhythm of nature. The bones of the dead reside in the sacred locale of the tribe, which helps define it as sacred. "Heaven" (the Happy Hunting Ground) is vaguely acknowledged but is not emphasized.

Deloria contrasts what he regards as the pre-Columbian's "healthy attitude toward death" with what he regards as Christianity's pathological obsession over it. Here, he highlights "the message of Christianity" as fundamentally flawed: "Death was early considered as unnatural to the creation and as an evil presence resulting from the disobedience of Adam in the Garden of Eden." As a result of early Christianity's death-denying message, that religion became wedded to an "overemphasis on eternal life." Over the centuries, "people became separated from participation in the life cycles of the natural world and death became something to be feared." For Deloria, it is one more sharp contrast between Indian religion and Christianity that reveals the latter in a bad light: "For the tribal people, death in a sense fulfills their destiny, for as their bodies become dust once again they contribute to the ongoing life cycle of creation. For Christians, the estrangement from nature, their religion's central theme, makes this most natural of conclusions fraught with danger."[9]

Deloria described the Indian identity as primarily with the tribe and with the sacred living space of the tribe and not with the individual. As a result, individual death is not overemphasized. The tribe lives on as the individual dies. A leaf falls from a tree that continues to live. Little has changed. The individual has meaning only as a contributor to the life of the tribe, not as a self-defining entity. He sees Indian "community religions" as fundamentally different from most variants of Christianity in not "abstracting a hypothetical individual from his or her community context." He reports that Indigenous religion teaches that the individual is not larger than nature and that the individual has responsibilities to both the community and the natural world that transcend personal desires and wishes. His advice to Christians is harsh: "Rather than attempt to graft contemporary ecological concern onto basic Christian doctrines and avoid blame for the current planetary disaster, Christians would be well advised to surrender many of their doctrines."[10]

Native American Christian Theology

Indigenous American Christian theologians, who agree with much of Deloria's analysis, need to be heard. Their collective insights derive from a shattered past. Similar to the rest of us, they are venturing into a most uncertain future. These fellow Christians tell us that we must join with them in a reconstruction of Christianity that emphasizes respect for the land. Unlike Deloria, they do not regard this projected new reformation of Christianity as a lost cause even before it begins. They call for a new Christianity focusing upon a new resurrection—a restoration of balance in ongoing natural creative processes. They envision a widespread religiously inspired respect for earth's rhythms overcoming our culture's current prima facie value of human expansion.[11]

Today, Indigenous American Christian theologians have embarked on a mission that begs us to reconsider long familiar theological constructs that they perceive have facilitated our current predicament. Similar to the Social Gospel theologians of a century ago, they want us to rethink our understandings of both "sin" and "salvation" in an effort "to return to a state of communitas." In Native traditions, they report, "the closest approximation of the Christian notion of sin. . . is a failure to live up to one's responsibilities to the community." Likewise, the closest understanding of "salvation" present in Native traditions is the sustainability and continuance of the tribe.

Similar to Deloria, Indigenous Christian theologians want us to rethink our emphasis on life after death. They report, "Although the stereotype of a 'Happy Hunting Ground' is well established, the continuation of personal existence after death has less importance in tribal societies than in Christianity." They want us to rethink our rigid monotheism. The Lakota notion of Wakan Tanka (often seen as equivalent to our God) is commonly expressed as "unity in diversity," but it is the diversity of Wakan Tanka as knowable physical and spiritual forces in a particular sacred location that is emphasized.[12]

These Christian theologians suggest we reconstruct the meaning of "creation" not as a one-time event but rather as an ongoing process. The pre-Columbian residents of North America were engaged daily in their physical/spiritual world order involving reciprocity as well as enjoyment of the fruits of nature. They regarded all created things as embodying a sacred energy, and they experienced a deep reverence for this totality, not merely for their own human existence in any superior or separated way. They were branded as "animists" because their attitudes did not conform to the religious categories of the missionaries who sought to force their beliefs into a realm of word constructs that bear no direct relationship to nature as experienced in unique spaces. In opposition to the traditional teachings of Christianity, these early Indigenous resisters did not think of themselves as privileged stewards of the whole. Rather they were both reverential of a mysterious spiritual power unifying all of the various parts of the whole and immediately aware of their obligations to it. Instead of fostering individual mastery, their "animism" encouraged a communal attitude relating them to tribal communities as well as all of nature.

Reflecting upon the interior perspective of Indigenous Americans, people holding a traditional Western worldview are challenged to question their deepest assumptions that have contributed to "a mentality of looking at nature as something to be conquered and subdued rather than as a living world that humans work with and within." With others, Indigenous American Christian theologians suggest that persisting in the familiar ruts of traditional axial religions is part of the unprecedented problem now facing us.[13]

According to Indian prophetic analysis, pre-Christian Europeans began the bad Western habit of objectifying the world as observers disengaged and separated from their natural context. This, Indigenous American Christian theologians observe, was the first step toward a worldview of external control and domination, ultimately including an assault on the natural order necessary for all of life. Among ancient Greek thinkers, Pythagoras initiated the Western tendency to divide body and soul, regarding the soul as divine and eternal and the body as from the Earth and therefore transitory and corrupt. Plato and the Gnostics who influenced early Christianity built upon this philosophical foundation that diminished earthly existence. Postexilic Hebrew religion contributed eschatological and apocalyptic tendencies to defer all meaning to a presumed end of time when the Kingdom of God would be revealed to a righteous remnant. These disparate influences shaped Christianity's subsequent "otherworldly disposition."[14]

Native Americans have different names for what Westerners call "God," but they are agreed concerning this highly mysterious God's essential nature, which is not that of a dominator or personal Lord who demands our submission. Rather, God is "the Sacred Energy, or Mystery or Power." The interior perspective of Indigenous Americans does not presume to define this power with any pretense of objective precision. But it is quite definite in its assurance that the appropriate way to view our human relationship to "God" is that of intimate sharing within this Sacred Energy. Their perspective is far more egalitarian (within a spiritual context of reverential wonder and respect) than is the typical Western perspective of hierarchical domination and control.

George Tinker is perhaps the principal Indian theologian of our time. He participated with others in writing the second foreword for the thirtieth anniversary edition of Deloria's *God Is Red*, proclaiming that work as giving voice to American Indian religious thought. The differing roles of Deloria and Tinker may be described in the familiar metaphor of "good cop/bad cop," with Deloria playing the latter role. Deloria first softens up Euro-American readers with his harsh claim that Christianity is irredeemable. Tinker, the "good cop," then follows with his assurances that Christianity is still salvageable. Malcolm X and Martin Luther King Jr. constituted a similar tandem during the Civil Rights Movement, although Martin never publicly collaborated with Malcolm, as Tinker has with Deloria. In reviewing Tinker's book *Spirit and Resistance: Political Theology and American Indian Liberation*, Deloria described their relationship this way: "Tinker's powerful and well-reasoned thoughts are expressed in a much kinder way than some of us are likely to do."[16]

Use of the term "Lord" is at the top of Tinker's suggested reforms. He points out that many disparate and quarreling groups within Western Christianity find an unfortunate area of agreement in the notion that "Jesus is Lord." That very linguistic construct, he emphasizes, encourages a bad tendency. Feminist Christian theologians, such as Rosemary Radford Ruether, have come to the same conclusion. Tinker relates his own perspective on the use of the word "Lord": "Many Amer-European Christians seem to feed on a hierarchical view of the world that has historically privileged and continues to privilege White people on this continent and in other Third World colonial contexts."[17]

Indigenous Christian theologians tell us that Christians must not only reconsider their linguistic (and mental) habits regarding Jesus Christ but also historical pretensions of Christian exclusivity. If religion is characterized by a rigid exclusivity, they emphasize, it becomes self-righteous, nationalistic, idolatrous, hateful, rage-filled, and ultimately destructive of both Self and Community. Tinker concludes:

> The colonizer churches themselves will necessarily have to rethink their notion of Christian exclusivity and make room for American Indian religious traditions as being potentially as powerful and salvific as the best vision well-intentioned peoples have for Christianity. . . . It should be possible today for a mutual respect to emerge that will allow Christians to acknowledge spiritual power and goodness of [other] religious traditions.[18]

Envisioning a New Mentality

Can Indian wisdom and Christianity be united in a workable way that holds promise for the future? This remains a key theological question for our age as it grapples with the realities of how human activities are destroying life-giving habitat. It is not now clear how the dominant culture will respond.

Historically the European invaders envisioned only two futures for indigenous peoples. Some, perhaps many, sought their elimination, and genocide was effectively practiced. The more "Christian" response called for their assimilation into Western and Christian ways. To ensure the success of this mission, Whites even took Indian children away from both their parents and tribal communities and placed them in boarding schools where they were denied the use of their own language and socialized into the alien, Western culture. This is not the kind of outcome that Indigenous Christian theologians have in mind.

Indigenous peoples have had to make many adjustments to the dominant culture, and some Native Americans have learned to work well within it, but success stories are not commonplace. The old cultures and traditions, so closely bound to the landscape, have been broken for most tribal peoples by forcing them to choose between reservations that cannot support traditional means of livelihood and an alienating urban environment. By and large, the current result reflects an unhealthy assimilation.

Native American authors describe the depth of the problem:

> The average yearly income [of Indigenous Americans] is less than half the poverty level, and over half of all Natives are unemployed. On some reservations, unemployment runs as high as 85-90%. Health statistics chronically rank Native Americans at or near the bottom. Male life expectancy is forty-four years, female forty-seven. Infant mortality is twice the national average. Diabetes run six times the national average; heart disease at about five times the national average; alcoholism five times the national average; and cirrhosis of the liver eighteen times the national average. Substance abuse, school dropout rates, suicide, crime, and violence are major problems among both urban and reservation populations.[19]

George Tinker sees no prospect for overcoming "Indian dysfunction" independent of the dominant society addressing its own "ecological dysfunction."

In short, modern pathologies exhibited among Indian populations are not their problems alone. The dominant culture that encourages these societal diseases needs to be changed.[20]

The question for Indigenous Americans is how they can reclaim the ancient wisdom of their cultures. Indians have internalized many negative perceptions of themselves that have been dominant in the broader culture for many centuries. Getting free of this form of mental bondage will be no easy task. For their part, Indigenous Christian leaders are seeking ways to look at Christianity beyond the categories and paradigms that helped the religion facilitate colonial oppression. This remains a work in progress.

The question for Euro-Americans is whether they can learn from an indigenous spirituality to bring about needed changes. In pre-Columbian days, native religions flourished in the context of a very different way of living than what is possible for most people today. Can the Indian mentality of being close to Nature be adapted by the dominant culture to address the Earth Crisis in meaningful ways? Indian theologians such as Tinker offer no simple prescriptions. Native commentators have long been recommending that whites need to listen to Nature in order to change their own dysfunctional habits of thinking and being. As these recommendations are now being heard, it is up to the hearers to decide how they should respond. As a teacher, Jesus of Nazareth never laid out clearly how to solve the multiple dysfunctions of his own time. Rather he gently nudged his hearers to consider new perspectives that they would have to wrestle with in order to make them interior realities for themselves. It is no different in our current situation. Native Americans cannot simply inject us with an Earth-friendly mentality as a physician might administer a curative potion. As has been true in all ages, we have to discover authentic religious truth ourselves.

As the Earth Crisis calls us all to live more responsibly, we must change many patterns of past behavior. It is clear that a great cultural shift will have to occur. People now wedded to a preference for individual freedom will have to change their orientation to one of individual and collective responsibilities. Indian prophets promise that individual identity will not be lost in this necessary reorientation. Native American customs of naming individuals for their unusual abilities or experiences demonstrate that any fear of obliterating an authentic individual self in this anticipated indigenously inspired transformation is unwarranted. Individual life must always be appreciated but in its way of contributing to the whole, rather than encouraging any and all personal desires.

Sioux religious traditions have long encouraged "vision quests" of individuals to discover their unique responsibility in contributing to the well-being of the whole.[21] Similar in some ways to the notion of the Christian "calling," the Indigenous American vision quest more intimately links individual destiny to that of both the community and the sacred Earth. As such, it has an intrinsic social integrity that is now required in our confrontation with a fractured and dysfunctional world disorder.

Conclusion

We are in a process of returning to an appreciation of Mother Earth. The human race's instinct for survival demands this. Our culture's environmental discourse amply demonstrates this, but for this process to be corrective, it must become more than intellectual sharing. Talk is valuable only if it leads to changed patterns of living and being. Scientific knowledge and philosophical insights alone cannot persuade us. Indigenous American commentators advise us that our daily religion must become experiential and communal and rooted in specific places if it is to become transformative.

In the past, religions have been remodeled when conditions required it. We have faith that humankind will come again to harmonize with the life rhythms of the Earth, restoring a balance that is under attack in our own time. Our future will require this restoration. Then we will know that "we are not larger than nature and that we have responsibilities to the rest of the natural world that transcend our own personal desires and wishes."[22] This is the interior perspective of Indigenous Americans that is offered to everyone.

Writing in a German theological journal in 1989, George Tinker regretted that Christianity had been forced upon his people. The resulting horror taught indigenous peoples who survived that something was amiss with refined Christian theologies that promised Indians salvation in the next world while ensuring only their destruction in the present one. Tinker concludes that ultimately the Christian missionaries failed in their cause of religious eradication, in that "Indians continue to tell the stories [of their ancestors], sing the songs, speak the prayers and perform the ceremonies that root themselves deeply in Mother Earth." And, he added almost as an aside, that his people "are actually audacious enough to think that their stories and their ways of reverencing Creation will some day win over the immigrants and transform them."[23]

Decades later, Tinker continues this theme with greater emphasis and elaboration. In his *Spirit and Resistance*, he states his goal as "to recapture something of the premodern, pre-1492 world as a vision" to guide all of humankind. Tinker calls for "dreaming a new future." He emphasizes that this new Christian theology will have to focus upon "the salvation of the communal whole (that is, the world)" and radically reject the "fracturing of the community into individual actors." "The space of our existence," he continues, will have to have a higher priority than "the time of our existence" in this new theology. A spatial emphasis alone, he advises, is capable of inculcating "the wisdom of living within limits." And a deemphasis of "the time of our existence" cannot but help weaken certain Earth-disrespecting aspects of Christian eschatological thinking.[24]

The Indigenous American perspective challenges Christian theologians to ponder their faith anew. And in doing so, hard questions must be addressed, especially regarding the Native American advice to highlight "the space of our existence." Spatial consciousness in and of itself is no panacea. The ideologies currently generating conflicts in Kashmir and/or Israel/Palestine have a spatial emphasis, at least to some degree. Likewise, the Nazi perversion of Christianity attempted to connect it with a particular land and people. Many negative examples exist of spatially oriented ideologies/religions that do connect people and land and use that connection to maltreat refugees and immigrants of other cultures who come to live among them. How can this evil be avoided if Tinker's advice is followed?

The Christian Bible advises that one can observe false prophecy by its fruits. Matthew 7:19 advised, "Every tree that does not bear good fruit should be cut down and cast into the fire." By this standard, traditional Christianity itself is at least in need of some pruning. The point is that any reformulations of the Christian message need to be tested by their fruits. Loving-kindness, long at the center of Christianity, needs to become the litmus test of any new constructions of it. Indeed, this attribute is reflected in Tinker's own accounting of spatiality within Indigenous American religious traditions:

> Perhaps the most precious gift that American Indians have to share with other peoples is our perspective on the interrelatedness of all of creation and our deep sense of relationship to the land in particular. We

are all relatives: from buffaloes and eagles to trees and rocks, mountains and lakes. Just as there is no category of the inanimate, there can be no conception of anything in the created world that does not share in the sacredness infused in God's act of creation.[25]

A reformed Christianity that incorporates a spatial emphasis in this manner is certain to avoid the chauvinism represented most perversely in the Nazi example.

We cannot adopt Indigenous American religions as our own. Their spiritual stories are not ours. But their mentality or interior perspective may inspire us.[26] Their example may assist us in our own "search for an intimate spiritual experience of the natural world."[27] Our troubled age is ripe for many transformations, including religious ones. Consumerism, the dominant secular religion of our age, is unsustainable. The natural order itself is rejecting it.[28] As the false promises of Consumerism are exposed on a global stage, religious sensibilities encouraging ecological health will touch hearts and minds as never before.

Native American Christian theologians point us toward new considerations. There are aspects of their theology that are antithetical to familiar Christian teachings, yet there is an opening in scripture: In John 16:12-13, Jesus reportedly advised his followers that better translations of his message would occur later when the Holy Spirit would help bring about an understanding of God's fullest intentions. We need not adopt completely the reforms suggested by Indigenous theologians, but we must work toward reforming Christianity to strengthen its capacity to preserve life in all of its rich diversity. If we do this, George Tinker's own prophecy of Indigenous advice eventually transforming us will have been fulfilled.

Further Reading

Peggy V. Beck, Anna Lee Walters, and Nia Francisco. *The Sacred Ways of Knowledge, Sources of Life.* Tsaile: Navajo Community College Press, 1996.

Vine Deloria Jr. *For This Land: Writings on Religion in America.* New York: Routledge, 1990.

Vine Deloria Jr. *God Is Red: A Native View of Religion.* Golden: Fulcrum, 2003.

Richard Erdoes. *Crying for a Dream: The World through Native American Eyes.* Santa Fe: Bear and Company, 1990.

Clara Sue Kidwell, Homer Noley, and George E. Tinker, eds. *A Native American Theology.* Maryknoll: Orbis, 2001.

George E. Tinker. *Spirit and Resistance: Political Theology and American Indian Liberation.* Minneapolis: Fortress Press, 2004.

Anand Veeraraj. *Green History of Religion.* Bangalore: Centre for Contemporary Christianity, 2005.

Bron Taylor, *Dark Green Religion: Nature, Spirituality and the Planetary Future* (Berkeley: University of California Press, 2010).

Questions for Consideration

1. Indigenous theologians claim that their religious traditions emphasize the particular, specific, and experiential rather than the general, universal, and philosophic. How is their orientation reflected in their emphasis of space over time? And in their deemphasis of God (or the Great Spirit)?

2. What aspects of American Indigenous religion do not welcome outsiders?

3. What aspects of Indigenous religion are most similar to Christianity?

4. Would a synthesis of Indigenous and Christian traditions be desirable? Given the distinct differences between the two, is such hybrid even possible?

5. Is Christianity capable of becoming an effective force in addressing the Earth Crisis? What aspects of the Christian heritage might reduce its effectiveness? What aspects might strengthen it?

SIX

Theological Response

John B. Cobb Jr.

In each of the four chapters that constitute the heart of this book, challenges are directed to Christians—some explicitly, some in more implicit ways. There are also suggestions of how progressive Christians respond. But a more developed statement of our response is also needed. This requires reflection about who we are.

In our previous book, *Resistance*, we considered our identity in relation to the culture of our time. When Christians have lived in cultures that were not influenced by Christian faith, they have always recognized a need to resist. But in cultures that understand themselves to be Christian, the note of resistance often fades to the margins. The liberal Protestants who are our recent ancestors in the United States found themselves in harmony with much of the cutting edge of their culture and so worked in it and with it. But as we analyze the dominant forces in our current society, even if the society thinks of itself as "Christian," we conclude that we need a different strategy. There is now much about the direction in which our culture is moving that, in the name of our scriptures and our faith, we must resist.

Of course, there is also much in our culture that we continue to affirm and celebrate. This is especially true in relation to the topic of this book. In the United States, our culture affirms and widely embodies a tolerance of diverse religious traditions that is an admirable move away from the dominant form of the Christian tradition in the past.

The move toward tolerance has characterized our American history and has been a part of the cultural development with which our liberal ancestors strongly identified. Of course, many horror stories can be told about the treatment of religious minorities in the past. But our national constitution forbade the establishment of a national church, and the states also rejected this approach in favor of equal freedom for all religious groups. Originally the religious groups in question were chiefly Christian. The various Protestant groups generally came to agreement that despite their differences, they did not condemn the followers of other traditions to eternal hell. Increasingly they defined themselves as legitimate alternative forms of Christianity. This attitude was grudgingly extended to Catholics, and for practical purposes, at least, the legitimacy of Judaism was also recognized. As a fuller and more complex religious diversity has appeared and been recognized, the great majority of Americans, Christians and others alike, extend an accepting attitude toward all, or almost all. Most of the resistance to this acceptance comes from sectarian Christian groups rather than from the culture. Progressive Christians celebrate this cultural development.

There have always been exceptions to this inclusive tolerance. These have varied in different epochs of American history. Until very recently the spirituality of Native Americans was not recognized as a valid form of religion. Currently, the most important issue is with Islam. The suspicion of Islam is not primarily theological. It is as widespread among secular people as among Christians. It has been fueled especially by the official account of 9/11 and the widespread association of Muslims with terrorism. We must not be complacent about the religious tolerance that characterizes American culture, but we believe that, despite its limitations, it is working now to increase acceptance of Islam as a valid form of religious life.

Nevertheless, progressive Christians are not simply a part of this cultural attitude. In both its secular and religious form, this culture tends to belittle the teachings of all religious groups. Either it assumes that, on basic matters, all religious groups are much the same, or it assumes that, in itself, what they teach makes little difference. We do not agree. Practically, we think that cultural tolerance needs to be undergirded by fuller information about, and understanding of, differences. Theoretically or theologically, as progressive Christians we think that the beliefs by which people live are of great importance, and we are convinced that it is important for us to rethink our own beliefs in light of what we learn from others.

As progressive Christians, we think in radically historical terms. In responding to Native American criticisms, we must confront the problems with this approach to understanding, and we will return to this later. But in understanding who *we* are and how *we* deal with what others have shown us about ourselves, we must think historically. Although contemporary historical thought is quite different from biblical thinking, it has its roots there.

In some ways historical consciousness is another feature of contemporary culture that we share. However, as Christians we employ historical thought differently from its dominant cultural use. That use objectifies everything, explaining it in terms of its historical location. The dominant culture's use of history to understand the various religions encourages an objectifying relation that works against personal commitment and involvement. In the university, to be a believer is considered something of a handicap for proper teaching about religions. For us the deepest purpose of historical understanding is to enable us to rethink our faith, not to diminish it. We believe a deeper understanding of history leads to living our faith rather than objectifying or distancing it.

However, our historical understanding also emphasizes the absence of any absolutes. Many forms of personal and social practice that have developed over the millennia can be considered "religious." None of these is perfect or final or should seek universality. There has never been an ideal Christianity. There is much to learn from every epoch and every Christian movement, but all have been, and ever will be, imperfect. The same can be said of other religious traditions.

We find much inspiration in the Hebrew scriptures. They are themselves historical through and through. They do not pretend to depict perfect people or a perfect society. They reflect the views of many people over many centuries. They disagree among themselves, and there is no reason for us to assume that any of the writers was without error. The later extreme ideas about their inspiration are not themselves biblical. Nevertheless, the scriptures encounter us with the challenge to confront our society with a call for justice and peace. They also bring us wisdom for living, comfort, reassurance, and inspiration. We agree with 2 Timothy 3:16 that "all scripture is inspired by God and is useful for teaching, for correction, and for training in righteousness."

As Christians we read these Hebrew scriptures from a point of view shaped by the New Testament account of Jesus and the response to him, especially as shaped by Paul. For us history has a center that throws light both on what took place before and how we are to live and think from then on. That some Jews thought that one particular Jew, Jesus, was the center of history distinguished them from other Jews. It led these Jewish followers of Jesus to accept Gentiles on an equal basis. This gradually brought about a separation, so that eventually the followers of Jesus were no longer accepted as Jews or wanted to be thought of as Jews. We are the heirs of that historically important event. We can appropriate the Hebrew scriptures only in light of that event. Obviously, today's Jews are heirs of those Jews who did not accord Jesus a central place.

The debate about Jesus was intense and sometimes acrimonious. As Christians we repent of much that our Christian ancestors said against those who continued the Jewish tradition. We deeply regret that the bitterness of the conflict is reflected in our New Testament, so that terrible sayings against Jews are part of our canon. Today we recognize that Jesus did not fulfill the expectations of a Messiah, so that the messianic claim by his followers is profoundly problematic. We can appreciate its rejection by the majority of the Jews, and we can appreciate also the values realized in the continuation of a Jewish community that long excised Jesus and his teaching from its tradition. Of course, we Gentile Christians are deeply grateful for those Jews who followed Jesus and welcomed us to join them. We make no judgment of superiority on our side, but there is no question about which side we are on. For us, Jesus is the center.

In arguing for this centrality, the church developed complex doctrines about what Jesus did and who he was. Some of them make little sense to us today. We deplore the fact that through long centuries, many Christians thought that correct beliefs about Jesus were more important than actually following him. Many of the horrors of our historical relation with Judaism and Islam resulted from this distortion. This does not mean that clarifying what Jesus accomplished and who he was are unimportant. But it is important as a guide to us in discipleship, not as a replacement for such discipleship. Most progressive Christians strongly favor the idea that God was incarnate in Jesus and affirm Trinitarian images. On the other hand, when commitment to any particular formulation leads to hostility against those who think differently or to cruel action, doctrine has ceased to play its proper role in directing our discipleship.

The realization of the many crimes committed in the name of Christianity has led many to distance themselves from the faith and the community that espouses it. That response is understandable. We do not condemn those who leave. We think that leaving may be better than the defensiveness with which some Christians respond to criticism.

But there is another response. For us for whom Jesus is the center, repentance is a central part of our faith. Jesus called us to repent because the *basileia theou* is at hand. That the divine "kingdom" or "commonwealth" is at hand is as hard to believe now as it was when Jesus proclaimed it. But like Jesus' first followers, we do get glimpses of the divine *basileia* in Christian communities and elsewhere, and we want to be a part of that new form of life and share it as widely as possible.

The repentance to which we are called now includes our communal sins as Christians as well as the personal ones that Jesus had primarily in mind. Repentance for communal sins is possible only for those who remain part of the community that has sinned. It does not mean primarily the acknowledgment of wrongdoing and expressing remorse, although it cannot take place without those elements. It means, primarily, changing direction. For us to repent, in the name of Jesus, of the historical crimes of Christianity as well as our personal failures in the name of Jesus can contribute more to the presence and coming of the divine commonwealth Jesus proclaimed than does abandonment of the Christian community and placing ourselves more fully in the secular world. For us, the fuller the repentance the more deeply we are expressing our discipleship.

We Christians have repented of much, and we continue to learn of more of which we should repent. This book is chiefly about repentance for our long history of exclusivism, in the sense of absolutizing our own position and judging all others inferior insofar as they differ from us. There is no doubt that we have done this. The fact that other traditions have done similar things in no way reduces the evil of our deeds. We have done immense harm to others, and in doing this we have replaced Jesus with an idol as the center of our history and our lives.

The purpose of this chapter is not to express recognition and remorse for our crimes, even those that still continue. It is to consider how, as we understand our place in history in light of the centrality of Jesus and seek to follow him in this new time, we can be informed and transformed by what we learn from other religious communities and our past history with them. What features of our teaching and general practice have caused us to sin against them? How can these be changed in light of our intention to be disciples of Jesus?

The Abrahamic Traditions

One point we made in our introductory chapter was that general statements about the relation of Christianity to other traditions do not take us very far. We hope that the four examples we have considered in this book display the need to consider each case separately. Christianity, Judaism, and Islam are sister traditions, all three of which claim Abraham as a forefather in the faith. Our histories extensively overlap and interact. But this has not made relations smoother.

The main problem has been our exclusivism. As long as we insist that we have the one truth, so that all who disagree are simply wrong, we will in one way or another continue to relate to Judaism and Islam in destructive ways. The damaging exclusivism in these cases has been with respect to Jesus. We have often held that a certain view of Jesus is essential to salvation. Accordingly, some have proposed that progressive Christians shift from Christocentrism to theocentrism. This would enable us to recognize that Jews and Muslims relate to the same God and that this is what is of crucial importance. We could relegate our relation to Jesus to secondary status.

For this to improve relations with Jews and Muslims, Jews and Muslims would need to make similar changes. Jews would need to relegate their relation to Torah to subordinate status and Muslims, the Qur'an. A few Jews and Muslims may be willing to take this step. We would then have a group of "progressive" Christians, Jews, and Muslims who shared in the view that the differences among the traditions are not important to any of them. Of course the vast body of Christians, Jews, and Muslims would ignore this new group. Or if, in the unlikely event that large numbers would follow those who are prepared to part this radically from their histories, much of what has been most valuable in all three traditions would be lost.

We do not believe that this belittling of what distinguishes us from one another is the best direction for progressive Christians to go. We do not believe that the important goals of harmony and mutual appreciation can be realized only when people limit their beliefs to that on which everyone can agree. Instead, we would emphasize that the problem is not that Christians center on Jesus, Jews on the Torah, and Muslims on the Qur'an. The problem has been that believers in each community have too often brought exclusivist assumptions and attitudes to their relation with others. Christians especially have thought that if they are correct to understand all of history and all of life in a way that places Jesus at the center, then Jews and Muslims must be wrong in not doing so.

This negative judgment of others need not follow. On the contrary, if we truly place Jesus at the center, we may be completely open to appreciate what happens in other communities with other centers. Indeed, we will find that closing ourselves to the possibilities that there are forms of wisdom and truth other than our own is not faithful to Jesus. His central "command" is to love God and to love our neighbors as ourselves. To love others is to be open to hearing their stories and respecting the wisdom they have gained. We may think that we have gained still greater truth from the story in which Jesus plays the central role, but Jesus warns us not to judge. It is the openness to hearing and appreciating, not the judging, that best expresses our discipleship to him.

Judaism

With respect to Judaism, the most glaring problem is that we follow Paul in believing that in Jesus we, and all who follow him, are freed from the Jewish law. We understand that law as a burden, and we would like for others to be freed from that burden. We think that there are Jews throughout the centuries who have found liberation in the Christian gospel.

But when we listen to the witness of many Jews, we learn that for them what appears to us as a burden is joy and fulfillment. Obedience to the law binds them to one another and to God. It gives rich meaning to their lives. What appears to us as liberation impresses them as loss of meaningful existence. Paul did not affirm that there was inherent value in *not* observing the law. He felt strongly that observing or not observing was a secondary matter for those in his communities. They were free to adopt either path. Since observant Jews do not press their style of life on Gentiles, their commitment to observing the law poses no problem for our acceptance and appreciation of their life and thought.

Of course, matters are not so simple. There are Jews who find the law oppressive, and there are forms of Judaism that greatly simplify it. Christians can certainly understand that choice and support it as well. The point is not that Christians should approve of one form of Judaism more than another. The point is that we can appreciate and learn from discussions about the law in the Jewish community without judgment.

Law in the sense of ethics plays a large role in the Christian community as well. Christians believe that faithfulness to Jesus in response to God's generosity to us involves freely adopting many of the principles laid down in the Hebrew scriptures. Most Christians give a place of special honor to the Ten Commandments. Some make a sharp distinction between the ceremonial and dietary laws from which they consider themselves freed and the ethical teachings that they fully accept and reaffirm.

For Paul the problem was legalism as such. The historical fact is that Christians have fallen into the legalism from which he sought to free us no less than have many Jews. Despite Jesus and Paul, most Christian communities have developed legalistic patterns. The Reformers saw this clearly in the church of their day and undertook to renew Paul's call for freedom. Luther was especially strong on this point. But this never meant indifference toward morality. And even among Lutherans a relapse into legalism can be observed.

Sadly, Christian legalism has often centered on gender roles and sexual behavior in ways from which the Torah is relatively free. Also, Judaism has learned ways of developing its law through discussions among rabbis, retaining their diverse interpretations within the tradition, as can be seen in the Talmud. Protestants often have greater difficulties in responsibly revising and developing our ethical teachings. Paul sharply contrasted his understanding of faithfulness to Jesus with the centrality of law in the Judaism of his day. The difference continues. But it would be a serious misunderstanding of historic reality simply to repeat Paul's affirmations about freedom from the law against bondage to it as if they described the relation of Christian and Jewish experience.

When it is a matter of asking what it means to order our lives in terms of the centrality of Jesus, we progressive Christians are properly more active participants in the discussion than when the question is that of evaluating Judaism. We have a responsibility to explain the teaching of Jesus and the theology of Paul to those who think that being Christian is a matter of obeying whatever laws are taught in their communities. As progressive Christians, we prize the freedom Paul proclaimed and do not want to fall back into the legalism he so strongly opposed. We hold fast to the Christocentrism that enabled us to be engrafted into the history of Israel's life with God while freeing us from all legalisms.

But for us to follow Jesus, and to be deeply influenced by Paul in doing so, is not to condemn those who center their lives in the Torah. We find that they have derived from their study and experience in this tradition a rich wisdom from which we have much to learn. They have much to teach us about the scriptures we share with them, and they contribute to the coming of the divine commonwealth. Through the centuries, on many matters relevant to that commonwealth, they have given extraordinary leadership despite their relatively small numbers and the many centuries of persecution at our hands.

The direction that Christians need to choose in our understanding of ourselves in relation to Judaism does not, therefore, entail any abandonment of Christocentrism. While Jesus is indeed the center for us, being faithful to Jesus does not call on us to condemn those who live out of other centers. However, this understanding is threatened if we turn Jesus from a human being, whose message and life provide for us the needed center, into a supernatural being. We can affirm the incarnation without doing this, but historically many Christians have viewed Jesus not as fully human but as God appearing to us in human form. The creeds held faithfully to Jesus' full humanity against those who sought to qualify it. They insisted that our recognition of God's presence in Jesus in no way conflicted with that humanity.

Sadly, in the post-creedal period, those who wanted to treat Jesus as metaphysically different from us gained the upper hand. They accepted the creedal affirmations that Jesus had a fully human mind, nature, and will, but they said that the "person" of Jesus was only divine. This can be understood as meaning that Jesus' "self" consisted only in God rather than in a human being in whom God was fully present. In both East and West the church began to speak of Jesus' humanity as *impersonal*, thereby losing the real depth of meaning of incarnation. Jesus came to be thought of as metaphysically different from everyone else. This encouraged a tendency to suppose that believers cannot approach Jesus directly but must ask his human mother to intercede with him on our behalf.

Progressive Christians side with the creeds in insisting on the full humanity of Jesus. We also affirm strongly that God was in Jesus. But since God is in all of us, God's presence in Jesus does not make him metaphysically different. Some of us emphasize that Jesus was peculiarly responsive to God's call and peculiarly informed in his life and activity by the presence of the Spirit. Others so describe the *way* Jesus shared our humanity and embodied the divine as to accent his difference from ourselves. But much as we emphasize the work of God in and through Jesus, we do not do so in a way that denies or belittles God's work in and through others.

At the general level of theological interaction it helps also that there is an increasing number of thoughtful Jews who now view Jesus and Paul in a positive light. These founders of our faith do not become central figures for these Jews, but as they share appreciation they can also share the distinctive historical understanding that they bring from their Jewish tradition. Christians have learned much from them about how Jesus and Paul and the early community of followers can be better understood in the setting of their own time.

The traditional Christian approach to the theological status of Judaism has been through the covenants with God. Christians have affirmed that God made a covenant with the Jews. They have also asserted that there is a new covenant with those who follow Jesus, whether they are Jews or Gentiles. The question has been how the new covenant relates to the old. Christians have often taught that it supersedes the old, rendering invalid the claims of those who hold to the old. This view has led to denying salvation to Jews and to efforts to convert them. When it has been combined with blaming Jews for Jesus' crucifixion, it has led to pogroms and prepared the way for the Holocaust, or Shoah.

Most of the major branches of the Christian church have now repudiated the supersessionist view and also the idea that the Jewish people are responsible for Jesus' execution by the Roman government. The validity of the covenant between God and Israel is unaffected by the new covenant. Each community has its particular opportunities and challenges, and each is chosen or elected to live out of its covenant.

Some Jewish thinkers are able to take pride in the way that, through Christianity (and later Islam), much of their heritage has taken root in large parts of the world. They may be even more sensitive than progressive Christians to the distortions that various forms of Christianity have embodied. But from their point of view, as from ours, Christianity and Judaism can be seen as sister traditions, each of which has made significant contributions and both of which have the resources to make others. At this point the strictly theological problems entailed in this relationship can achieve a fairly happy resolution without diminution of the distinctiveness of either community.

However, today we recognize a particular problem that threatens the progress we have made in mutual understanding and appreciation. The millennia-long persecution of Jews at our hands has left many of them feeling that we Christians cannot be trusted. They know that very few Christians truly and deeply understand what the experience of the Shoah meant to the global Jewish community. Unfortunately, however committed we personally are to never allowing Christian anti-Judaism a foothold in the church, and however clear the official statements of our churches now are, it is difficult for us to know whether, as a whole, we Christians are now truly worthy of Jewish trust. This lack of trust leads many Jews to intense concern to have their own secure country where they are always welcome. Progressive Christians understand this desire, and we unequivocally support the existence of the state of Israel.

Now we find ourselves in an acute bind. Even at best, the establishment of a Jewish state in Palestine could not have occurred without a high price being paid by Palestinians for the sins of Europeans and Euro-Americans. Most Christians, including liberal ones, underestimated this cost from the beginning. Regrettably, the mutual animosities engendered by the way the new state was established have brought about levels of suffering on the part of the Palestinians that few foresaw. Of course, the Palestinians and neighboring Arab states are not innocent bystanders in the terrible events that have occurred in Israel/Palestine. But the Palestinians are basically victims of American policies, and the injustices inflicted on them are often magnified by the decisions of Israel itself.

We continue to affirm unequivocally that the Jewish people have the right to a state, and we understand and respect something of the intensity of their concern for its security. But we also affirm the aspirations of the Palestinian people and the depth of their resentment of losing their homes, their livelihood, and their dignity, as well as members of their families. Too often our government's support of the policies of the government of Israel leads to further, unnecessary suffering of the Palestinian people. That form of support we oppose.

In one sense, this is a quite separate question from our relation to Judaism as a sister Abrahamic tradition. But for many Jews the centrality of Torah includes the centrality of God's gift of the whole of the land we call Palestine to the Jews. It is then difficult for these Jews to distinguish our criticisms of the policies of the government of Israel, aimed at realizing that gift, from the Christian attacks on Judaism under which they have suffered so long. Our criticisms heighten their suspicion that we are not to be trusted, that underlying our apparent repentance is continuing anti-Judaism. This problem is intensified because most Jews understand the recent history in Israel/

Palestine in ways that give extensive moral justification to actions of the Jewish state that many progressive Christians condemn. Accordingly, in their ears our criticisms sound biased.

Accordingly, progressive Christians are caught between two evils. There is the evil of silence in the face of massive injustice to Palestinians, much of it supported and even financed by our government. There is the evil of heightening Jewish anxiety that their Christian friends cannot be trusted and thereby driving them to more stringent efforts to safeguard their new state, often at still greater cost to Palestinians.

Fortunately, there are many Jews who are deeply concerned for justice to the Palestinian people and who believe that the most hopeful future for Israel lies in generosity to those who have paid the price for making the state of Israel possible. Perhaps our role is largely offering support to this segment of the Jewish community.

Islam

The challenge of Islam is similar with respect to Christology, but it differs in other ways. Muhammad was aware of Jesus and of Christianity. If it had not seemed to him that the doctrine of the Trinity undermined the unity of God, and that the doctrine of incarnation turned Jesus into a deity, he might have accepted Christianity. As it was, he remained generous toward Christians. Also, the Qur'an presents Jesus in exalted ways. The Sufis were freed by this appreciation of Jesus to give him an important role in their form of Islam.

Muslims feel that they have built on Christianity and gone beyond it. If being a Christian in fact entailed tri-theism and treating the human Jesus as if he were a separate God, progressive Christians would agree that the Qur'an's insistence on the unity of God and the humanity of Jesus were gains. I have explained that for progressive Christians, the form of Christianity rejected by Muhammad is a distortion. As we agree with Jews that Jesus was not the messiah they had reason to expect; so we may agree with Muslims that some common Christian formulations of Christology have seriously threatened the unity and uniqueness of the one whom Jesus addressed as "abba." But just as the acknowledgment of the justification for the rejection of Jesus as messiah does not settle the deeper issues that divide us from Judaism, so also the acknowledgment of Muhammad's good reasons for rejecting the distorted form of Christianity he encountered does not go far to settle the issues that have separated Christians and Muslims through the subsequent centuries.

Christians have often compared Jesus and Muhammad, much to the disadvantage of Muhammad. On this basis they have judged that Islam fell back from the heights to which Christianity had arisen. But this comparison does not do justice to the issue.

First, although Muhammad is much admired by Muslims, Islam does not claim that he is the incarnation of God or that his person is the final revelation of God. He is not even the center of history. Muslims understood that through him, God revealed the divine will for humanity in the writings that became the Qur'an. The supernaturalism that is too often part of the Christian description of Jesus pertains, in Islam, not to Muhammad but to the Qu'ran. Progressive Christians cannot follow such ideas, and we hope that the tendencies now developing toward historical criticism of the Qur'an will flower. We do not believe that authentic Islam depends any more on treating the Qur'an as supernatural than authentic Christianity depends on such treatment of Jesus.

Second, Christians should consider seriously the Muslim claim that Muhammad is the culmination or "seal" of the prophets. Since Jesus also plays the role of prophet, this is a clear claim to superiority. Just as Christians for many centuries claimed to supersede Israel; so Islam, at least implicitly, claims to supersede Christianity. Rather remarkably Muslims have not acted as badly on their supersessionist claims toward Christianity as Christians did on theirs toward Judaism. But, however kindly the manner of the claim, Christians cannot accept it. Jesus is not, in our view, superseded by a greater prophet.

Indeed, many Christians balk at considering Muhammad a prophet at all. For us, in general, the prophets are those like Nahum, Amos, Jeremiah, and Isaiah, who spoke truth to power. Jesus represents for Christians the culmination of *this* prophetic tradition. It is not clear that Muhammad belongs in this list at all.

But there is another way of thinking of the prophets. For many Jews, Moses is the greatest of the prophets and David also counts as such. In other words, the greatest prophets may be those who led the people in battle and governed them, as well as taught them. It can be argued that the true spiritual leaders must show how the whole of life is to be lived, and that includes its political and even military dimensions. In Christian communities, there are governments and wars, but Christians differ drastically on how to relate Jesus' message to these major characteristics of history. Moses and Muhammad, on the other hand, not only brought God's law to the people but also defended them, led them, and ruled them justly.

This difference in the roles of Jesus and Muhammad points to a deep difference between Christianity and Islam. Jesus is a source of ideals that judge all human societies, calling for a realm that can never be fully realized in this world. Muhammad aimed to make this world better even by force of arms. The history of Christian thought includes all sorts of reflection relating the teaching of Jesus to the realities of political and military life. Islam has the example of one who embodied the connection. This involved actions that we cannot associate with Jesus. But these are actions of the sort that rulers, including admired Christian rulers, perform.

Which is better? For those of us for whom Jesus is central, the former is better. We progressive Christians are committed to living in the tension between the ideal embodied and taught by Jesus and the demands of life in this sinful world. We find the revelation of God's purpose for the world in Jesus rather than in the political and military actions of Moses and Muhammed.

However, we must acknowledge that the struggle to relate Jesus' teaching to life in the real world has been a difficult and perplexing one and that the results have been highly ambiguous. For those who look to Muhammad as the greatest of the prophets, the relation between teaching and practice is much closer and more immediately realizable. Surely both have their advantages – and their problems and limitations. Progressive Christians can understand and appreciate the preference for a political and military figure, even if we cannot share it.

Even though Jesus' message gave very little guidance for the ordering of ongoing society, Christians long believed that it was incumbent upon them to Christianize all aspects of their lives and their society. This was true through the Reformation and even into the early part of the modern epoch. But it was also possible to think of Jesus' message as dealing with only certain dimensions of life, leaving business, professions, government, and the military outside its purview. In recent generations, most Western Christians have allowed secular thinkers and practitioners to take over most of this territory.

In Islam we are confronted with a community that has retained characteristics that were once those of Christianity as well. The secular world objects strongly to a religious institution that claims all of life as its province. Many contemporary Christians are likewise disturbed. Progressive Christians are disturbed by some of laws and practices that are imposed when a country is organized on traditional Islamic principles. Christian leaders made serious mistakes. The church claimed too much authority, and its power corrupted it. Secularization has brought gains as well as losses. The situation in Islam reminds us of both the strengths and the failures of our own past. We do not want to return to that past, and we see many problems in contemporary Islamic practice.

Nevertheless, progressive Christians see something positive in this understanding of a religious tradition. It has the potential of a unified vision that orders life to the service of God and the world instead of to wealth and power. We have moved to a stance of resistance toward much of modern culture, and we see Islam as also resisting much that needs to be resisted. That it also resists much that we believe to be desirable is also true. Once again, we can recognize profound differences. We continue deeply committed to living in the tension brought into the world by Jesus. We respect and appreciate those who follow different paths. In encountering them we can be inspired to find new ways of resistance in our own tradition.

Buddhism

In the highly diverse world of the past fifty years, there has been a major movement from the traditional religious communities to the secular world. Many people seem to feel no need for the sort of life-orientation provided by these communities. On the other hand, many people are hungry for religious communities that provide more of a shelter from the secular world than do the old-line Protestant churches, and mega-churches and some very conservative forms of evangelical Protestantism have benefited. There are other seekers who are more concerned for spiritual depth in their personal lives, and some of these turn to one or another of the religious traditions. Probably the largest beneficiary in the West of the recent resurgence of a private spiritual quest has been Buddhism, especially in its Zen and Tibetan forms. Among converts to Buddhism are many former Christians.

For a century or so, those seeking to pursue an inner journey could find extensive resources in mainstream Protestantism. At one level there were the disciplines of regular church attendance, family devotions, and private

Bible-reading and prayer. At another level, this private prayer could move into mystical depths. However, in the second half of the twentieth century, the formal disciplines of frequent church attendance and family devotions markedly declined, and those who pursued spiritual disciplines were left largely to their own resources.

At the same time, many people became aware that in other religious traditions the individual pursuit of spiritual depth had been richly developed. This had been far more central to the life of India than in the West. China also has produced profound forms of spirituality. As Americans studied the traditions of Southern and Eastern Asia, they discovered that there were ways of being religious quite different from the Abrahamic ones. Representative teachers of these other traditions came to the United States and found enthusiastic reception. After a century of Christian missions to the non-Christian world, the tide turned.

In countries where these other traditions have long been practiced, they have many accretions that prevent them from being very attractive to seekers in those countries. Among Buddhist immigrants from Japan to the United States, there remains a close connection between Buddhism and Japanese culture. But as Japanese and Tibetan missionaries bring Buddhism to the United States, where Christianity suffers from its own cultural accretions, they often offer a Buddhism that is relatively free at least from the more distorting historical accretions it had acquired in their home countries. For example, the close connection between Buddhism and funerals and memorial services, so important to Buddhism in Japan, has not been part of the Buddhism brought to the United States by Japanese Buddhist missionaries. Zen missionaries took the forms of meditation now practiced in Japan mainly by monks and adapted them to Euro-American lay people. Thus the spiritual disciplines that they offer can be experienced in their purity. They can accomplish much for their practitioners and often quite richly reward their quest.

In presenting a culture-transcending religious practice, Buddhism has a great advantage over Christianity. A practice such as Zen meditation is wordless and seeks to weaken the influence of language on the practitioner. Christian worship is full of words that cannot be separated from their historical use and meaning. Christianity, which understands Jesus as the incarnation of the word of God, has no wordless core. The Christian focus on Jesus cannot separate him from his cultural context, or if it does, it reimages him in another cultural context. As a historical tradition, Christianity can develop in many different cultures, but it can only exist in cultural forms. Hence, Western Christian missionaries have inevitably presented a gospel that has been enculturated. What they strive for at best is indigenization of the gospel in the host country. This process is far more complex than teaching a meditation technique that is largely separable from the culture in which it has developed.

In this book we have chosen Buddhism as representative of the spiritual traditions of South and East Asia, and have dealt especially with its Japanese form. We do not claim that the challenge to Christianity coming from Buddhism is the only one posed by this large family of traditions. Far from it. However, Zen Buddhism serves well as an example of the sort of challenge and stimulus to new thought that the religious traditions of India and East Asia offer.

Progressive Christians have great appreciation for Buddhism. We admire those who practice Buddhist meditational disciplines faithfully and judge that they benefit from these. We recognize that our churches in general have not developed comparable disciplines. We know that we have much to learn. We are glad that Christians can practice these disciplines while remaining Christian.

The challenge of Buddhism is severe for those who think of Christianity as "a religion" and of religion as "spiritual practice." Where those assumptions are in place, it is clear that Christianity does not measure up. Conversion to Buddhism is the appropriate move. But progressive Christians do not understand Christianity in this way.

Christianity certainly has a "religious" dimension and recognizes that people benefit from regular participation in spiritual practices. But the heart of Christianity is discipleship to Jesus. Jesus' message includes encouragement to pray—and specifically to pray for the coming of the divine commonwealth, which is central to Jesus' proclamation. As disciples we are called to bring into being communities in which, in some measure, that commonwealth is realized and to extend it as we can to more and more of life and society. Spiritual disciplines are to be evaluated according to their contribution to this goal. On this basis, the evaluation of Zen is mixed.

The Buddhist claim, and certainly the Zen one, is that enlightenment leads to wisdom and compassion. To whatever extent this happens, Buddhist meditation certainly contributes to the Christian goal. But the spiritual depth attainable by Zen meditation does not have much to do with historical under-standing or social analysis. Zen was practiced by samurai in order to improve their skill as swordsmen. Musicians find that it enhances their skills. This is all fine in itself. But in general, the purposes for which Zen is practiced are not determined by Buddhist teaching or meditational styles. Progressive Christians define themselves largely by the purpose of following Jesus.

This is not to say that the effects of Zen practice are entirely neutral. Many psychotherapists have found that it is highly beneficial for their patients. Yagi testifies to how it freed him from useless and destructive guilt. Its personal effects enable people to retain their equanimity and inner peace regardless of what is transpiring externally. But Zen practice does not of itself lead to critical response to those events. Even the greatest Zen masters in Japan gave considerable support to the militarization of Japan and its imperial efforts.

In China, Korea, and Japan, Buddhism has generally been given a lim-ited niche and not looked to for comprehensive guidance. Accordingly it has not developed a social ethics or guidelines for national policies. Fortunately, through the dialogue with Christians, this situation is changing. Future gen-erations of Zen leaders may offer a much broader vision for their followers.

The examples of Buddhist use of meditation that progressive Christians are likely to find most attractive come from South Asia, where Buddhists have been more closely related to political power and action. The remark-able Buddhist activist Sulak Sivaraksa of Thailand has organized Buddhists internationally under the heading of "socially-engaged Buddhism." This is a group with which progressive Christians can partner with enthusiasm. In Sri Lanka, Sri Ariyaratne has envisioned a healthy future for his country, and especially for the rural villages, based on traditional values deeply influenced by Buddhism. He has many followers who work in these villages in ways that progressive Christians can only regard as highly positive. Before going to their work, they spend several hours in meditation. The goal is to prevent egoism from distorting what they do. Any of us who have worked in justice-oriented groups can recognize the need to deal with the desire for power or for appreciation or for self-justification.

Both Christians and Buddhists seek to overcome egoism, understood as self-centeredness and selfishness. There is certainly much overlap in their concerns, and Christians can highly appreciate and admire the spirit and attitude of many Buddhists. However, Buddhist and Christian strategies are different. To risk oversimplifying it, Buddhist practices are designed to *overcome* the self or to enable one to recognize that there is no self. Christian practices are designed to overcome the *centrality* of the self.

From the Buddhist point of view, the Christian approach seems somewhat superficial, and many Christians agree to this appraisal. However, the Christian approach has immediate and direct social effects. Central to Christian teaching is that we should love others as we love ourselves. This does not eradicate the self, but it directs both feelings and actions away from preoccupation with oneself. Of course, there are many "others," and growth in love is both in the quality of the relation and in the breadth of extension. That we are also to love God completely implies that the extension of love to God's creatures should be universal. Christian spiritual disciplines are likely to focus on self-examination with respect to motives and actions.

The emphasis on difference should not lead to underestimating the similarity of results. If the self is overcome, and if that results in complete nondefensive openness to all, this leads to universal compassion. The universal, nondiscriminatory compassion toward which Buddhism moves and the universal concern for the well-being of others toward which Christianity moves have a great deal in common. But that does not mean that they are identical.

The situation is different with respect to the understanding of what is thought of as ultimate in the two traditions. Buddhists identify their ultimate as Buddha nature, emptiness, or *dharmakaya*—or *pratitya samutpada*, which is sometimes translated as "dependent origination." It is beyond all characterization, demanding nothing, favoring nothing, affected by nothing. It is, of course, not "a thing," and can be described simply as "nothing." Zen teachers usually called it "emptiness." Masao Abe often renamed it "emptying" in order avoid the notion that it has any sort of substantive existence. It is instead the ongoing process of ridding one's experience of given content so as to be completely open to whatever presents itself. In India, it replaced Brahman and Atman, which were usually depicted as the underlying substance of all things and the underlying substance of the self. Buddhists asserted that nothing underlies the flow of events. These events are all instances of dependent origination, that is, new events coming into being out of old ones.

This may all be true, and Buddhists have shown that the existential realization of oneself as an instance of such origination, lacking all substantial existence, can have profound positive effects. But this is not what is meant by "God" in the Jewish, Christian, or Muslim scriptures. Buddha nature is "beyond" any distinction between good and evil, right and wrong, better and worse. The God spoken of in the scriptures of the Abrahamic traditions transcends conventional notions of right and wrong, but remains very much concerned with the deeper meaning of these distinctions. Paul's concern is with the *true* nature of righteousness, and his emphasis on freedom from the law in no way implies lack of concern for the righteousness at which the law aims.

Again, it is important to emphasize that Buddhism's ultimate transcendence of involvement in the world of moral judgment and decision does not lead to less moral behavior. It does lead to less focus on questions of morality. Buddhist psychological analyses are richer and more useful to psychologists than anything found in the Christian tradition. But Buddhists have not given equal attention to the analysis of morality. The universal compassion in which enlightenment results expresses itself in spontaneous acts benefiting others rather than in calculations that balance good and bad consequences of a particular course of action or in obedience to a priori principles.

This is not to say that Christian history knows nothing of the enlightenment of which Buddhists speak. But the roots of that kind of understanding and experience are to be found chiefly in Neoplatonism. This was admired and appropriated by many Christians, much as Buddhism is now admired and appropriated. But the mysticism of the *via negativa* is evaluated by the church from the perspective shaped by the Bible, with its central focus on a God who is closely bound up with judgments of right and wrong. Those, such as Meister Eckhart and Paul Tillich, who focus their attention on the God or Godhead who is beyond the God of the Bible do not speak for the mainstream of the church, whose worship cannot be understood in those terms. Worship and prayer are far more characteristic of Christian practice than the attempt to empty oneself through disciplined meditation.

In the traditions of India and China there is room for both God and an ultimate such as Buddha nature or Brahman. In the West, Thomas Aquinas developed the notion of Being Itself, but to avoid a duality of ultimates, he tried to identify God and Being Itself. Meister Eckhart recognized their difference and distinguished them by calling Being Itself the Godhead. Unfortunately, Christians in general have hesitated to accept a clear distinction of this sort. In the twentieth century, Martin Heidegger emphasized that Being as such cannot be God, while leaving open the possibility that there is also God. Paul Tillich and John Macquarrie renewed the identification proposed by Aquinas, but whereas in his writings this often means attributing to Being

Itself the characteristics associated with God, they identify God with Being Itself, while recognizing that this means freeing "God" of these biblical and traditional characteristics.

Progressive Christians differ in these matters. But in general they are open to the reality of what mystics of the negative way teach us and of that to which Buddhists point us. We do not believe that affirming a primary concern for God and our relation to God exclude this recognition. But we do not abandon our interest in the God of justice and of love proclaimed by the Hebrew prophets and by Jesus. We appreciate the value to be found in realizing the ultimate nature of ourselves as instances of Being Itself or of dependent origination, but for us this is not central.

Fortunately, within Buddhism as well there is some recognition of another reality besides the wholly characterless one of which I have spoken. In the Mahayana form of Buddhism, in addition to *dharmakaya*, there is also *sambhogakaya*. That is, in addition to Buddha-nature simply in and of itself, there is Buddha-nature *for us*. Whereas the former is beyond all characterization whatsoever, the latter is characterized by wisdom and compassion. Whereas some forms of Buddhism, such as Zen, are condescending toward those who look religiously to the *sambhogakaya,* other forms of Buddhism think that Buddha *for us* is supremely important *for us*.

Buddha for us has much of the character of the one whom Jesus called *abba*. Buddha nature as it relates to us is infinitely wise and compassionate. The Bodhisattvas who represent it, give themselves wholly to our enlightenment. We can turn ourselves to them for help. Among Buddhist denominations in Japan, Jodoshinshu, or the Pure Land denomination, especially emphasizes that we are enlightened only through a power not ourselves. Its message is enlightenment by grace through faith rather than as an achievement of personal discipline. Buddhists do not use "God" as the way of identifying this gracious reality, but the parallels between some forms of Buddhism and some forms of mainstream Christianity are close, just as the parallels between other forms of Buddhism and forms of Christianity informed by Neoplatonism are also close.

Native American Spirituality

In every part of the world, human beings once functioned as one animal species among others. Of course they functioned quite distinctively because of their extraordinary capacities to use tools and weapons and their ability to communicate linguistically in very complex ways. But for hundreds of thousands of years they lived with other species on an Earth that supplied their needs. They moved in limited geographical areas with a keen awareness of the landscape, of the biota, and of the seasons. Their cultures, including the more recognizably religious aspects of these cultures, reflected these relationships and expressed reverence for the nature that nurtured them.

This deep feeling of kinship and reverence has persisted among some indigenous people to the present. In the United States it survives among Native Americans. But what we generally call "civilization" is closely connected with a progressive alienation from the land. The other animals are viewed as subordinate creatures to be managed and exploited for our human benefit and enjoyment. Attachment to particular landscapes came to be regarded as sentimental in the belittling sense of that term. The land is viewed as space to be occupied and as providing natural "resources" for the human economy.

There is a long history of how this change came about—a history we cannot rehearse here—and some elements of connection to other creatures and to the land remain in everyone. But there is no question but that there was a profound difference in these respects between the indigenous people of what is now the United States and the European invaders. The latter saw the natives' failure to tame the wilderness and build cities as showing that they were "uncivilized." The fact that they lived with the other creatures *within* nature rather than dominating and exploiting nature meant that they were not fully human. Since they did not "own" the land, they could be forced to move off of it so that civilized people could use it. Belden C. Lane provides a fine statement of the consequences:

> In much of Jewish and Christian theology, the freedom of the transcendent God of history has regularly been contrasted with the false and earthbound deities of fertility and soil. God has been removed from the particularity of place, extracted from the natural environment. Hence, the tendency in Western civilization has been toward the triumph of history over nature, time over space, male dominance over female dependence, and technical mastery of the land over a gentle reverence for life. In this artificial schema, God has often been viewed as a Lord of times but not of places—involved in mighty acts but not

so much in the quiet energies of creation. The result has been rampant secularization of nature and activism of spirit in Western life, leaving us exhausted in our mastery of a world stripped of magic and mystery.[1]

The natives, on the other hand, were appalled at the total irreverence of the Europeans toward the land. They suffered immensely at the hands of the Europeans partly because of their views of civilization and the practices that flowed from these. But even beyond their own interests, they saw that the forms of "civilized" exploitation of the land were unsustainable, that in the end the Europeans would destroy themselves. Today it has become clear that they were correct, and we can only appreciate their continuing efforts to point us in a different direction. We can only marvel that after centuries of appalling mistreatment, often amounting to genocide, the heirs of indigenous traditions can still seek to help Euro-Americans find a way forward.

As progressive Christians we want and need to listen carefully to what indigenous people tell us. Their proposals are couched in terms of the distinction between basic orientation to time and basic orientation to space. There is no question that the invaders of North America and those who drove the natives repeatedly off of their land were overwhelmingly oriented temporally rather than spatially. Even among Europeans they were the ones who were most ready to turn away from the familiar landscapes of their homes in search of better lives in a new land. They were the Americans who were most willing to leave the settled areas of the East to move West to "tame" more land.

But the matter before us is not simply the self-selection of the least settled Europeans to face and destroy the indigenous peoples of this continent. Whether as individuals most of them were Christian is another question, but all of them had been shaped by a Christian culture. That culture supported, and even celebrated, their willingness to leave the established civilization to subdue other regions and add them to Christendom. And Christian teaching accepted and even nourished these views. It was time-oriented.

This can be seen in many ways. Christians often understood themselves to be pilgrims on this Earth. This world was not their true home. That home, Heaven, was their destination. Attachment to the particularities of this Earth was not encouraged.

The Bible itself is organized in a temporal way, beginning with the creation of this earth and ending in a new heaven and a new earth. Much of it is devoted to the history if Israel. Israel's religious leaders interpreted the present in terms of what had happened in the past. Of course, this past was "mythical" in a broad sense, but the stories were told in a way that gave them a meaningful sequence. Most of them did not begin with "once upon a time." One can reconstruct the sequence of historical events as they were understood in Israel, and much of this overall account still fits the best we know about history today. Christians understand themselves as heirs to this long history mediated through Jesus and Paul. The further history of the missionary enterprise and the establishment of the church is important for later Christian self-understanding. Progressive Christians understand ourselves to be heirs of all that history, and to be called to rethink our faith in view of the ever-changing historical situation. We are as deeply immersed in the time dimension as any Christians have been. Being "progressive" only deepens the importance for us of our historical consciousness.

If Native Americans were now calling us to abandon our time-orientation in favor a space orientation, we would not be able to respond. It is precisely our historical consciousness that now enables us to see the terrible mistakes we have made and to begin the long and difficult process of repentance. We are open to the wisdom of our Native American friends for historical reasons. We keenly regret that it has taken us so long to recognize the profundity of their understanding.

Our historical consciousness now enables us to see that there is no necessary conflict between historical consciousness and spatial orientation. Indeed, the Bible provides us an example of synthesis. The historical consciousness of Israel did not reduce the attachment to the land that Israel had, through historical events, been given. Indeed, historical consciousness was important to the return to the land on two occasions. It is important today.

One way in which ancient empires controlled conquered people was to carry the leaders into exile, that is, to separate them from their familiar landscape. In many instances within a generation or two they ceased to identify with their ancestral homes. But life in Babylon did not weaken the attachment of the Hebrew exiles to Jerusalem. They retained the attachment through their historical memories. Again, Rome exiled many Jews from Palestine in the second century c.e. Most Jews lived elsewhere for eighteen centuries. But they did not forget the land.

These historical facts suffice to show that time- and space-orientation can belong together in mutually reinforcing ways. But it does not provide an altogether positive model for Christians. Our sense of the Holy Land led

Christian armies to fight Muslims for centuries to gain control. Finally to have abandoned the religious need for such control was surely a gain. The religious passion for the land of Israel on the part of contemporary Jews leads to profoundly unjust treatment of the previous inhabitants.

In European history, the shift of primacy from Christian faith to nation states has been accompanied by a renewed emphasis on the motherland or the fatherland. History has not been ignored, but national leaders often emphasize the close connection to the land. People are roused to fury by the sense that alien forces are on their sacred soil. The consequences have often been terrible.

Clearly space-orientation in itself does not solve the problems brought about by time-orientation. We must consider the different forms of both. The time-orientation cultivated by progressive Christians is geared to enabling us to recognize our past mistakes and crimes and to be open to new ways of expressing our discipleship. We need that type of time-orientation if we are to learn from the wisdom of indigenous people. The space-orientation we need is one that is immersed in the land and its biota without a special focus on who the people are who should be sharing that land with the other creatures. This orientation leads to concern for the land for its own sake rather than for its possession by one group or another.

Since the 1970s Christians have been looking at the Bible with new questions. We have noticed that it addresses the issue that now confronts us. In the first creation story, God sees that the land and its biota are good quite apart from any human presence. In the second story, the role of human beings is to tend the garden. When human sin causes God to send a great flood, God makes provision for saving not only human beings as a species but all the other animal species as well. God's care for all the creatures is celebrated. All living things praise God. Human beings are an especially wonderful part of a good creation for which we also have particular responsibilities.

The limitation of the theology drawn from these themes is that it remains detached from particular landscapes or localities. The indigenous thinkers show us how we can be universal *and* particular, in that they affirm that wherever people are they should truly inhabit the particular land where they find themselves. As we have seen, this note is prominent in the Bible with respect to Jerusalem and the land of Israel. Christians need to transfer those feelings to whatever piece of the Earth they inhabit, without giving up the general conviction that every part of the Earth glorifies God.

Because we are so time-oriented, we need to retell our history. The histories we have inherited, already from the Bible, tend to treat the land chiefly as the location of human action. But there is a deeper history—the history of the Earth and its creatures. This also appears in the Bible, but it has been almost entirely dropped in later historical thinking. It has just begun to reappear in recent years.[3]

Perhaps the most important achievement to date is that of Thomas Berry and Brian Swimme in *The Universe Story*. Locating ourselves in the context of that story leads to the recognition that the changes human beings are causing on the planet are analogous to those that mark the great geological ages of the past. Berry and Swimme locate us (hopefully) at the beginning of the ecozoic age. This account has moved tens of thousands of people to re-envision themselves and to begin to live in terms of what Thomas Berry calls the "Great Work."

This broad sweep is being supplemented here and there by histories of culture and religion that show how these are shaped by changing natural conditions, many of which, in turn, are the result of human action. Anand Veeraraj has contributed to this work in his *Green History of Religion*, which gives special attention to developments in ancient Mesopotamia. We need also histories of local areas in which the land and its life are co-present with human action.

In short, the way ahead for progressive Christians does not lie in finding a compromise between space-orientation and time-orientation. We are committed to time. But if we deepen our understanding of history so that it ceases to abstract human beings from the rest of the world, if we tell our story in such a way as to see how our acts change the land and the landscape and how the changes of land and landscape profoundly change us, we will, through our time-consciousness, redevelop a strong space-consciousness. This process has already begun, forced upon us by awareness of the ecological crisis. This crisis has prepared us to listen with great seriousness to the wisdom of indigenous people, and especially to those from whom we Euro-Americans took the land we now claim as "ours."

Conclusion

Progressive Christians know that we have much for which to repent. Future church historians may view the last decades of the twentieth century as the time of repentance. On a remarkably large scale, the churches have begun to free themselves from their anti-Jewish teachings, from their anti-sexual teachings, from their exclusivism, from their patriarchalism, and from their anthropocentrism. Progressive Christians view these and other forms of repentance as working together to bring into being a form of Christianity that is more faithful to Jesus. On all these fronts we have a long way to go. Perhaps the last is the one on which we have the farthest yet to go and is, at the same time, the most urgent of all. We are greatly helped by interacting with those who have preserved the wisdom that we lost long ago and who are still willing and able to share.

A new book by two progressive Protestant women is richly suggestive of where our historical consciousness may now lead us. *Saving Paradise*, by Rita Nakashima Brock and Rebecca Parker, shows us that for the first millennium of its life the focus of Christianity was on the possibility and reality of paradise in this world. Whereas the language of "divine commonwealth," by which we have translated the *basileia theou* proclaimed by Jesus, highlights human relationships, "paradise" locates them fully within the wider natural context, and this context appears in early Christian art. The Christians who proclaimed paradise, and who found something of paradise in their world and especially in their churches, were not ignorant of evil or free of suffering, but they attended to what expressed God's presence in the world. The suffering and dead Jesus did not appear in their art.

In the second millennium, however, especially in the West, the crucified Jesus became central to Christian experience. The world in which Christians lived was viewed in its loss of paradise and its immersion in evil. Brock and Parker write: "In exile and always in search of paradise, Western Christianity has made humanity's location in time and space a problem. Preoccupied with being *lost*, Western souls are anxious for home, for grounding, for meaning, and for escape from present life which can never measure up to our imaginary goals."

They see Western passion for economic growth, colonialism, and imperialism as expressive of this rejection of what is already given. "What we need now is a religious perspective that does not locate salvation in a future endpoint, a transcendent realm, or a zone after death. . . . Histories of harm are all around us, forces of evil operate within and among us, and yet everywhere the bushes are on fire, the risen Christ is with us on the road, the Spirit rises in the wind, the rivers of Paradise circle the earth, and the fountain of wisdom springs up from the earth we tread, from this holy ground."[2]

Glossary

Abrahamic Religions. Judaism, Christianity, and Islam. All give a prominent role to Abraham (Ibrahim); as such, they are often collectively termed as the Abrahamic Religions.

Adversus Judaeos literature. The body of early Christian writings depicting Jews as rejected by God.

Agnostic. A person who does not think that human beings can have knowledge about the existence or nonexistence of any godhead or gods.

Allah. This is an Arabic word meaning God. Muslims use this term, as do Christian Arabs.

Animism. A term derived from the Latin word *anima*, meaning breath or soul. Animism is the belief that natural objects and phenomena are spirit-filled.

Anthropocentrism. A cultural/religious orientation that puts human beings first and foremost above all other considerations.

Atheist. A person who does not believe in any godhead or gods.

Bahá'í. The Bahá'í faith is a monotheistic religion founded in nineteenth-century Persia (Iran).

Bible. The sacred collection of scriptures recognized as "holy" by Jews and Christians. However, Christians define and interpret the Bible differently than Jews, and within Christianity, Catholics and Protestants define the

Bible differently. No one translation of the Christian Bible is universally regarded among Christians as authoritative.

Bodhisattva. An enlightened being in Buddhism, who out of compassion forgoes nirvana in order to save others.

Brahma. A mortal creator god associated with the two major personal godhead representations of Hinduism: Shiva and Vishnu.

Brahman. The name given to the impersonal universal godhead of Hinduism influenced by the **Upanishads** (see below). Though similar to Brahma, Brahman means something completely different.

Brahmanism. The religious practices and beliefs of ancient India as reflected in the Vedas, ancient holy scriptures in Hinduism.

Brahmin. A member of the highest caste in Hinduism.

Caliph. A successor to the Prophet Muhammad. The last caliphate ended with the Ottoman Empire's demise at the end of World War I.

Caste system. There are four major castes in Hinduism that define each individual's dharma, or occupational role.

Church. A religious organization based upon the teachings of Christianity. No one church is universally regarded among Christians as authoritative.

Cosmic Buddhas. Just as the historical Jesus is projected into the unrestricted heavenly realm as the Cosmic Christ, so Mahayana Buddhism projects the historical Siddartha Gautama into the unrestricted heavens as multiple Cosmic Buddhas. Several principal Cosmic Buddhas are Amida Buddha and Maitreya.

Covenant. A binding spiritual contract between two parties. In Judaism, the special relationship between God and the Jewish people. In Christianity, the special relationship between God and the People of God.

Decalogue. The 10 Commandments appearing in Exodus 20.

Deicide. The killing (murder) of God. This accusation was leveled by Christians against Jews for centuries and became one of the major elements in Christian anti-Judaism and systematic persecution.

Diaspora. The body of Jews (or Jewish communities) outside Palestine or modern Israel.

Eightfold Path. A Buddhist disciplined regimen that is designed to assist the seeker in finding enlightenment. This path recommends restricting behavior, speech, and ultimately thought processes in clearing away ignorance.

Enlightenment, the. An intellectual movement in Western civilization in the eighteenth century C.E. that emphasized individual liberty, equality of individual rights, and rationality over tradition.

Eschatology. A branch of theology concerning the end of historical time. All major world religions have unique and particular claims regarding the end of time.

Exclusivism. A characteristic found in major world religions that claim ultimate truth not to be found elsewhere. Jewish exclusivity is founded upon the 613 laws of the Torah. Christian exclusivity is founded upon the unique nature of Jesus Christ, born of a virgin and resurrected from the grave. Islamic exclusivity is founded upon the Qur'an, regarded by Muslims as the inerrant word of God.

Exile. There have been several major forced exiles of Jews from their homeland. The first involved the Babylonian Captivity in the sixth century B.C.E. Later forced exiles (following the failed Jewish uprisings against Roman authority in 70 C.E. and 135 C.E.) had a long-lasting impact up to modern times.

Filioque Controversy. A theological dispute in Medieval Europe over whether the Holy Spirit proceeds from God the Father and Christ the Son or from the Father only. The Western Church maintained the former, and the Eastern Church the latter dogma.

Five Pillars of Islam. Muslims focus upon behaviors more than belief, suggesting that true belief is reflected in one's behaviors. Five behaviors valued above all others are 1) declaring that there is only one God (Allah) and that Muhammad is his prophet, 2) praying five times daily, 3) fasting during the daylight hours of the month of Ramadan, 4) giving alms to the poor equivalent to 2.5 percent of one's total assets on a yearly basis, and 5) going on at least one pilgrimage to Mecca (where the Ka'ba is located). The Five Pillars help keep Islam a religion defined by regular practices and personal sacrifices.

Four Noble Truths. Buddhist precepts that hold that craving or desire is the source of human suffering, which can be overcome by following the Eightfold Path.

Genocide. The extermination or mass destruction of a community, people, or nation. Also see **Shoah**.

Gentiles. A term first used by Jews for persons who are not Jewish. In modern times, Mormons also use this term for persons who are not Mormons.

Gnosticism. A religious movement occurring in the Near East before, during, and after the life of Jesus. Its adherents claimed to have special religious knowledge (gnosis) about eternal life. Beyond this one tenet in common, gnostic groups were quite dissimilar in understandings.

Gospel. A Christian term meaning the "good news" of Jesus Christ. The first four books of the Christian New Testament are collectively called Gospels.

Guru. A Hindu, Sikh, or Buddhist religious and spiritual teacher.

Hadith. A body of stories and anecdotes relating to the Prophet Muhammad and his contemporaries. Together with the Qur'an, the Hadith constitute the written sources used to determine Muslim orthodoxy.

Hajj. The annual pilgrimage to the Ka'ba in Mecca. In each Muslim's lifetime, the ideal is to go on this pilgrimage at least once.

Hellenism. The principles and ideals associated with classical Greek civilization.

Hinayana. A derisive term used by Mahayanists, meaning "the small raft," describing an insufficient vehicle for transporting most of humankind to enlightenment. Hinayanists prefer the term Theravada (The Way of the Elders) to describe their own form of Buddhism.

Holocaust. See **Shoah,** below.

Humanism. A belief system that exalts human needs and interests. Its growth since the Renaissance has served to emphasize anthropocentric tendencies within Christianity.

Ijma. Agreement among the learned scholars of Islam, the principle whereby religious beliefs become articles of faith. "My people shall never be unanimous in error," said the Prophet Muhammad.

Ijtihad. In Islamic law, the analysis of problems not covered precisely in the Qur'an, the Hadith, or the scholarly consensus called the ijma'.

Imam. An Arabic word meaning "leader." In Sunni Islam, the Imam is the person who leads Friday prayers, a relatively minor role. In Shi'a, the term Imam is used to refer to a descendent of the Prophet Muhammad who was reported to have gone into occultation (spiritual hiding) and will return at the end of time. Also in Shi'a, a religious leader of especially exalted status—such as the Ayatollah Khomeini, who was thought to be in spiritual communication with the Hidden Imam—can also be called Imam.

Inclusivism. The view that one religion alone is true but that others outside that faith may find God.

Indigenous Religions. A wide variety of human belief systems explaining the origins and meaning of life. Common attributes are the predominance of animistic and polytheistic sensibilities and a close association with Nature and the sentient beings and objects found within it, all of which are deemed alive and interrelated. These religions have their origins before recorded time.

Islamist. An Islamic revivalist movement, often characterized by moral conservatism, literalism, and militant resistance to the current dominance of Western modernism. Often called Islamic Fundamentalism.

Jerusalem. A city that for different reasons is holy to Jews, Christians, and Muslims.

Jesus. A person who for different reasons is holy to both Christians and Muslims.

Jihad. An Arabic word meaning struggle. Islamic resistance to forces hostile to God is seen as fully appropriate and necessary, whether these forces manifest themselves in general society or in the interior of one's own soul. The latter is commonly called the Greater Jihad.

Judaizer. A party of Jewish Christians in the Early Church, who held that circumcision and the observance of the Mosaic Law were necessary for salvation. During the Middle Ages and after, this term was used for Christians who continued to observe some Jewish customs and beliefs (often secretly).

Ka'ba. The cube-shaped building in Mecca that is regarded as the holiest site in all of Islam. It is the object of the annual pilgrimage, and the worship center to which Muslims turn in prayer five times daily.

Koan. A paradoxical riddle or anecdote that has no rational solution. Koans are used in Zen Buddhist meditation as a device to break through the inadequacy of human logic.

Kristallnacht. Often translated as the night of the broken glass, November 9-10, 1938, when synagogues and Jewish-owned businesses throughout Germany and Austria were destroyed and burned, accompanied by the arrest of thousands of Jews. A precursor to the Shoah.

Logos. A Greek term, translated as "word," which the Gospel of John uses to refer to Christ, who was God manifested in the flesh.

Mahayana. A Buddhist term meaning "the large raft." As the most prominent form of Buddhism, Mahayana prides itself in being a large enough raft for all of humankind. It does not require that every seeker of enlightenment become a monk, as does Theravada (Hinayana).

Mandala. A graphic cosmic design used in both Hinduism and Buddhism to focus the mind during meditation.

Mantra. A repeated word or phrase used in both Hinduism and Buddhism to focus the mind during meditation.

Marcion. A second-century Christian philosopher/theologian who taught that the god of the Old Testament is not the true God, and that the Old Testament should be rejected by Christians. His views, though influential during his lifetime, did not prevail, and he was condemned as a heretic.

Messiah. In Judaism, the anticipated leader and liberator of the Jewish People. In Christianity, Jesus Christ.

Modernity. A cultural orientation (associated with Western civilization over the past two centuries) hostile to tradition-dependent values and in favor of accentuating equal human rights, scientific progress, and especially individual freedom.

Monotheism. The belief that there is only one true God.

Mosque. A Muslim temple or place of public worship.

Neoplatonism. A philosophical system originating in the third century c.e., founded chiefly on Platonic doctrine and Eastern mysticism, with later influences from Christianity. **Nirvana.** A Buddhist term meaning "to extinguish." Extinguishing human desire or craving is the highest goal of Buddhism.

Orthodox Judaism. Viewed as the only authentic form of Judaism by those who rigorously follow the 613 laws of the Torah. Today, this form of Judaism has more influence within the state of Israel than any other form. It is criticized by non-Orthodox Jews as encouraging self-segregating practices that prevent Jews from assimilating in non-Jewish countries.

Panentheism. The idea that all things are in God, thus contributing to the divine reality.

Pharisee. A member of an ancient Jewish sect that emphasized strict interpretation and observance of Mosaic law in preparaton for the coming of the Messiah.

Pluralism. The religious belief that all major world religions are equally valid and lead to God.

Pogrom. An organized mass slaughter of a minority, especially of Jews.

Polytheism. A belief in multiple gods.

Pope. The Christian Bishop of Rome. The head of the Roman Catholic Church.

Protestant. A member of a Christian set of churches whose faith and practice are founded on the principles of the Reformation.

Psalm. A sacred song or poem in praise of God, as found in the Bible's Book of Psalms.

Qur'an. Sometimes written as Koran. Literally, it means "recitation." The holy book of Islam consisting of the revelations given by the Angel Gabriel to the Prophet Muhammad.

Reform Judaism. The form of Judaism most widely practiced in the United States. It was established in nineteenth-century Germany in an effort to promote assimilation of Jews into the wider society. It seeks to retain the high ethical tone of Judaism while not adhering to the restrictive nature of Judaism's 613 religious laws.

Reformation, the. The European Christian reform movement that established Protestantism as a major branch of contemporary Christianity.

Righteousness. The quality or condition of being upright, moral, and just.

Roman Catholic. A member of the Christian church that looks to the Vatican for spiritual leadership.

Sabbath. A day of rest and worship: Saturday for Jews; Sunday for most Christians.

Samsara. The endless cycle of birth, suffering, death, and rebirth emphasized in both Hinduism and Buddhism.

Satori. The term used in Zen Buddhism for enlightenment.

Shari'ah. Islamic law. The complete way of living as a Muslim, adaptable in each Muslim community based on the Qur'an and Hadith.

Shekkinah. In Jewish theology, a visible manifestation of the divine presence.

Shi'ite. A follower of the Islamic group known as Shi'a, or literally "the party" of Ali, the fourth Caliph. This version of Islam derives from the early history of the Islamic community and is especially prominent in Iran and Iraq. It emphasizes that true authority in early Islam came from those who were related by blood to the Prophet Muhammad. In most countries, this is a minority view within Islam.

Shintoism. A religion native to Japan, characterized by veneration of nature spirits and ancestors.

Shirk. A Muslim term meaning "association of anything that is not God with God." Idolatry.

Shoah. Hebrew for "catastrophe." The Jewish Holocaust at the hands of the Nazis during World War II.

Shura. Arabic for consultation. In pre-Islamic Arabia, the various tribes selected their leaders and made major decisions after appropriate consultation. The Qur'an requires this in Islam.

Siddartha Gautama. The historical Buddha.

Sikhism. A religion blending Hinduism and Islam that was founded in India during the sixteenth century C.E.

Social Gospel. A Protestant Christian reform movement most prominent in the late nineteenth and early twentieth centuries C.E.

Stupas. Burial shrines for portions of Siddartha Gautama's ashes. Gautama, the historical Buddha, insisted that his followers not worship him but rather seek their own enlightenment. Nevertheless, after his death he has been revered in pilgrimages to numerous stupas located throughout south Asia.

Sufis. Islamic mystics. The word derives from suf (rough wool), as that was the material that the early Sufi ascetics selected for their garments. The Muslim Prophet Jesus is their model.

Sunni. A follower of Sunna, the "beaten path." The overwhelming majority of Muslims worldwide are Sunnis. Unlike Shi'ites, Sunnis find no betrayal in the early government of Islam and believe that Muhammad's intention was not to have blood lineage define authentic leadership within Islam. They emphasize that Muhammad's true intent was to minimize tribal or blood loyalties and instead exalt the Ummah, the entire Muslim community.

Supersessionism. This theological term derives from the Latin *supersedere* (supersede, take the place of, replace) and refers to the early Christian claim that the Jewish rejection of Christ erased the ancient Jewish Covenant with God and made Christians to be the People of God in their stead. Supersessionism is today rejected by most mainline churches.

Synagogue. The place of worship for a Jewish congregation.

Synoptic Gospels. The first three Gospels (Matthew, Mark, and Luke) in the Christian New Testament, that describe the events in Christ's life from a similar point of view, are in contrast to the Gospel of John.

Tao. In Taoism, the Tao is the ultimate reality that is the source of being, non-being, and change.

Temple, the. Refers to a series of Jewish holy structures located on the Temple Mount in the old city of Jerusalem. The last Temple was destroyed in 70 C.E.

Theist. A person who believes in one or more gods.

Theodicy. A theological explanation for human suffering.

Torah. In Hebrew, "teaching" or "law." A term that most specifically refers to the first five books of the Bible, wherein the 613 religious laws are contained. More broadly, the term can also be used to refer to the Jewish Bible as a whole. More broadly still, it can also mean the whole body of the Jewish sacred writings and tradition including the oral tradition.

Trinity. A Christian concept referring to the mysterious union of Father and Son and Holy Ghost in one Godhead.

Ulema. Learned scholars in Muslim tradition and canon law.

Ummah. The Muslim community.

Upanishads. Hindu scriptures, dating from 800 to 599 B.C.E., constituting the culmination of ancient Vedic religion on the Indian subcontinent. The Upanishads encourage the believer to aspire to self-realization through intense meditation about the union between Self and Godhead (Atman/Brahman). This ideal was later nurtured within Buddhism, albeit in ways completely dissimilar to Upanishadic teaching. In contrast to the Upanishads, the Abrahamic religions have generally placed a higher value on changing the world.

Vatican. The Holy See; the central governing body of the Roman Catholic Church, surrounded by Rome and yet a sovereign entity recognized by international law.

Wahhabism. A conservative and highly restrictive version of Islam founded on the Arabian peninsula in the eighteenth century, c.e. The twentieth-century discoveries of immense reserves of petroleum in Saudi Arabia, the area where Wahhabism dominates, has served to propagate Islamic Fundamentalism throughout the world in modern times. Today Wahhabism is one facet of a broader movement called Salafi Islam, Islamic Fundamentalism having its origins in nineteenth century Egypt.

Yin/Yang. An ancient Chinese belief system that instructs that good and evil are not separated but rather are intertwined, with one having no existence or definition without the presence of the other. This philosophy also emphasizes that nothing is good or evil, fortunate or unfortunate, in itself, and that such determinations can only be made within ever-evolving contexts. The fluidity of this system was adopted by Mahayana Buddhism to help break the human mental habit of craving specific outcomes.

Zazen. Seated meditation, the practice that most closely characterizes the discipline of Zen Buddhism.

Zealots. An ancient Jewish sect in Judea that was prominent during the life of Jesus of Nazareth and that fought to the death in the war with Rome that ended in 70 c.e.

Zionism. A policy for establishing and developing a national homeland for Jews in Palestine.

Zoroastrianism. A religion founded by Zoroaster in sixth century b.c.e. Persia (modern-day Iran), emphasizing the struggle between good and evil and an end to history when good will triumph.

Notes

Introduction

1. We explained our understanding of "progressive" Christianity much more fully in the foreword to *Resistance: The New Role of Progressive Christians* (Louisville: Westminster John Knox, 2008).

Chapter One: Rethinking Christian Faith

1. This chapter is the outgrowth of an unusual number of contributions. We acknowledge with special appreciation the assistance of David Chappell, Zayn Kassam, Michael Kuhlwein, and James A. Nelson.

2. Judaism, like other religious traditions, has its system of historical dating. Because the Christian system of Before Christ (B.C.) and Anno Domini (A.D.) is so well established, and since no other system would be more neutral among religious traditions, many who want to overcome triumphalistic Christian rhetoric now propose that we retain use of the familiar dates but describe them differently—as Before the Common Era (B.C.E.) and the Common Era (C.E.).

Chapter Two: Jews and Christians

1. I am indebted for the following account to Dr. Gordon Douglass of Pilgrim Place, a participant in the Claremont Interfaith Exchange from its beginning.

2. See the chart in Raul Hilberg, *The Destruction of the European Jews* (New Haven: Yale University Press, 2003), 5.

3. Rosemary Radford Ruether, *Faith and Fratricide: The Theological Roots of Anti-Semitism* (New York: Crossroads, 1974), 184.

4. Jules Isaac, *The Teaching of Contempt* (New York: Holt, Rinehart and Winston, 1964), 21.

5. James Carroll, *Constantine's Sword* (Boston, New York: Houghton Mifflin, 2001), 272.

6. George Foot Moore, *Judaism*, I (Cambridge: Harvard University Press, 1966), 84.

7. *Homilies 1 and 3*, quoted in Edward H. Flannery, *The Anguish of the Jews* (Mahwah, N.J.: Paulist Press, 1985), 51.

8. *Homilies of the Resurrection*, 5, ibid., 50.

9. *Sermon on the Cross, 3:10,* ibid., 52.

10. See John Chrysostum, *Discourses against Judaizing Christians,* trans. Paul W. Harkins (Fathers of the Church, vol. 68; Wash., D.C.: Catholic University of Am. Press, 1979).

11. *Reply to Faustus,* ibid., 53.

12. Mary Boys, *Has God Only One Blessing? Judaism as a Source of Christian Self-Understanding* (Mahwah, N.J.: Pualist Press, 2000), 161.

13. Ibid., 168, n. 29.

14. Ronald J. Allen and Clark M. Williamson, *Preaching the Gospels without Blaming the Jews, a Lectionary Commentary* (Louisville: Westminster, 2005).

15. Peter the Venerable, quoted in Flannery, *Anguish of the Jews,* 94.

16. Ibid., 101.

17. Cf. Boys, *Has God Only One Blessing?,* for a new version of these ancient symbols.

18. Carroll, *Constantine's Sword,* 323.

19. Ibid.

20. Ruether, *Faith and Fratricide,* 206.

21. See Heiko A. Oberman, *The Roots of Anti-Semitism in the Age of Renaissance and Reformation* (Minneapolis: Fortress Press, 1984).

22. Quoted by Daniel Goldhagen, *Hitler's Willing Executioners,* in Carroll, *Constantine's Sword,* 428.

23. Heiko A. Oberman, *Calvin Studies* VI, 3.

24. Ibid.

25. See the beautiful film on Le Chambon by Pierre Sauvage, "Weapons of the Spirit," and the book by Phillip Hallie, *Lest Innocent Blood Be Shed* (New York: Harper, 1994).

26. Oberman, *Initia Calvini: The Matrix of Calvin's Reformation,* 142. I am indebted for these sources to Jane Douglass of Pilgrim Place, Claremont, CA.

27. Oberman, *Calvin Studies* VI, 3.

28. Comment made at a Jewish-Christian meeting of Catholic and Jewish leaders in Chicago, March 20, 1999; quoted in Carroll, *Constantine's Sword,* 376.

29. See David Kertzer, *The Kidnapping of Edgardo Mortara* (New York: Knopf, 1997).

30. Quoted in Carroll, *Constantine's Sword,* 459.

31. For an extensive account, see Jean-Denis Bredin, *The Affair: The Case of Alfred Dreyfus* (New York: George Braziller, 1986).

32. Elie Wiesel, *Night* (New York: Bantam, 1982), 32.

33. See the chapter by Eva Fleischner, "The Shoah and Jewish-Christian Relations," in *Seeing Judaism Anew,* Mary C. Boys, ed., Sheed and Ward, 2005), 3–14.

34. Guenter Lewy, *The Catholic Church in Nazi Germany* (New York: McGraw Hill, 1964), 264.

35. Michel Marrus and Robert O. Paxton, *Vichy France and the Jews* (New York: Schocken Books, 1983), 201.

36. Cited in Greenberg, "Cloud of Smoke, Pillar of Fire," in Eva Fleischner, ed., *Auschwitz: Beginning of a New Era?* (New York: KTAV, 1977), 11–12.

37. The literature on the rescuers is today voluminous, and still growing. We cite here only one example, the story of the French village of Le Chambon-sur-Lignon already referenced: Philip Hallie, *Lest Innocent Blood be Shed*.

38. Cf. Richard Rubenstein, *The Cunning of History* (Indianapolis: Bobbs Merrill, 1966).

39. Affirmation 7.

40. Krister Stendahl, in "Judaism and Christianity, Romans 2: A Plea for a New Relationship," in *Meanings* (Minneapolis: Fortress Press, 1984), 221.

41. Ibid., 223, italics in original.

42. *New York Times*, 3/27/2000.

43. For a devastating critique of Roman Catholic efforts at reform, see Daniel Goldhagen, *A Moral Reckoning: The Role of the Catholic Church in the Holocaust and its Unfulfilled Duty of Repair* (New York: Knopf, 2002).

44. Mary C. Boys, ed., *Seeing Judaism Anew: Christianity's Sacred Obligation* (Lanham: Sheed and Ward, 2005).

45. Ibid, xiv.

46. Michael S. Kogan, *Opening the Covenant: A Jewish Theology of Christianity* (New York: Oxford, 2008).

47. Ibid., 212.

48. See the *National Catholic Reporter* of 9/19/08 for an article on this issue, and Eva Fleischner's letter to the editor in the *National Catholic Reporter* of 10/17/08.

49. Quoted in "The Spirit Level: Amos Oz Writes the Story of Israel," *New Yorker* (November 8, 2004): 85. All other quotations from Amos Oz are from the same article.

50. In "Spirit Level," 95. See also *Tikkun* 20/1 (Jan/Feb 2005), especially 10.

51. See *Network News* (Fall 2004): 19–21. For the more recent developments (at the time of this writing) see the following: "Divestment: an Exchange," in *Christian Century* (February 8, 2005): 30–38, and "The Divestment Debate," *Tikkun* (Mar/Apr 2005): especially the piece by Michael Lerner (33–35, 38–43).

52. Quoted in Richard Harries, "Israel in Christian Thought," in James Parkes, *End of an Exile: Israel, the Jews, and the Gentile World* (Marblehead: Micah, 252).

53. Ibid., 260.

54. Stendahl, *Meanings*, 229.

55. Ibid., 94.

56. Evangelical Lutheran Church of America, *Talking Points on Jewish-Christian Relations*.

57. Quoted in Eva Fleischner, *Judaism in German Christian Theology* (Metuchen, N.J.: The Scarecrow Press, 1975), 128.

Chapter Three: Islam and Christians

1. Hans Küng et al., *Christianity and World Religions: Paths of Dialogue with Islam, Hinduism, and Buddhism* (Maryknoll: Orbis, 1986), 55–56.

2. Ibid., xiii, xv.

3 Samuel P. Huntington et al., *The Clash of Civilizations? The Debate* (New York: Council on Foreign Relations, 1996), 12.

4. Ibid., 50–52.

5. Aslan, Reza, *No god but God: The Origins, Evolution, and Future of Islam* (New York: Random, 2006).

6. *Los Angeles Times*, July 2, 2005, E13.

7. In addition to this primary Islamic schism, there are also other groups that are covered elsewhere in the paper, such as Sufis and Wahhabis. Directly pertinent to the Sunni-Shi'ite schism is the fact that Shi'ites are likewise divided into several principle groupings known as Seveners and Twelvers. The differences between these Shi'ite subgroups are not explored in this paper as they are not essential for a progressive Christian understanding of Islam.

8. In an effort to curb Reformation violence, the right of princes to determine the religion of their territories was firmly acknowledged in the Peace of Augsburg (1555). In Great Britain, questions regarding the religious identity of the monarch (and head of the established church) produced wars (both external and within the kingdom) well into the eighteenth century.

9. This statement must be qualified by the realization that not all Sufi orders are quietist in orientation. Sufism is a highly inventive religious phenomenon that has resulted in many variants that do not fit the norm described here.

10. Christians may argue that in their understanding, Jews are "people of the Bible," but Jews hold no similar understanding of Christians. And the treatment of Jews by Christians throughout most of their shared history belies any notion that Christian acceptance of Jews as "people of the Bible" has had much practical value.

11. Brian Brennan, "The Jesus of Islam: Christians Have More in Common with Muslims Than They Realize," *National Catholic Reporter* 41 (June 3, 2005): 15.

12. Küng, *Christianity and World Religions*, 33.

13. Progressive Christians currently sense that this norm is under attack in American culture. Nonetheless, the tradition of no establishment of religion within the United States is strong and will most likely successfully resist any and all attempts to undermine it.

14. Paul A. Winters, ed., *Islam: Opposing Viewpoints* (San Diego: Greenhaven, 1995), 116, 118. For a very readable and brief explanation of *ijtihad* and its history, see Irshad Manji, "From Books to Virgins," *Los Angeles Times*, November 6, 2005, M3.

15. See Gordon Douglass and Ward McAfee, "Consumerism," in John B. Cobb. ed., Resistance: The New Role of Progressive Christians (Louisville: Westminster John Knox, 2008), 55–74.

16. Pope John Paul II, "Address of Pope John Paul II to the Participants in the Colloquium on 'Holiness in Christianity and Islam,'" May 9, 1985. This

development built upon a statement in Vatican II (1962–1965): "Upon the Moslems, too, the church looks with esteem. They adore one God, living and enduring, merciful and all-powerful, maker of heaven and earth, and speaker to humans. They strive to submit wholeheartedly even to his inscrutable decrees."

17. *Los Angeles Times*, June 27, 2005, A12.

18. "A Common Word Between Us and You" initiative began in 2007 when 138 Muslim scholars from around the Islamic world called upon Christians to start a process of historic reconciliation between the two communities. The initiative emphasized that Christians and Muslims make up almost half of the world's population and that reconciliation between the two communities is essential for world peace. Jews have responded to this initiative in positive ways. In August 2008, Yale Divinity School hosted a conference bringing together over 150 Muslim and Christian scholars, intellectuals, academics, and religious leaders to discuss how Muslim-Christian relations may improve. Former British Prime Minister Tony Blair has also entered this arena, establishing the Tony Blair Faith Foundation, the purpose of which is to make common faith traditions a positive force in bringing about world peace.

19. Progressive Muslims usually prefer to use the word "surrender" instead of "submission."

Chapter Four: Buddha for Christians

1. Before statehood, Hawaii—dominated by Asian cultures and Asian religions—was placed under the Foreign Mission Board instead of the Home Mission Board by the Southern Baptist Convention.

2. The historical novel, *The Sea and Poison (Umi to Dokuyaku)*, by reknown Catholic novelist Shusaku Endo, graphically described this secret project of the Japanese army. It is available in English translation. My home in Fukuoka was about four miles from Kyushu University. In exchange for receiving documentary results of all these toxic biological human experiments, the American Occupation Forces promised not to prosecute Japanese scientists and military officers directly responsible for these crimes against humanity.

3. Pain is physically unavoidable. But suffering is avoidable mental stress.

4. David J. Kalupahana, *Buddhist Philosophy: A Historical Analysis* (Honolulu: University of Hawaii Press, 1976), 44–55.

5. Leo D. Lefebure, *The Buddha and the Christ* (Maryknoll: Orbis, 1997), 5. Other options on dates are offered by Andrew Skilton, *A Concise History of Buddhism* (Cambridge: Windhorse, 2004), 19. Modern scholarship has shown little consensus for Buddha's dates, differing over a hundred years.

6. Most likely his father, instead of being a king, was the presiding ruler of the oligarchy governing the Sakya clan-based republic. Some clan-based republics in the Himalayan foothills were not swallowed up yet by the rising new monarchies arising in the central Ganges basin. *Concise History of Buddhism*, 19.

7. Ibid., 19–24.

8. Many insightful monks, of course, see beyond party-line propaganda that excludes women and laymen.

9. This is in contrast to theravada which offers no saviors, not even Gautama Buddha. Gautama Buddha instructed his monks not to depend on him, but to work out their own salvation by their own practice. This is radicalized in Lin Chi, the founder of Rinzai Zen in China. His famous slogan proverb is: "If you meet the Buddha, kill him." That is, it is better to kill the messenger and fulfill his message, than to worship the messenger and forget the message.

10. The owner of the Japanese Canon camera company is a devotee of Kannon, the Bodhisattva of Compassion. Canon is the Westernized spelling of Kannon, whose name means the Bodhisattva "Who Listens to the Groanings of All Suffering Beings."

11. A Buddhist priest explained how a male Buddha could so easily become female. He said it was a matter of lowering truth to the level of human understanding. Of course, there is no male or female in the world of Buddhas.

12. "All past, present, and future Buddhas live this Perfection of Wisdom and attain supreme, perfect enlightenment. So know that this Perfection of Wisdom is the holy mantra, the luminous mantra, the supreme mantra, the incomparable mantra by which all suffering is swept away. This is totally true. Proclaim this Perfection of Wisdom mantra and say, *'Gate, gate, paragate, parasamgate, bodhi svaha.'*" Closing lines of the Heart of the Perfection of Wisdom Sutra.

13. They become ten syllables when read in Japanese as *namu myo-o ho-o renge kyo-o.*

14. Impossible to back-slide in Pure Land, *fu-tentai* 不転退.

15. Speakers at graduation ceremonies speak of *tatta ikkai dake no tootoi jinsei* ("this one precious chance at life)".

16. Andrew Skilton, A Concise History of Buddhism (Cambridge, England: Windhorse Publications, 2004), 121–27.

17. Ibid., 131.

18. Ibid., 134.

19. The book is available in most university libraries.

20. For an academic description of tantric literature explaining sexual intercourse as spiritual practice, see ibid., 140–41.

21. Shingon and Tendai are Vajrayana in Japan. They both have rejected sexual practices in the training of monks. Japanese society would not tolerate them. Tachikawa, a Shingon sect, is infamous for their past sexual practices.

22. A man is shot with a poisoned arrow. The feather in the tail of the arrow could occupy our time and attention. What kind of bird did this feather come from? What kind of tree did the arrow come from? If we allowed ourselves to be occupied with such curiosities instead of hurrying to find a doctor, the man would die. We must not be distracted by theoretical questions and focus on the mission at hand— the practical problem of relieving suffering.

23. Buddhists duck for cover at the charge of male chauvinism. Male domination and patriarchal systems are far more extreme in Buddhism of Southeast Asia

and East Asia. Traditionally, the most senior nun must subject herself to the authority of the lowest ranking monk, even someone ordained just yesterday.

24. "If God is defined primarily as cosmic compassion and wisdom, then some Buddhists . . . may be inclined to say they believe in 'God'. . . . On the other hand, if God is a supreme personal being who created the universe, lives in heaven, watches over me, and knows my thoughts and actions, then Buddhists clearly do not believe in God," Ken Tanaka, *Ocean: An Introduction to Jodo-Shinshu Buddhism in America* (Berkeley: Wisdomocean, 1998), 26.

25. In the hymn of praise celebrating the drowning of Pharaoh's army is the startling sentence: "The LORD is a man of war; the LORD is his name," Exodus 15:3.

26. Some scholars say that there was no conquest. They claim that some Canaanites actually joined the Israelites to form the Confederation of twelve tribes. But that is not the theme of our present Book of Joshua.

27. Losers becoming winners and winners becoming losers is the clear framework for the New Testament Beatitudes in Matthew 5.

28. Redeemability is the foundation for all evangelism, pastoral ministry, peace and justice projects, and world missions. So Yin Yang with its framework of redeemability is a better fit for the message of Jesus. In Yin Yang, Good can become Evil, and Evil can become Good. People committed to Good fall into temporary Evil; people committed to Evil often find themselves doing momentary good. Nobody is all Good or all Bad. So the path is repentance, confession, and rededication. Christianity crusading for Good has at times committed massive evil—in the Crusades, in the persecution of Jews, in the near genocide of American Indian tribes, in the demonization of Hawaiian religion, and in the brutal enslavement of Afro-Americans. All this fits better in the ambiguous framework of Yin Yang that opens up possibilities of redeemability. Walter Wink confirmed Yin Yang as the appropriate framework for the gospel of Jesus in his book *The Powers That Be* (New York: Galilee, 1999).

29. Ibid., 97.

30. Herbert Nearman, Shobogenzo: *The Treasure House of the Eye of the True Teaching* (Mount Shasta, CA: Shasta Abbey Press, 2007), 23, Nearman provides a slightly different English translation than what appears here.

31. Masao Abe lectured from Philippians 2:5-11 to eminent Christian theologians at the Second International Buddhist-Christian Conference at Hawaii Loa College in January, 1984. Hans Küng was there to state his objections to "self-emptying" as a key to Christology.

32. John B. Cobb Jr. and Christopher Ives, editors, *The Emptying God: A Buddhist-Jewish-Christian Conversation with Masao Abe on God, Kenosis, and Sunyata* (Eugene: Wipf and Stock, 1990).

33. From unpublished lectures I heard by Dale Moody at Southern Baptist Theological Seminary in Louisville, Kentucky, 1965–1972.

34. The first step toward ancestor worship was benign. Public services were held in 706, during the reign of Chung-tsung, in which Buddhist monks honored deceased emperors by vegetarian meals and incense burning. These services that spread throughout the empire did not involve ordinary citizens. Through the forty-nine-day services, however, ancestor worship entered every Chinese Buddhist household.

35. See Dickson Kazuo Yagi, "Protestant Perspectives on Ancestor Worship in Japanese Buddhism: The Funeral and the Buddhist Altar," *Buddhist-Christian Studies* 15 (1995): 43–60. Shin Buddhists are perhaps the only Buddhist denomination that consistently rejected ancestor worship syncretism.

36. The Amakusa government and Catholic devotional literature list thirty-seven thousand martyrs. Some conservative scholars reduce the number down to seventeen thousand.

37. For the persecution era, see Otis Cary, *A History of Christianity in Japan* (North Clarendon: Tuttle, 1976, 1909). See also Masaharu Anesaki, *History of Japanese Religions* (North Clarendon: Tuttle, 1975, 1928), 240–58. For recent reference, see Kazuo Kasahara, ed., *A History of Japan* (Tokyo: Kosei, 2002), 435–40.

38. A few Christian groups went underground and survived intact for six to seven generations. After 217 years, some of these underground Christians came out to greet Catholic missionaries when they first returned in 1855. They are known as "hidden Christians," or *Kakure Kirishitan*. See Kasahara, 437–40.

39. Ibid., 342–44.

40. Fumio Tamamuro, "Local Society and the Temple-Parishioner Relationship within the Bakufu's Governance Structure," *Japanese Journal of Religious Studies* (2001) 28/3–4, 261–92. See also Nam-lin Hur, "The Rise of Funerary Buddhism in Tokugawa Japan," *Death and Social Order in Tokugawa Japan: Buddhism, Anti-Christianity, and the Danka System* (Cambridge: Harvard University Asia Center, 2007), 1–30.

41. A rapidly growing fad of the past twenty years in Japan is to have Christian weddings. Since there are not enough Christian churches or ministers, any Caucasian can be hired as a "fake priest" by wedding business companies.

42. When the Zen master was leaving the monastery to officiate at a memorial service, I challenged him, saying, "Why are you doing ancestor worship, which Buddhism denies?" He thought for a while and answered, "We have to eat, too."

43. When the Mount Hiei Tendai headquarters seminary opened three spots for incoming freshmen from non-priest families about twenty-five years ago, it was front-page news in Japanese newspapers.

44. I sat weekly with a group of laymen sitting with monks-in-training at a Fukuoka monastery. Over a period of six months, never did any priest come over to the laymen's lounge to say even one word to encourage us in sitting. How outrageous!

45. In their zeal for laypeople, outstanding leaders have come to the West. Many Zen Centers in the United States are directly founded by inspired masters of

Sanbo Kyodan and their dharma heirs, including the Diamond Sangha in Honolulu, the Zen Center of Los Angeles, and the Yokoji Zen Mountain Center in Southern California.

46. Honolulu has the large Kotohira Jinja Shinto Shrine near the airport. Across the Pali is the magnificent Byodoin Shinto Shrine, a copy of the famous Byodoin in Japan. On the Big Island there is a small Shinto Shrine less than a mile from my family home. This Shinto presence, however, is infinitesimal compared to the enthusiastic and successful transplanting of Japanese Buddhist faith and temple institutions in Hawaii and the West Coast. In the Japanese phone book in Los Angeles there is not even one phone number listed under Shinto. What is visible is the Shinto-related Konkokyo religion in Boyle Heights (Los Angeles) and in San Francisco.

47. In the headquarter temple of Nishi Shin Buddhism on Pali Highway in Honolulu, I attended the funeral of a distant relative. To my surprise, no one on the program called out to address the deceased by name, saying, "I am speaking to the spirit of Mr. Tanaka." No one talked directly to the dead to praise him, to scold him for dying so early, and to bid him sayonara as they always do in Buddhist funerals in Japan. Buddhism in Japan must accommodate such heretical practices of ancestor worship out of consideration for the strong feelings of the family of the deceased. But second- and third-generation Japanese Americans in the United States are no longer sure what is Japanese custom and tradition. The Buddhist priest, then, is almost completely free to do a purely Buddhist funeral in the United States. Nobody spoke to the dead.

48. Sallie B. King, "Contemporary Buddhist Spirituality and Social Activism," *Buddhist Spirituality; Later China, Korea, Japan, and the Modern World*, Yoshinori Takeuchi, ed. (New York: Herder, 1999), 457.

49. "Sarvodaya" is a word coined by Mahatma Gandhi that means "well-being/enlightenment of all." "Shramadana" is "the sharing of labor and resources." Both words together mean "sharing of labor and resources for the enlightenment of all," ibid., 70.

50. Today Sarvodaya Shramadana is active in over 11,600 villages. Ariyaratne's writings are available in the seven volumes of *Collected Works* published by Nandasena Ratnapala. See A. T., Ariyaratne, "Sarvodaya Shramadana's Approach to Peacebuilding," *Buddhist Peacework: Creating Cultures of Peace*, David Chappell, ed. (Somerville: Wisdom, 1999), 69–77.

51. Ariyaratne, 70.

52. King, 457–59, 471.

53. Ariyaratne, 71.

54. King, 357–59.

55. Acharn Sulak Sivaraksa, "Buddhism and a Culture of Peace" in *Buddhist Peacework*, 39–46.

56. Sulak Sivaraksa, www. sulak-sivaraksa.org.

57. King, 461–64.

58. I sat next to young Vietnamese nuns at a large public reception for Thich Nhat Hanh in 2006 at Loyola Marymount University. When I asked, they said they were from a Thich Nhat Hanh sangha in Southern California.

59. Ibid., 464–67.

60. Seminary professors at Bishops College, the main seminary of the Church of North India in Calcutta, hung their heads in shame as they explained to me why Christians failed to welcome Dalits more enthusiastically. High caste Christians feared that a flood of Dalits would make it unlikely that other high caste Indians would become Christians. Others complained that the primary concern for economic-social benefits made suspect their conversion motivation. On the other hand, the most convincing reason why Ambedkar converted to Buddhism, instead of Christianity, is that Buddhism was an Indian religion. In the past three decades, however, great numbers of Dalits have been converting to Christianity. Christian converts have grown to such numbers that radical Hindus in several states, such as Orissa, have installed anti-conversion laws relating to Christianity.

61. Dhammachari Lokamitra, "The Dhamma Revolution in India," in *Buddhist Peacework*, 29–30.

62. Lokamitra, 31–35.

63. King, 472–73.

64. Ibid., 466–67.

65. Ibid.

66. Makiguchi and Toda created the *Soka Kyoiku Gakkai* (Value Creating Education Society), which proclaimed a "human revolution" of individuals and society promoting social and religious reform through the practice of Nichiren Buddhism. While the government promoted education to mold obedient subjects, they sought to empower ordinary people to become self-reliant individuals.

67. These vows are recited at many Mahayana gatherings. They are carved in Chinese into the gigantic wooden pillars at the entrance of Hsi Lai Temple in Hacienda Heights, Los Angeles.

Chapter Five: Indigenous American Religious Advice

1. In this essay, terms such as Indian, Native American, and Indigenous American will be used interchangeably, a style used by the Indigenous authors cited here.

2. Mary Evelyn Tucker, "The Ecological Spirituality of Pierre Teilhard de Chardin," *Spiritus, A Journal of Christian Spirituality* 7 (Spring 2007): 16.

3. Ritual is an important part of Indigenous religion. Practitioners of Indigenous American religious ceremonies, dances, and rites are generally averse to sharing the deepest meaning of their faith traditions with outsiders. While there are some Indian New Age religious entrepreneurs eager to inform those who are hungry to learn tribal ways, they are regarded as charlatans by the elders who maintain these traditions. Vine Deloria Jr. has provided a cursory review of preferred religious practices among various North American tribes in his *For This Land, Writings on Religion in America* (New York: Routledge, 1990): 122–25. Richard Erdoes, *Crying*

for a Dream: The World through Native American Eyes (Santa Fe: Bear and Company, 1990) is another attempt to communicate Indian experiential religion in writing and accompanying photographs. Also see Peggy V. Beck, Anna Lee Walters, Nia Francisco, *The Sacred Ways of Knowledge, Sources of Life* (Tsaile: Navajo Community College Press, 1996).

4. Vine Deloria Jr., *God Is Red: A Native View of Religion* (Golden: Fulcrum, 2003), 81, 94.

5. Ibid., 99.

6. Ibid., viii.

7. Ibid., 89.

8. Ibid., xii, 146, 154, 288–289, 295.

9. Ibid., 152, 162, 167, 169, 171, 183.

10. Ibid., 195, 197, 285, 292.

11. Clara Sue Kidwell, Homer Noley, and George E. "Tink" Tinker, eds., *A Native American Theology* (Maryknoll: Orbis, 2001), ix, 33–34; Norman W. Jackson, "Native American Theology and the United Church of Christ," *Prism: A Theological Forum for the United Church of Christ*, 5 (Spring 1990): 74–79; James L. West, "Indian Spirituality: Another Vision," (Presented on September 26, 1986, at the theological conference "Patterns of Faith: Woven Together in Life and Mission" at American Baptist Seminary of the West, Berkeley, California).

12. Kidwell, Noley, and Tinker, eds., *A Native American Theology*, 19, 55–56, 61, 105, 150.

13. Ibid., 34–36: Rosemary Radford Ruether, *Integrating Economism, Globalization and World Religions* (Lanham: Rowman and Littlefield, 2005), 17.

14. Kidwell, Noley, and Tinker, eds., *A Native American Theology*, 39; Anand Veeraraj, *Green History of Religion* (Bangalore: Centre for Contemporary Christianity, 2005), 218–221, 249.

15. "Good cop/bad cop" is a psychological device used in police interrogations involving a team of questioners. The bad cop attacks and condemns, while the good cop plays a much more friendly role. The goal of both policemen is to get the person being questioned to cooperate.

16. George E. Tinker, *Spirit and Resistance: Political Theology and American Indian Liberation* (Minneapolis: Fortress Press, 2004).

17. Kidwell, Noley, and Tinker, eds., *A Native American Theology*, 68–69.

18. Ibid., 84.

19. Ibid., 178–179.

20. Tinker, *Spirit and Resistance*, 4–5.

21. Deloria, *God Is Red*, 196.

22. Ibid., 285.

23. George E. Tinker, "Gerechtigkeit, Frieden und die Integrität der Weinachtsbäume," *Ökumenische Rundschau* 38 (April, 1989): 180.

24. Tinker, *Spirit and Resistance*, 20–27, 85, 98. In the early days of Christianity, "the time of our existence" did not characterize the faith that expected that the

age would soon end with Christ's return. As centuries turned into millennia, Christian eschatological thinking came to be characterized by "the time of our existence," a situation in which ultimate meaning is deferred until the end of time. See footnote 24 for an explanation of how indigenous people experience ultimate meaning in each day's existence on Earth.

25. Tinker, *Spirit and Resistance*, 45.

26. As the stories of indigenous American religion are rooted in specific places, they are not universal in their application. They directly communicate only to the tribe that reveres them. These stories are not transportable to outsiders. However, the mentality underlying these stories can inspire outsiders to develop something similar. To begin to understand the Indigenous mentality, one should review Mircea Eliade's classic work *Cosmos and History: The Myth of the Eternal Return* (Princeton: Princeton University Press, 1954/2005). Primitive peoples, Eliade emphasized, do not live in historical or profane time but rather in eternal time in which archetypal sacred moments punctuate daily activities such as eating, grooming, hunting, reproducing, and living in close association with the specifics of Creation known in one particular place. The stories and rituals of Native American religions are designed to recreate this mentality for their participants. Christian language holds the potential to reactivate a similar mentality. For example, Christ is commonly referred to as the tree of life, a metaphor that suggests eternity is present to us each day and need not be delayed until the end of the age. Within Christian history are memories of communities that found eternal life in sacred rituals available within this earthly existence. While we cannot simply copy Indigenous American rituals, we can look back into our own experiential religious past to reawaken a sense of eternity in the processes of a sustainable Creation. Even in recalling our own religious past, much re-envisioning will necessarily have to occur, as the awareness of our circumstances is dissimilar to mental states that existed long ago. The search for authentic religion is necessarily a never-ending process actively engaging the seeker. Receiving an awareness of eternity in the present moment can never be a wholly passive experience.

27. Tucker, "Ecological Spirituality," *Spiritus*, 7 (Spring, 2007): 15.

28. Lester R. Brown, *Plan B 3.0: Mobilizing to Save Civilization* (New York: Norton, 2008), 283; also see the essay by Gordon Douglass and Ward McAfee "Consumerism" in John Cobb et al., *Resistance: The New Role of Progressive Christians* (Louisville: Westminster John Knox, 2008), 55–74.

Chapter Six: Theological Response

1. Belden C. Lane, *Landscapes of the Sacred: Geography and Narrative in American Spirituality* (Baltimore: Johns Hopkins, 2001), 23.

2. Rita Nakashima Brock and Rebecca Parker, *Saving Paradise: How Christianity Traded Love of This World for Crucifixion and Empire* (Boston: Beacon, 2009), 417.

3. For example, see *The Earth Bible Series*, 5 vols., Norman C. Habel, general editor (Cleveland: The Pilgrim Press 2000-2002).

Index

supersessionism, 45, 50, 61, 73, 81, 194, 197, 222
sustainability, 127
synagogues, 12, 47, 49, 73, 223
synoptic gospels, 13, 16, 49, 223

Talmud, 29, 192
Taoism, 35, 223
Temple (Jewish), 28, 47–48, 50, 101, 223
Ten Commandments, 192
terrorism, 90–91, 126
Theravada, 34, 137, 158
Thich Nhat Hanh, 159–160
Three Marks of Existence, 135
Tibetan Buddhism, 140, 160–161
Tinker, George, 178, 180, 181
tolerance, 186
Torah, 11, 29, 47–48, 93, 190, 192, 223
Trinity, 23, 53, 123–124, 145, 188, 196, 223
trust, 195 (also see dialogue)
Tucker, Evelyn, 171
Turkey, 115

ulema, 101, 111, 123, 223
ummah, 96, 100, 223
United States, 116, 195
unity, 126–127
Upanishads, 143, 223
usury, 54

Vatican, 63, 66, 71–72, 224
Vedanta, 31
virgin birth, 23, 104
Vishnu, 32
vision quests, 181

Wahhabism, 116, 224
Wailing Wall, 115
West Bank, 115
Wiesel, Elie, 65
Williams, Roger, 26
Wise, Isaac Mayer, 27
women, 108–110
World Council of Churches, 37, 68
World War I, 115
World War II, 133, 155

Yazid, 98–99
yin yang, 147–148, 224
yoga, 32

Zealots, 47, 93, 224
Zen Buddhism, 34–35, 123, 134, 200, 202
Zionism, 65, 76, 224
Zoroastrianism, 93–94, 224